D1549125

An Eye for Movement

Warren Lamb's career in Movement Analysis

Told in transcripts from interviews, extracts from
his diaries and published works, by Dick McCaw.
This book complements the DVD ROM
"Decision Making and Movement Pattern Analysis"

Published by
Brechin Books Limited,
6 Brechin Place, London SW7 4QA

First published 2006 by Brechin Books Limited,
6 Brechin Place, London SW7 4QA
www.brechinpublishing.co.uk

Copyright © Dick McCaw 2006

ISBN 978-0-9540284-1-1
0-9540284-1-4

Typeset in Avenir Roman by Chichester Typographic,
Chichester, Sussex

Printed in England by RPM Print & Design, Chichester, Sussex

Dedicated to Mac and Sheila McCaw

It has been my single biggest stroke of luck
to have parents who have never failed in their
support throughout my career.

An Eye for Movement

CONTENTS

PART THREE ~ THE DEVELOPMENT OF A METHOD: 1950 – 2000

THE INTERVIEWS

PART FOUR ~ WARREN LAMB'S METHOD DESCRIBED IN DEPTH

THE INTERVIEWS

ILLUSTRATIONS

An Eye for Movement

W arren Lamb has been writing about movement for the past sixty years. This book offers a survey of those six decades of reflection. The late 1940s are represented by excerpts from his diaries which offer us a vivid picture of his life and activities at the Art of Movement Studio in Manchester, and his work in the factories with the movement genius Rudolf Laban, and with Frederick Lawrence, a far-sighted management consultant. In the 1950s he wrote a five-hundred page study of movement provisionally called *Movement and Personality.* Although unpublished, it is an important document in that it contains 'everything that I knew about movement and movement analysis at that time'. The 1960s are represented by three books, *A Kinaesthetic Approach to Piano Technique* - written with pianist Ronald Meachen in 1962/3 but only published in 2003 – and his ground-breaking *Posture and Gesture* in 1965, the only published book that he authored alone. The end of the 60s were marked by a third book, *Management Behaviour,* this time written with David Turner. The end of the 1970s saw the publication of another co-authored book, *Body Code,* written with Elizabeth Watson. Finally in the 1990s he embarked on an autobiographical reflection which was to be entitled *The Movement Man.* Eden Davies made rough edits of five chapters from the projected fifteen, but it remains unpublished.

The body of this book consists of interviews that I conducted with Lamb between December 2003 and August 2006. To understand the purpose of these interviews and indeed the relationship between this book and the accompanying DVD ROM, I need to go back a little in time. In Spring 2001 I began studying movement with one of Rudolf Laban's pupils, Geraldine Stephenson (whose DVD ROM will be available through Brechin Books from December 2006). She has known Warren from when they both enrolled at the Art of Movement Studio in 1946 (she in September, he in November). We all met for dinner in early 2003 and very quickly I became interested in the idea of documenting his work. All the previous documentations that Peter Hulton (Director of the Arts Documentation Unit) and I have made together have used film footage taken of teachers at work in the studio. Until my first interviews with Lamb, I had no idea what his Movement Pattern Analysis (MPA) entailed, therefore he simply began talking to me about his work. By mid-2004 we agreed that the only way to capture the essence of Movement Pattern Analysis was for Hulton to film the entire process of Lamb making an MPA of me.

After filming the various stages of the MPA process I started to understand this complex and subtle process much better. I started to grasp Lamb's extraordinary claim that it was possible to understand how a person makes decisions by watching how he or she moves: not any form of athletic or aesthetic movement – but the tiny, involuntary movements that one makes whilst sitting in a chair being interviewed. Setting aside the improbability of anyone being able to detect or record such movements (surely the point is that you *don't* move when sitting down), how on earth can anyone propose to relate the very complex and conscious mental process of decision-making with the casual and meaningless movements one makes in everyday life? Things were made even more difficult because he had been right in his assessment of how I go about the process of decision-making! Indeed, he was absolutely spot-on in his assessment of me. Thus our conversations between June 2004 and the present day have had one purpose - to get Lamb to explain to a layman (myself), in the simplest terms possible, how he arrived at his method, and how it works. As I listened to him over these months it became clear why he has written so many books on the same subject – it is extremely difficult to describe physical movement in words. In a single movement there will be six or seven different processes at work: however, writing and speaking only allow a description of one process at a time. It is so much simpler to *show* the movement at work, rather than talk about it. The job of the DVD ROM is to show how Lamb creates an MPA, the job of this book is to explore how he arrived at this method, and to outline some of the assumptions – cultural, psychological, aesthetic, educational, philosophical - that underlie his approach. In some ways this is the last telling of the story about movement that Lamb has spent his life writing.

This book is structured along two axes: the first is chronological and follows his development in the late 1940s through to the present day. The second axis is one of depth: at first his ideas are described in outline, and later in much greater depth and detail. Part I is a chronology of his early life, Part II outlines the thinking developed at this time. Part III returns to the chronology of his later life while Part IV offers a much closer analysis of his mature approach to Movement Pattern Analysis.

It is important to remember that the bulk of this book consists of interviews, and because I wanted Lamb to express himself informally, it means that occasionally he will use technical terms that require further elaboration. It is for this reason that I have written short introductions to each part of the book, outlining the arguments to come, highlighting important developments and discoveries, drawing upon his writings (published and unpublished) or writings about him. In this way I hope to give the reader a means of arriving at the answer to that question – How can decision-making be related to everyday movement?

Warren Lamb's Publications

In a conversation in March 2006 when we were discussing his publications, Warren Lamb gave an account of his continuing attempts to get his message across to a wider public.

It's often said that people have a book in them just waiting to come out. I think that I did have a book in me going right back to my teenage years. Had I gone to University instead of the Navy in 1941 I would have read English Literature. My father was really responsible for getting me interested in literature. He read a lot of books himself and encouraged me to read all the classical authors. Had I not met Laban and got into the movement work I might have tried to write a novel or something. As soon as I got into the study of movement I started to write about it. I suppose that I just had to keep on writing. Since I thought it was something great I wanted to communicate this to the world. I don't think my writing is good. I often say that if somebody can write, it doesn't matter what they're writing about, you will enjoy reading it. Much depends on the environment in which they write.

'Motivating by Strategy', an important article published in Management Today in 1984 was massively rewritten. The deputy editor spent hours and hours changing my original script, the result being much better than the original. However much I rewrite it doesn't get any clearer. I have been very conscious of my inability to write clearly and in a way that provides a pleasurable experience for the reader. Whether I could have been a successful novelist I very much doubt.

This was quite significant in that it was the only article published in the management world where I make the link about Action Profiling and decision-making in a significant sense. I insist that what MPA does is to improve the decisions that people, particularly those with big responsibilities, have to make. We want to make known to them that it influences the strategies that they think are right for whatever they are managing.

In an earlier conversation he talked about his landmark book, *Posture and Gesture* (1965), and his last published book written with Elizabeth Watson, *Body Code* (1979), making no reference to his third published book, *Management Behaviour* (1969) co-written with David Turner, nor to his earlier or later unpublished writings. Lamb is surprisingly cavalier about his writings: it was in July 2006 that he announced that he had 'found' the manuscript of a book entitled *Work and Play*, and it was only when reading Kestenberg's *The Meaning of Movement* that I found a reference to yet another unpublished manuscript, *Movement Assessment.* For clarity's sake I will list his book-length writings:

1954 – 56	*Movement and Personality* (unpublished)
1961	*Movement Assessment* (unpublished)
1962 – 63	*A Kinaesthetic Approach to Piano Technique* (with Ronald Meachen)
1965	*Posture and Gesture*
1969	*Management Behaviour* (with David Turner)
1979	*Body Code* (with Elizabeth Watson)
1980's	*At Work and at Play* (unpublished)
1990's	*The Movement Man* (with Eden Davies) (unpublished)

Although Lamb made no reference throughout our conversations to *Movement and Personality* or *The Movement Man,* I feel that these are important documents and, since they have never been published, I will quote from them in my introductions.   Although Lamb has written a vast number of articles, these have usually been to promote rather than to explain or explore the philosophical underpinnings of his work.

> Concerning my articles, there was an article published in 1953 called 'A Yardstick for Personality' that really got my career started. I would never dream of publishing an article with that title now, since personality is such a vast concept. However that article produced more than 30 enquiries and I turned seven of them into clients. I benefited from the fact that this was the first business magazine to appear in England at that time: maybe that drew more attention to my work (see page 143).

> I wouldn't think that my articles would be so useful since they were mostly designed to sell my method. However I think you could see a development in my books, from *Posture and Gesture* to *Body Code.* The attempt in the second book was to make the method more understandable. I wanted to get across to a bigger public. I thought that almost everyone could be interested in learning how movement could be studied. So I wrote it and touted it among lots of publishers all of whom rejected it. I happened to mention it when I was having dinner with a client, Peter Watson and his wife Elizabeth. She said that she'd be interested in reading it. She then came back saying that it was very interesting but just needed rewriting. She deserves to be credited as co-author because she did completely rewrite it. She made it really quite entertaining. However Routledge didn't really market it, so it was only a reasonable success. It was published by Princeton books in America where it did much better.

Eden Davies has also used a lot of my materials very intelligently in her book. I now work through other writers rather than writing myself. Carol Lynne Moore has a book – Movement and Decision-Making - coming out [It was published in Summer 2005] which incorporates some of my ideas.

Warren Lamb's Philosophy of Movement and Education

It is surprising that more attention has not been paid to the study of movement. Perhaps one reason is that the various systems that do exist all attempt to label certain movements as having certain meanings. Thus we learn, for example, that a man who holds his cigarette one way is secretive and a man who holds his cigarette another way is open. This sort of naivety fails when put to any test. There is nothing in the present study which attempts this sort of labelling, nor is it akin to graphology, phrenology or any other interpretative system. The analysis of movement can be used as a tool by practitioners of various disciplines, but it does not impose any one viewpoint or cult of its own. [*Kinaesthetic Approach*, p. 74]

It is really fascinating what movements people do with their bodies. To convey that fascination and to teach people to find it for themselves has always seemed to me a worthwhile aim. Like most things in this life that are worthwhile, it involves a lot of struggle and hard work. Before the fascination can be found the rules have to be learned. They consist above all of segregating the recording of a person's movement (and notating a record rather than making a video is essential) from the attempt to attribute a meaning to that movement. [*The Movement Man*, Chapter 3, p. 24]

This paragraph contains so many of the elements that constitute Lamb's approach to movement. Firstly, it was clear throughout our conversations that Lamb remains quite as fascinated by movement now as he was when he first began his researches into Laban sixty years ago. His enquiry is very much still open and live. The second thing of note is his commitment to teach people to find movement 'for themselves'. Laban believed that everyone had their own unique gift for movement and his summer schools and classes used to attract a huge variety of individuals. Lamb has embraced this inclusive (indeed I'd go so far as to call it a 'democratic') approach to teaching movement. Lamb is more interested in how a person composes a movement, rather than the movement taken in isolation. In the third and fourth sentences we can sense the balance of enthusiasm and rigour in his approach. He admits that an untrained eye could not detect or understand these everyday movements. Lamb's enthusiasm is much needed to encourage students to persevere in what is a fiendishly difficult and elusive field of study.

Already in his first writings – *Movement and Personality* - he notes how few good books there are about teaching movement. Even when there are books, they tend to be too preoccupied with technique – how to do gymnastics, or succeed in sport, or excel in ballet – rather than with an education of the person, of the self, by means of movement. This distinction between learning skills and acquiring a wider education is something to which he will return throughout his reflections upon movement. Lamb is ahead of his time in demanding a more body-based understanding of education and learning: Physical Education it is not a question of teaching students what to do with their bodies but of how to learn *through* their bodies, or, to be more specific, through developing their kinaesthetic sense ('the study of the sensation of movement').

> Writers such as Lange, Dewey, Nunn have been followed by many educationalists keen to promote more attention to the non-academic side of education. They argue that young people should be educated to a mature mastery of the use of their bodies and that this equips them better for their academic work. From this point of view the study of movement from the purely physical aspect, as in the old Physical Training, has given way to increasing study of the sensation of movement ... [*Movement and Personality*, pp. 1 - 2]

We shall see how Warren and other members of the Art of Movement Studio struggled with finding a category for Laban's concept of creative movement: many people teaching the 'old Physical Training' regarded both Laban and his students with great suspicion. Physical Education was based on a very old-fashioned idea of pedagogy – drilling the students - and indeed of the body as something that needed to be drilled, dominated and trained, like a wayward plant. Neither Laban nor Lamb started out with the idea that the body is something that needs limiting through discipline, but that it can be a tool by means of which we can learn about ourselves and our relations with others and with our natural and cultural environment. According to them the body is something to be listened to, something you can listen with; thus physical education is about acquiring the disciplines that can help develop one's awareness.

Lamb states the purpose of *Movement and Personality:* 'This book puts the focus on the independent study of movement sensations and attempts to explain the contribution which an objective knowledge of them can make.' He then ties in this kinaesthetic sense or movement sensation with 'the broadest sense of learning' [Ibid., p. 2]. In the following page he links this development of the kinaesthetic sense with the study of personality - 'No two people move in exactly the same way and no two personalities are exactly the same.' [3] Here, in a nutshell, he has outlined the work of the next fifty years. It is no great leap from the question, 'How do you link movement and personality?' to the question, 'How do you link movement and decision-making?' The connection between how we move and who we are (as personalities) was something that Laban proposed and Lamb spent all of his adult life exploring. One page later we see Lamb asking whether, 'Is it possible to have movement tests comparable to intelligence tests? What are quantitative variations in movement?' [Ibid., p. 4] In four pages we have touched on some of the themes that are central to Lamb's approach to teaching and learning movement. I shall elaborate on each of these themes, drawing on his early study for illustrations.

I want to start with the last question he posed: Why is our sense of movement not tested? Later he would demand why we don't have Action Quotients to put alongside Intelligence Quotients: 'perhaps soon there will be comparable tests designed to measure their Action Quotient. Such an Action Quotient would be a measure of the sensitivity or awareness of the kinaesthetic sense.' [Ibid., p. 44] It is not that Lamb is some romantic anti-academic; he is simply demanding that the study and measurement of movement aptitude be accepted as something equally serious and useful as intellectual accomplishment. But behind this seemingly narrow polemic against the limits of a purely academic education, there lies a series of much broader questions about personal development, about the purpose of education, and the assessment of aptitude.

I would argue that Lamb's philosophy of education hasn't changed greatly over the years – all that has changed is the means of delivering it. We have seen him quote Dewey above and he echoes her again in the following statement:

> The people most in need of education of the senses are those who habitually reply, 'I don't mind', or 'It doesn't matter' to any question requiring an expression of their taste. [Ibid., p. 26]

Therefore one important dimension in what Lamb will call our 're-education' is to develop a sense of discrimination.

> When, from his own individual effort, a person can renew and revive his use of the sense of sight, then he is exercising greater discrimination in respect to his sight; he learns how to use part of himself better; a sort of increased personal efficiency. [Ibid., p. 14]

In his belief that one can live a richer life through a broader education he echoes Moshe Feldenkrais, another great educator of the whole person. Feldenkrais advises that learning entails 'time, attention, and discrimination', and to discriminate 'we must sense', and sensing cannot be developed 'by sheer force' of will.

> The exercises here are intended to reduce effort in movement, for in order to recognise small changes in effort, the effort itself must first be reduced. More delicate and improved control of movement is possible only through the increase of sensitivity, through a greater ability to sense differences. [*Awareness Through Movement*, p. 59]

Like Feldenkrais and Dewey, Lamb argues against a system of learning and examination which relies simply upon the memorisation and recall of knowledge.

> An examination only fixes the memory faculty at a particular instant in time. The capacity to apply the knowledge memorised depends upon individual aptitudes. [*Movement and Personality*, P. 53]

Lamb warns against stereo-typed attitudes towards theory and practice.

> The distinction of theory and practice is a misleading one; the kinaesthetic sense can be stimulated much more by a sensitive teacher of history than an insensitive teacher of gymnastics. [Ibid., p. 58]

This is not something new: Lamb is as equally opposed to people who teach academic subjects by rote as he is to sports or gymnastic teachers who demand the mindless repetition of exercises. He observes that when a child is forced to run round the pitch 30 times before practising this 'induces in him a benumbed mental attitude'; so when he starts to work on finer aspects of technique 'his eagerness to apply his latent talents has been subdued' [Ibid., p. 62].

> A sensitive trainer may even teach him how to run so that it is relevant to his football. Without such good fortune the boy may be unable to regain the sense of meaning needed for the ballwork. He finds himself doing the same thing over again; making the same mistakes. [Ibid., p. 62]

Whether being asked to run around a pitch or recite one's 'times-tables', the result is the same: a form of education that is meaningless and consists in unregenerative repetition. Worse than being meaningless, it dulls the child's eagerness to develop a curiosity about themselves and the world. As Feldenkrais puts it: 'Learning in the most general sense, is acquiring new responses to stimuli.' [*Body and Mature Behaviour*, p.38]

There are other forms of education or training that are equally meaningless. He considers how one trains animals and people to perform in the circus. Train a horse to fox-trot on its hind legs and it will return to its habitual way of walking on all fours after the dance: this is a trick that is completely isolated in its life. Lamb offers a comparison: 'Gymnastic feats like double somersaults are, for the great majority, a trick, as meaningless to them as doing a fox-trot with its hind legs is to the horse.' [*Movement and Personality*, p. 94] He goes on to argue that 'a skill achieved without forcing carries qualities of co-ordination which will be of significance in other situations whereas a skill achieved only through forcing is fixed upon its object and has no worthwhile 'carry over'. [Ibid., 95] Feldenkrais argues that we develop through learning in an exponential pattern: by learning we bring into play more parts of the brain, thus stimulating growth and increasing the capacity for more learning.

> the human brain is such as to make learning, or acquisition of new responses, a normal and suitable activity. It is as if it were capable of functioning with any possible combination of nervous interconnections until individual experience forms the one that will be preferred and active. [Ibid., p.40]

Lamb wants an education that enables a student not to reproduce the same thing over and over again, but, as Feldenkrais indicates, to create new things.

> The ability to compose a run, jump and turn, in a disciplined form, suggests that the skill of running or jumping or turning could be adapted to an everyday situation. [*Movement and Personality*, p.97]

This brings us back to the example of the history-teacher who possesses more feeling for the kinaesthetic than a gung-ho gymnastics teacher. The attitude that 'toughness and robustness, for example, developed through gymnastic feats and games makes men tough and robust in "life"' [ibid, p. 99] simply results in a coarsening rather than a quickening of our sensitivity – it results in muscle-bound and inflexible human beings. Lamb is seeking a training whereby a person is equipped to 'adapt his attitude to each situation which confronts him' [Ibid., p.102].

He develops this argument by giving the example of a civil servant who didn't make full use of his potential in his job. Lamb argues that his career decisions might have been more informed had he been more 'aware'. 'The criterion is the degree of awareness and, of course, this does not necessarily mean a degree of ambition.' [Ibid., pp. 74 - 5]

> The education of the senses which enables this realisation of potentiality makes life richer and more enjoyable. [Ibid., p.75]

Education is not something that happens just at school – it is, or at least should be part of our continuing everyday lives. The fault doesn't just lie with schools that offer a limiting concept of education, that limits the potential of its pupils, but also with psychology: 'The great discoveries of psychological research during the last fifty years have almost left untouched the question of realisation of potential capabilities.' [Ibid., p.76] Lamb sees that neither education nor psychology have furnished us with the means of getting the most out of ourselves and our lives. Without the full exercise of our senses through acts of discrimination we live less-fulfilled lives because we fail to understand all that we can be as individuals who are unique:

> Conscious knowledge of these distinctions can help a person to know what his individuality is; what it is which distinguishes him from the rest of mankind. [Ibid., p.86]

However, when it comes to creating individual profiles and personality assessments Lamb is modest in his claims:

> So it is a bold and foolish assessor, whatever his technique of observation or testing, who claims to be able to assess people's character or to be able to give a character reading. All that can be attempted is some relative quantitative and qualitative analysis which is again made relative to the situation. [Ibid., p.126]

This is consistent with his approach to examinations and tests. Beginning with *Movement and Personality* (which he proposed retitling *Analysis for Personality Assessment*) and all through his career we will find him rejecting the very notion of a test. A test is too limiting because it sets out in advance what can be learned about someone – it offers a limited and limiting picture of what it is to be human. When Laban and Lawrence changed their Personality Assessment to a test, Lamb resigned in protest. When his partners in Action Profiling chose to offer Tests rather than Profiles, Lamb resigned – from his own company! – in protest. Lamb is interested in what the person can become through developing a greater awareness of movement – he is against any form of education or examination that will limit a person's capacity for growth.

PART ONE ~ EARLY DAYS AT THE ART OF MOVEMENT STUDIO

Introduction to Part One

In this section Lamb reflects upon his life after he was demobbed from the Navy in 1946 at the age of 22; how he became interested in the work of Rudolf Laban; and how this took him to Manchester to study at the recently-opened Art of Movement Studio. These autobiographical reflections are followed by his memory and his assessment of Laban, as a teacher of movement, as a healer, and as a profound and provocative thinker about the meaning of human movement. This section ends with excerpts that Lamb has made from diaries written between 1947 and 1949 which, despite their fragmentary nature, offer a vivid account of his life and activities.

In the autobiographical sketches, *The Movement Man,* written in the mid-1990s he offers a few more facts about his early life.

> I discovered when I was 23 that I wanted to study movement, that it was a fascinating subject and one for which I had some sort of aptitude. The interest arose from my involvement in amateur dramatics which led to a fortuitous meeting with the man who became my inspiration and mentor, Rudolf Laban.
>
> I had recently been demobilised from the Royal Navy at the end of World War II and was unsettled about my choice of career. I went to study with Laban and after a few months saw his surprised reaction at the depth of understanding I had of the subject. I feel that in the subsequent 45 years or so I have succeeded in conveying that depth of understanding to only a few people. Few recognise the immense scope of the subject or the value of studying it as a discipline in its own right.
>
> One problem may be that the concept seems too broad. Claiming to be a 'Student of Movement' seems dangerously like claiming to be a 'Student of Life'. But when we talk of movement we mean this in its strictest sense. If a person moves his arm forward, for example, there is no question that it can be observed as forwards and not sideways or upwards, and if the movement also accelerates or decelerates this, too, can be observed. Elementary observation indicates the way movement can be studied as a practical discipline, it is a simple, logical step to the observation of more and more complex forms of movement. The genius of Rudolf Laban was that he codified the components of movement in a way which has made such a disciplined study possible, exemplified, for example, by his creation of a notation for recording movement now known as Labanotation.

Right from the beginning of my time with Laban I wanted to be multi-disciplinary - to apply movement study as a common denominator to many different activities. It surprises me now, in view of the difficulty we had in gaining acceptance for Movement Study, that I was able to work in so many fields, be treated with reasonable respect, and even be paid. My job in those early days was to observe movement, to use Labanotation to record it, and to explain what I had observed.

Soon after meeting Laban I announced to my astonished parents that I had resigned from Lloyds Bank and enrolled at a place called the Art of Movement Studio. They were incredulous and, of course, tried to persuade me to cancel the whole project, my mother wrote me a note saying that she had often supported me against the wishes of my father, but this time she believed he was right and she implored me to think again.

I had always been restless as a bank clerk, perhaps because I arrived there by default. The day Britain declared war on Germany, 3rd September 1939, I was about to return to Wallasey Grammar School for two years to study for university entrance. In a fervour of patriotism I tried to enlist, but at sixteen I was too young and so I decided I might as well get a job. My father had been unhappy working in a shipping office and advocated banking or insurance. I could not understand the difference, but he explained that banks and insurance companies were far superior to shipping offices. A few applications quickly led to a job and I found myself commuting by ferry across the River Mersey to a big block of offices, the local HQ of Lloyds Bank. A year or so later I managed to get into the Royal Navy, and five and a half years after that, my romantic patriotism assuaged, I was back at the bank and very restless.

It is in the nature of young people to be restless and returning to my old job was the simplest option while I looked round for something else. But I threw myself conscientiously into the work and did well. I was in the Executor and Trustee Department of the Bank, which I thought a degree more special than the banking side. It had its amusing moments, particularly the work relating to the law of trusts. I recall that when only sixteen I was going through a deceased person's possessions and discovered a set of obscene photographs!

But in the end it was an office job. Had I known then that a lowly bank clerk can rise to be Prime Minister as John Major has done, I might have been inspired to stay as I was already active in post-war politics as a member of the Young Conservatives, and helped Ernest Marples to be elected to Parliament. Amateur drama also consumed a lot of my spare time and had any talent been recognised perhaps I would have been tempted to make the theatre a career. Fortunately I was realistic enough to see this was not the case, but it was through drama that I met Laban, and after that I had no time for politics. Everyone is tempted to look back and speculate "What if..." When I do so I view my bank job with much more respect than I did at the time.

It would seem to me, however, that through all these early years before I entered the world of Laban, I had a natural kinaesthetic appreciation, a faculty for looking at the world in terms of movement. It accounts for my immediate response to the nature or Laban's work, and the instinctive feeling that this was to be my career.

Memories from school days and the war years come back to me now essentially in terms of movement more than anything else. The frequent beatings I had from F.L.Allan, Head of Wallasey Grammar School for making jokes at the expense of student-teachers, meeting my first girlfriend on a country walk, helping an elderly lady whose house had been bombed, a Chief Petty Officer panicking on board ship in the Mediterranean, the soldiers I met in Cairo prior to the Battle of Alamein - the list is endless - and all recur in my mind as pictures of movement. They are like dance sequences to me. I cannot remember the words spoken, or details of the scene or the names of the people, but I could easily recreate the 'choreography' of the event. In order to describe them adequately I would need to write them down and for this it is necessary to understand movement notation.

For example, I recollect the choreography of the Headmaster wielding his cane on my hand with a slow lifting then aiming, a quick eye movement and a carefully measured increase in pressure. Then there was the rising, free-flowing approach of my girlfriend; the darting movements of the lady whose house had been bombed followed by a flexible slumping; the sharp angular movement and erratic floor pattern of the Chief Petty Officer; the swaying then flinging then emphatic clanging of the group of soldiers - all these I could easily recall and record in musical notation score, just as musicians are able to record in musical notation sounds or tunes which they have carried in their heads for years.

Laban's recommendation that I should enrol at the training centre recently set up by his student Lisa Ullmann, while he himself devoted time to my training, had to be implemented. My war service gratuity, all £62 of it, would pay for one and a half terms' fees. So I arrived one bleak November day at the shabby room above a noisy printing shop in the drab, war-damaged All Saints area of Manchester, which served as home for the Art of Movement Studio. Over the next three years I experienced more creativity, imagination, thrill, vision and excitement than I have known since even from arts establishments housed in luxurious buildings with lavish facilities.

In chapter three of *The Movement Man* Lamb reveals that when setting up the Art of Movement Studio (AMS) in Manchester, Laban and Lisa had wanted to call the studio 'The Basic Movement Studio', but the name 'Basic Movement' had already been registered by someone else.

> What's in a name? In this case, I think a lot. The concept of movement being an 'art' is very different from being 'basic' and might have encouraged an impression of its being effete, arty, fanciful. When I heard about this some time later I thought it a pity that the magnificent concept that movement is a common denominator, and that we can all gain from training in movement had been partially lost by this change of name. [3 -4]

This change from Basic to Art is important for a two reasons. Firstly, Laban had always insisted that the course at the AMS was what might be called a Foundation Course in movement, *after which* students could then specialise. Secondly, Lamb has always striven to demystify the field of movement study, and to deal with everyday movements.

Chapter Eight offers a significantly more detailed account of how Laban helped Lawrence over what would now be described as the Post-Traumatic Stress Syndrome that he suffered, following his fighting in the First World

> Laban's capacity as a healer arose not from any mystical talent or religious 'laying on of hands', but from his penetrating recognition of the essence of a person's individuality. Like so many people before him, especially women, Lawrence felt here was someone who thoroughly understood him and on whose every word he was prepared to act. It made him, as it had others, feel much more of a whole person - less fragmented, more sure of himself, realising a greater potential for what he would do with his life. [Chapter 8, pages 5 - 6]

He also guesses at what Laban might have thought of him developing the work on Industrial Rhythm into the Board Room

> Whether Laban would approve of my having taken movement study into the managerial field I doubt. He had still hoped for a resurgence of movement choirs bringing thousands of workers together for soul-uplifting movement and dance experience, restoring their sense of individual dignity. Mine was a different vision - establishing the common denominator of movement so that its disciplined study could contribute to a wide range of human activity. [Chapter 8, p.12]

Finally I want to cite a passage which argues for the continuing importance of Laban's (and his own) ideas, and the need for them to be understood and acted upon in the 21st Century:

> Much of my life's work has been dedicated to helping people become aware of their distinctive pattern of movement so that they can, truly, be free. I think the times are right for a new Laban, or perhaps a recognition of what he promoted. A greater appreciation of the importance of movement to our physical well-being would mean a lot of both physical and mental suffering could be avoided. Most people have to endure a restrictive environment to some degree. Requirements of work, climate, economy, responsibilities confine all but the most fortunate to some extent. ...An understanding of our own particular movement requirements would help each of us to strengthen our identity.' [Chapter 8, p.14]

Although the diaries at the end of Part I consist of very short, often ungrammatical or unfinished sentences, they really should be read with some detail. There are several very important themes that are dealt with in these notes. Firstly, there are reflections upon education: he argues (as he will argue at greater length in *Movement and Personality*) that education is not a linear development, but that this line needs to broaden in the middle, and then narrow and focus upon a particular specialisation. There are valuable descriptions of what and how Laban, Lisa Ullmann and Sylvia Bodmer taught, including specific exercises, notes for improvisations, and principles of movement. Again and again we see these teachers stress that they are imparting ideas and principles, but that these don't add up to a System. We are given an insight into a developing approach to education, not some finished programme that was being rolled out for the nth time. He touches on the tension between the students there for the One Year course in Physical Education, and those there on the Three Year course in movement. There are also notes about his own development as a teacher – Lamb wrote down with care Laban's detailed criticisms of him. Finally, there are vivid descriptions of life at the Studio. Maybe these diaries should be read again after having read through the whole book – then the references and ideas will have more meaning and life.

THE INTERVIEWS

i.   *Finding out about Laban and the Art of Movement Studio*

Just at the time that World War II had ended and nothing much was happening I'd got interested in drama and a group of us got into doing Shakespeare and stuff in the hanger of the aircraft carrier on which I was serving. I didn't really look upon myself as a talented actor or with any potential as an actor but I carried on after I was demobbed. There was a group in Liverpool which really did extremely good work and one of the people there, Edna Green, had been interested in Theatre Workshop. We went to this lecture on the work of a man called Rudolf Laban and though I didn't know anything about him I became fascinated by what was being said, particularly the notation that seemed to me to be a very significant achievement. Edna and I did quite a lot of research over the next few weeks. I was avidly going to libraries, looking up books where we could find any reference to Laban, and talking to the people in Theatre Workshop. I remember reading about him in Coton's book *The New Ballet* (1946). I increasingly got the impression that this was a man who was highly revered. I learned about what he had done in Germany and the more that I studied the more impressed I became.

Edna and I also went to a weekend course by Theatre Workshop at Ormesby Hall in North Yorkshire. They had been offered accommodation by a man who was the epitome of Colonel Blimp – at the very opposite end of the political spectrum to Theatre Workshop! His wife, Ruth Pennyman, was the one interested in theatre and who had persuaded him to take in Theatre Workshop. It was a very uneasy arrangement, but Theatre Workshop had the space to run courses, although eventually the colonel did force them to leave. At that course I did learn a lot more about Laban. I remember talking with Howard Goorney and Ewan McColl, and learning about Laban's teaching of movement in theatre, his reputation in Germany and what he stood for. I should say that I had some very interesting conversations with Joan Littlewood and McColl. I can't remember anything specific that I took from the Theatre Workshop conversations but feel sure that they will have said that here is a man of great achievement, with a lot to offer the world, who should be better known. All that made a great deal of sense to me - I was looking for confirmation of what I had found in those books I had read.

Of course, before I went to meet him I had no idea about the industrial work – that came as a complete surprise – and, naturally, I had no idea that there might be a career here. I think I was impelled by a feeling that in Laban there was something truly original. Maybe I needed something new and original; I think I am attracted to things that are a bit different from the routine.

ii.   Laban in England – from Dartington to Manchester

I met Laban at the offices of Paton, Lawrence and Company in Manchester. It was because of Frederick Lawrence that Laban moved to Manchester. He was actually both an engineer and an accountant. His consultancy company was a success in the late 1920s and '30s and he was invited to Dartington to advise them on some of their enterprises – mainly horticultural and agricultural, along with packing of produce. He must have been doing some form of motion study.

Dartington really was the launch pad since that is where they met. I don't know how Laban started taking an interest in what the workers at Dartington were doing in their various enterprises. He had been interested in Germany in crafts, so that was already in his range of interests. Whether he asked the Elmhirsts if he could start taking observations of the workers at Dartington I don't know. Somebody suggested that he might meet with Lawrence, and they met at Dartington and Laban started giving advice about picking cherries. The problem had been that after a time the cherry-pickers tended to get dazed, so he recommended something that made it possible for them to avoid that. Then Lawrence started introducing Laban to other clients, the Mars Bar factory, the Manchester Ship Canal – they worked together during the Second World War. He created the opportunities for Laban to go into factories. He firstly created a method called 'Lilt in Labour' which then became Industrial Rhythm.

iii.   Frederick Lawrence – his philosophy and outlook.

Lawrence was a farsighted man and started his consulting firm in 1923. He was, I think, probably the first management consultant to set up in England, although some had already existed in America. However he was not a good businessman in the promotional sense. He formed what was really the first business school in England but didn't promote it and since such schools weren't understood in England at that time, it lasted about a year or two and then closed shop. He did many advanced things but wasn't very good at marketing: things might have grown more rapidly had he been.

Lawrence confined himself pretty much to the field of industrial business but his vision did inspire and give confidence to Laban, certainly in the first year or two of their meeting. I think they met first in 1942. I am sure that Lawrence's support was very important for Laban. Lawrence formed an important part of creating such organisations as the Laban Guild, the Art of Movement Studio, and he was on the Trust that was formed at that time to buy the property at Addlestone where the Studio moved in 1953, and then to Goldsmiths in 1973 when Marion North took over its direction.

I used to spend a great deal of time with Lawrence and regret having lost touch with him in the years leading up to his death in 1982. I regret that more has not been done to acknowledge the part that he played and to recognise him. The moment he had been introduced to Laban at Dartington he could see the respect he commanded with the Elmhirsts – Leonard and Dorothy - and he immediately saw the potential of Laban's ideas. By the time I had come on to the scene there was no doubt about his dedication to Laban.

I only met Lawrence after I had enrolled in the Art of Movement Studio and was already studying movement. He really had a vision of what Laban's work could contribute to the world. Particularly, he was interested in industrial engineering and method study. He had on his staff three or four industrial engineers who were particularly involved in method and work study. At that time the work of the American management consultant Taylor[1] and that of Gilbreth[2] was influential in this country. Gilbreth had developed a form of notation that was called 'Therlbigs', which is his name spelt backwards. This described the operations that workers performed - for example transport load, grip, release and such like - for which signs were given and thus developed into a notation. It was dedicated to reducing a manual job to the smallest number of units, cutting down the amount of activity, because it was believed that the briefest and shortest time in which the operation could be performed meant greater productivity in the course of the working day.

Laban proved that this was not really the case, because very often production was interrupted by the workers having to take time off, suffering from stress, reporting in sick, absenteeism increased, labour turnover was very high. Laban proved that when workers could embody their individual rhythm into the operation, even though they may take a little longer, production would increase over time, because there would be less stress, less absenteeism and less labour turnover. One would have to say that Lawrence was at the root of this vision because it was he who directed Laban into this type of method study. Much of that is still incorporated into what industrial engineers do. Of course the work that Lawrence was involved in at that time was primarily repetitive work which doesn't exist so much now as a result of automation. Nevertheless, there are certain types of production such as food preparation where

---

[1] Taylor, Frederick Wilmslow (1856 – 1915) was the first to make a scientific study of industrial production, publishing The Principles of Management in 1911.

[2] Frank Bunker Gilbreth (1868 - 1924) was born in Fairfield Maine and became a proponent of Taylorism. With his wife and collaborator, Lillian Moller Gilbreth, he sought to understand the work habits of industrial employees and to find ways to increase their output. His method was founded on trying to identify 'the one best way'. He also used a motion picture camera, which was calibrated in fractions of minutes to time the smallest of motions in workers.

there is a lot of repetition. With so much manual work being outsourced to China, India and other places and where the workers have to labour from early in the morning to ten at night one wonders how those Asian workers are coping with the sorts of problems that Laban addressed in his work with Lawrence.

Lawrence's staff regarded him as 'a bit off his rocker' for engaging Laban, as one of his engineers put it. They were all mesmerised by Laban as everyone was, given his guru-like character. But I found it a hostile environment when I was alone with any one of these engineers. When Laban was around they were polite, but otherwise they were really very demanding in an aggressive way: they would want to see what I was noting and what it meant. They asked questions in a very sceptical manner.

Among the sceptics at Paton-Lawrence was Daniel Ellis, one of the engineers, whom I shall describe later. He was very much a Type A personality – someone driven to go for his objective with aggressive single-mindedness. Such people are prone to have heart attacks. Type B personalities tend to be less aggressive. This corresponds very nicely to the difference between those where effort as opposed to shape predominates. I talk about Effort Assertion: and those who are type A do take more initiative from Effort than they do from Shape. Type B people who take initiative for structure, appropriateness and who are less aggressive tend to be more shape-oriented. Another man called Carslake was less aggressive, though he was very sharp and intelligent and he and I worked together quite a lot on team-building.

That was very difficult for me for a year or two, after which they all became enthusiastic supporters of the work. That gave me quite a lot of confidence. Lawrence was farsighted and also perceptive. He looked up to Laban a lot and felt that Laban had helped him. He had had a hard time as an officer in World War I and suffered some kind of trauma as a result of the horrific experience. He believed that Laban helped him to handle this trauma. This was another example of Laban's healing power and no doubt assisted in them becoming good friends – they became very close. There's no doubt that Lawrence could see a great deal of potential in Laban's ideas. They wrote a book together – *Effort* (1947) which is usually accepted to be mostly Laban's but I think that Lawrence had certainly a very big hand in advising and correcting it. I heard someone say that Lawrence hung on Laban's every word but I don't think that this was the case: he would have probably contributed quite a bit in discussions with Laban.

Of course, accountancy was also part of Lawrence's skills: he was what was then called a 'cost and works accountant'. The Institute of Cost and Works Accountants has since merged with the Institute of Chartered Accountants. MacDonald and Evans published his book called *Marginal Costing* which revolutionalised costing and the principles that he outlined in it are still in application. Thus he was also a visionary in the field of accountancy.

Lawrence took offence very easily. Anything that he felt was critical of him was regarded as an insult. It was this that killed the work that Ellis and I were doing at Glaxo, and most successfully so. A follow-up in similar Glaxo factories looked a distinct possibility and the company had become a long-standing client. Lawrence met with the Chairman of the company, a man called Wilkins, to discuss the proposal to develop the work, but something must have been said to upset him, because there was a row and that ended everything. He was very touchy and took offence a couple of times at things I had said, though I had had no intention of offending him.

iv.   Working with Daniel Ellis at Paton Lawrence

Figure 1: Ellis (centre) and Lamb (right) with a client at Paton Lawrence

Daniel Ellis, an Industrial Engineer, was brought up on stop-watch studies, and aggressively pursued increased productivity from the employees of client companies. Ellis was outspoken in his scepticism of everything to do with Laban and openly referred to Lawrence as being "round the bend" in attempting to introduce Laban's work into industry. However, he was loyal. When told that a Laban apprentice was coming on the scene to make assessments of people in client companies for which he was responsible, he gulped but complied.

One of my first assignments was with Broadhead & Graves, a manufacturer of fine worsted material in Huddersfield. So Ellis and I found ourselves driving from Manchester over the Pennines in his ancient, underpowered car, with him fretting and cursing because we were so slow climbing hills. New cars were still almost impossible to find so soon after World War II. He barked challenging questions at me about how was I supposed to help him, and how was he supposed to introduce me to the client, what was this "movement stuff" I was supposed to do, how could it contribute anything and how on earth could a student from a place called The Art of Movement Studio know anything about industry? He could understand learning to be a "ballet dancer" (this with an explosive sneer) although, personally he had no time for ballet, but what did that have to do with people running looms or administering an office?

I was ill-equipped to answer these questions having had less than a year's training much of which was of no relevance to this new challenge. Obviously Laban believed in throwing people in at the deep end. I had been sent on account of a paper I had presented at the end of only my second term at the Studio, in which I surprised Laban by my depth of understanding of his Effort teaching. Armed with this understanding and with clip-board at the ready I plunged into the weaving shed and started observing the workers using Effort "graphs" (a form of notation).

Periodically Ellis pounced, looking over my shoulder and demanding, "What had I got?" and "What did it mean?" Away from the noise of the weaving shed which made conversation impossible, I tried to explain that this worker was different from that in the way he handled threads. Ellis wanted to see. So back to the shed we went and I pointed out the differences, hoping the workers were doing more or less the same movements. Ellis thought perhaps he did see something, but still had an element of doubt.

I could ask questions too. For example, was a highly Directing Effort needed to place the thread (I would demonstrate), how much pressure was required in tying a knot, was speed important - in brief what were the essential movements without which the job could not be done? These were expressed mostly in phrases of combined movements. From the beginning I was against giving a generalised description. Most Laban students would define movements only according to his Eight Basic Efforts (see p.67). I felt it was necessary to be more precise in movement descriptions for industrial purposes. Working with Ellis a detailed specification of the job was drawn up and this could then be related to my observations of the workers. Their movements were classified according to Laban's categories of Functional Actions, Shadow Movements and Body Attitude. I think I used aesthetics more than anything else to determine which of the workers' movements fitted most closely the movements in the job specification, and wherever necessary my observations and findings were subsequently checked by Laban.

There was a sufficient element of science about it to appeal to the engineer in Ellis, although I am sure in the end he was won over mostly by the accuracy of my assessments of any worker's productivity, and the fact that it was based purely on movement observation. We disagreed on the Motion Study principle of training workers to do the absolute minimum movement required by a job, and I think I eventually convinced him that some workers could be more productive by including in their total bodily rhythm or phraseology some movement which he would have regarded as unnecessary and therefore to be eliminated. This point became more significant later in the case of workers doing highly repetitive operations.

It was also at Broadhead & Graves where Ellis was putting in a new costing system that he asked if I could advise on the suitability of an Office Manager. He knew that Laban had offered assessments of managers and I was certainly prepared to have a go. I used the concept of Attention/Space, Intention/Weight and Decision/Time to ask questions about what was required. I probably amassed about forty or fifty requirements of the job, all in movement terms. This exercise set the pattern for my general practice and all subsequent specifications I drew up would be at least this length. I observed the Office Manager on the job and made my analysis of him. I was pleased to find later that I made the same analysis from observations taken at an interview. I matched my observations against the specification and offered Ellis advice on the man's relative strengths and weaknesses for the position. Ellis was so impressed he always subsequently called on my advice in appointing key people in client companies. I gained a lot of confidence, and I had made the vital jump from observation and assessment of manual workers to the observation and assessment of managers.

Another job that Ellis and I did together was with Glaxo at Barnard Castle. There were about 300 women doing about 25 different operations in the filling and packaging department. Many of the operations were highly repetitive; I remember one required an operator to do nothing more than press caps on vials of penicillin as they passed by. I made observations of all 300 or so workers and specifications of the 25 operations. On the basis of matching the one with the other we reallocated a majority of the 300 women to different jobs. This was done overnight and was met with the resistance to be expected to such major change. We persisted, however, and everyone settled down, achieving an increase in output of over 30%. While critics attributed the increase to the effect of giving a lot of attention to the workers in this case the increase was actually maintained.

Ellis eventually became a great supporter and advocate. He asked to play a part in the foundation of the Laban Guild and offered his services as an administrator to a number of Laban activities, even though he continued to challenge me. His death was a great loss to the cause.

v.   Meeting Rudolf Laban

Laban advised that I should enrol in the Art of Movement Studio which had been newly established by his pupil Lisa Ullman and that he would take an interest in me. I did that immediately. What I hadn't realised was that he had there and then earmarked me as a potential apprentice in the Industrial work. He didn't pick me from hundreds of potential apprentices, he just saw a potential in me. He and Lawrence were looking for someone for that work, I came along, and they took me on. Whether he initially saw any special talent in me, I don't know. He probably thought that I was a raw character that he could train and develop me into suiting his needs. It was a question of supply and demand: I was the only person in the supply chain that was around. Maybe he did see something in me – he did have a very penetrating understanding of people's capabilities and potential. Maybe he summed me up pretty quickly as somebody who could be trained.

Laban did have a reputation for being able to understand people almost at a first glance. Women particularly felt that he had penetrated into their innermost being in the advice that he gave them and that he had understood them in a way that nobody else had understood them. That gave him something of a guru-like manner. And he himself believed himself to be a healer. There are stories of Laban being able to get people to move, almost like Christ, and they were cured. Mary Wigman[3] in her writings has referred to Laban's talents as a healer. This was always present in his manner – it was part of his charisma I suppose. In my work with him I recognised his manner but I certainly didn't want to emulate it, and had no ambition to be a guru. I wanted to have a practical understanding of movement and to be able to demonstrate through observation and analysis whatever meaning can be extracted from movement. Laban's pronouncements were accepted as coming from the Master and it is true that they were often very penetrating. What Laban did through his perception I do through hard work!

---

[3] Mary Wigman, (1886-1973), was born Karoline Sophie Marie Wiegmann, on November 13, 1886 in Hannover, Germany. In 1910, she enrolled in School of Rhythmic Gymnastics at Helerau (outside of Dresden) where she studied with Émile Jaques-Dalcroze. At the age of 27 (in 1913), Mary began studying dance at Monte Verita under Rudolf Laban. Soon after that she began creating her own choreographies which won her the reputation of being a pioneer of ausdrückstanz, or expressionist dance.

Coming back to Laban as a guru, I also believed him to be a genius but that said, I didn't worship him, I didn't hang on his every word. A lot of what he was discussing seemed to me to have a great deal of mystique about it.   A word he used a lot was Cosmos. He would talk with me quite a lot about his Space Harmony research, and he really believed that he was touching on something that was of immense, epoch-making significance and that nobody else would have much of a glimmer of what he was talking about. This seemed a bit superior and far-fetched to me. I got the impression of a man who explored and rambled in a way about all sorts of things, many of which were mystical. Nevertheless he came out with some brilliant ideas in what he conceived to be possible, like his Notation. He was extremely creative. It seems a little extreme to put it in this way, but out of a lot of waffle would come these incredibly brilliant and penetrating ideas and concepts, all of which if adopted, could enhance people's experience. It seemed to me that people did not understand movement as much as it would be helpful for them to do.

The question of Laban having had any connection with the Nazis never arose when we were with Laban at the Studio. Remember that these were the immediate post-war years and there were still a lot of people who had been bereaved and had suffered a lot. So you would have thought that there would have been a lot of ready objections to Laban, had there been any evidence of his Nazi-leanings. We all had the impression that he was a refugee from the Nazi regime. One reason it never arose was that Laban seemed to be such a ray of light, offering a future, and creativity. He was somebody who gave people hope and confidence in the future. I really believe that he was naïve enough to think that he could influence the Nazi leadership into his way of looking at life, movement and individual creativity.

Remember that Manchester in 1946 was still a very bomb-damaged city. The area of All Saints where the Studio was situated was very close to an area that had been almost completely destroyed. There was very much an environment of struggle: rationing was still on.   The premises that they took in Oxford Street, was a slum and almost derelict. In this post-war environment of struggle and reconstruction with people trying to repair their lives, Laban seemed so poised and above it all. Laban himself had experienced things which could have rendered him bitter, but he never displayed this. I never detected this. He used to fall ill quite frequently but never showed any bitterness.

vi.   Life at the Art of Movement Studio

Lisa Ullmann wanted to train people and she and Laban set up the Art of Movement Studio. As they were living in Manchester because of Lawrence, that is where it was based. Laban himself had no formal role and refused to allow the Laban Diploma, coveted by students in Europe between the two World Wars, to be awarded. When I arrived a few months after it opened there were about twelve students from assorted backgrounds. Fees were £32 a term.

The Other Students

Sally Archbutt	Hettie Loman
Rome Bell	Maureen Myers
Molly Burn	Geraldine Stephenson
Joan Carrington	Claire Sumner
Ronnie Curran	Meggie Tudor-Williams
Mary Elding (Watkins)	Veronica Tyndale-Biscoe

Ronnie Curran

Most of my student contemporaries had a more direct interest in dance. Some were aspiring professional dancers, such as the only other man in the group, Ronnie Curran. He had been trained in ballet, was outstanding in his performance of the Scottish sword-dance, and had been selected by Lisa Ullmann as a dancer of potential distinction. Compared with him I felt awkward and cumbersome. It is a testimony to Laban's concept of "movement as a common denominator" that in the course of time my inferiority complex melted away in favour of an understanding that we could both dance, only differently. Laban claimed that everyone can dance, we only need to search for the form most appropriate to us individually. Hence he believed in teaching a wide range of styles, even including folk dance.

Geraldine Stephenson

It took a little time once there, however, to appreciate the importance of movement as a common denominator, or to understand Laban's principle "You train with me for three years in movement then you decide whether you are most fitted for work in dance, other aspects of the theatre, education, therapy or industry".

The achievements of my contemporaries at the Studio in the late 40s and early 50s demonstrate the wisdom of that principle. Geraldine Stephenson was a good example. She was a conscientious graduate of the Bedford College of Physical Education where, being a ladies' college, folk dancing was on the curriculum. Laban's principles were introduced and their dance syllabus renamed "Modern Dance". Geraldine came to the Art of Movement Studio as a student and found herself doing a lot of teaching. Had she not enrolled with Laban she would probably have become a physical education teacher instead. As it happened, she had her basic movement training and gravitated towards the theatre. She developed a repertoire of beautiful solo dances which she performed extensively. She also produced many pageants and acquired a reputation as a choreographer for many theatre, film and TV productions.

Valerie Preston Dunlop

Valerie Preston came a bit later, April 1947 I think, because I remember thinking of myself as a fairly experienced student when she arrived. In my own case I wasn't aspiring to become a dancer, but I did become a member of Hettie Loman's dance group, but more by accident than design, because I happened to be a man who was around the place.

The Curriculum

During my six months initial training at the Studio I valued the teaching of Lisa Ullmann particularly. Any concentrated teaching by Laban of me happened on the job rather in the Studio. It was a very flexible curriculum. The curriculum seemed to consist of whatever talent the students at the Studio fortuitously had. Laban recognised this talent and then you had to apply it. For example, Geraldine Stephenson knew something about anatomy so then we had Anatomy in the curriculum, otherwise it wouldn't have been there.

Everything that they taught in relation to movement either came under the heading of Eukinetics (Effort) or Choreutics (Shape). My use of Choreutics is simplistic because I had been earmarked by Laban as an Efforts man. That did influence me in my comprehension of Choreutics, though I do remember doing studies utilising the three-ring and such like. We were asked to create a choreography on a particular theme, and then re-introduce it in another level, high or low. I remember Lisa and Laban sitting in rather an intimidating way watching our pieces.

Eukinetics and Choreutics would very rarely come together - they were more or less kept separate - except for anything that we did on the Diagonal Scale. This was very complex as it had six different processes going on. I like teaching the diagonal scale precisely because there is so much in it. I once taught a three-week course in America during a Summer School and we spent most of it doing the diagonal scale in various forms. This was an experiment to see if we could make it into a sort of religion! It is interesting to note that Laban was influenced by Gurdjieff[4] (see p.32) – who really did mix religion and movement – and at the Art of Movement Studio we were all encouraged to read his books. He believed that learning Folk Dances was good for learning about different cultures. We also had Observation.

The Teachers

Rudolf Laban

His pride of bearing was evident in everything he did, especially at the Studio. In contrast to the fame and extent of power he had enjoyed in Germany here was this truly great man, one of the few really creative geniuses the world has produced, teaching in a drab slum area of Manchester and living in a modest terraced house. Yet wherever he went, even among people who did not know his background, he was received as someone of weight and substance. He made pride seem a virtue rather than a deadly sin. This was a quality which translated into inspiration in his teaching. It was evident particularly when he adjudicated students' work. We would present our Choreutics or Eukinetics study to Laban and Lisa sitting together, he proud, dignified and restrained; she effusive, compassionate and eager. Laban would pronounce. Lisa would jump up and demonstrate. Between the two of them my experience was to go away immensely inspired with new understanding.

Laban was much less effective when he chose to lecture rather than demonstrate or adjudicate. He would sometimes go on for three hours or more and the notes I conscientiously made read now as he sounded at the time; poetic, mysterious, with an indication of profound meaning, but without making that meaning clear - at least not to this student.

Laban was a very demanding teacher in his way of getting what he wanted and he did believe in a form of training that approached military drill. I remember him teaching the diagonal scale on one occasion for three hours on end. We were just having to float and punch and glide and slash, and all the while he would be shouting, 'More strength, more strength!' Very often he would come and get hold of you – something that one couldn't do these days. But Laban would get hold of people and try and get them to do the movement that he wanted. He seemed to succeed in doing this. With most people it defeats its purpose, the touch changes what one is doing. But Laban seemed to be able to get into the movement, so that you didn't feel that this was an imposition, something that you wanted to shake off. Lisa Ullmann would do that too and I certainly felt that with her it was an imposition, but Laban seemed to do it in a very heightened, intensive way which you could follow quite spontaneously. But during this three hour session that I was mentioning, everybody was exhausted, they were dropping as he started shouting louder and louder. There was something Teutonic about him. He did put you under pressure to do what he wanted.

[4] Gurdjieff, Georges Ivanovich (1872? – 1949), was a Greek-Armenian mystic and developed his own style of movement. A little like Laban he claimed that the teachings were based in his early experiences and travels, and contain truths and ideas found in other ancient religions and teachings relating to self-awareness in one's daily life and humanity's place in the universe.

Laban was consistently supportive except on just the odd occasion when he would burst out. It was sparked if he felt that anyone was getting a little too big for their boots or if someone criticised him. There were moments when we did feel that we weren't getting what we'd paid for, when neither Laban nor Lisa would turn up. I remember there was an American girl called Caroline Maldorelli. She complained about something and Laban jumped on her, saying that she didn't know anything, that she had no future, and so on. He did the same with Mary Wigman many years earlier – he pounced on her saying that everything she did was unharmonious; but such was her respect for the man that she weathered it. She didn't allow it to influence her. But Caroline Maldorelli left the next day; she went back to America. Apart from these occasional outbursts he was always very supportive, enlightening and helpful. Whenever he spoke to you, you felt that he was saying something meaningful and significant.

There are two contrasting theories on his part. On the one hand was the idea that everybody moves differently and should be encouraged to handle every situation or job in their own way, and thus encouraged to discover what their own way was. On the other hand, of course, if you are wanting to be professional then you really need to train for three years before you can really find what your own way is. So in the context of professional development you had to do the movements according to what he laid down and the standards that he was applying. I completed my three years with him in 1950.

Lisa Ullmann

Lisa Ullmann was very much more down-to-earth, but like Sylvia Bodmer, she was very movement-alive. She was quite bubbly but she did keep you very much focused on what she wanted – quite the opposite to Sylvia. If you had been asked after a class what you had done you would be able to spell out that this was done, and that it was related to that, and then a new element was introduced – and so on. It was practical in that respect. She was a wonderful teacher. Her classes were some of the most inspiring that I have ever attended. Her teaching was inspirational. She would give you specific guidance on what you could do and why and how you could make it better.

Lisa made her own contribution to the teaching at the Studio. I disagree with Valerie Preston-Dunlop's biography of Laban where she claims that Lisa could never do a thing unless she had notes and instructions from Laban: that's not true. Maybe Laban might give Lisa some ideas to pursue but she was herself very creative in how, as a teacher, she developed those ideas. I think that Valerie found a lot of notes that Laban had written for Lisa, but that doesn't prove either that she followed them, or that she didn't give lessons without notes. I'm sure she had lots of ideas of her own. She had a mind of her own. Lisa was extremely loyal to Laban but she would disagree with what he said – perhaps not publicly but certainly in smaller groups. She would question and was quite a stimulus to Laban in that she helped him develop his own ideas. I think we should recognise her as making a much greater contribution than Valerie Preston-Dunlop has presented.

Lisa would take over from Laban whenever he took ill. I often enjoyed comparing Lisa and Laban. He would sit there very charismatic and aristocratic, extremely poised. If there was a judgement following a piece of work that we had done, his opinion could be damning but it didn't give you much help other than knowing that it was good or bad. Lisa would come running up and indicate how something that you'd done could have been done better or differently so as to be better. Lisa was very responsive to what the students were doing, while Laban tended to be his dignified, aristocratic self, making judgements and prescient points. Lisa was much closer to the students, getting hold of them and moving them. We were manhandled quite a lot.

Sylvia Bodmer

A teacher everyone loved equally with Lisa was Sylvia Bodmer, a former student of Laban's and a dancer from pre-war Germany. Her intensity and participatory zeal was almost overwhelming, and often she inspired students to go beyond their imagined capabilities. Sylvia was a loquacious, very active teacher and was almost air-borne in the way that she taught. She created an environment in which you felt that you were almost floating and flying as you responded to her ideas. Sylvia was most entertainingly wild. You couldn't help but be fascinated by her. There was never a dull moment with her. It was mostly bewildering, but also remarkably enjoyable. You never knew quite what was being expected of you but what eventually emerged was extremely pleasurable and fun. I think to pass a test on what you had done with her and learned would be extremely difficult!

Summer School at Dartington Hall

While at Dartington Laban and Lisa Ullmann started Modern Dance Holiday Courses, a vehicle for inviting people to come together and dance for the joy of it rather than for theatrical presentation. I attended one and made my first visit to Dartington in the summer of 1947. As a relative newcomer to the world of dance, I was inspired by the experience. Much of the time we were able to work outside in the beautiful grounds which formed the ambience of Dartington. The charisma of Laban, and the teaching talent of Lisa Ullmann, all combined to create a truly exceptional experience. In the half century since then I have attended many movement courses of one sort or another, and although sometimes the teaching has been good, rarely has the experience come close to that imparted by Laban and Lisa Ullmann working together.

With the influence of Laban and that of Jooss[5] still very much alive, Dartington provided the ideal environment for gaining movement experience, for thinking in terms of movement, for enhancing the kinaesthetic sense - all the things which I have since grown to believe are vital elements of the teaching of movement. It belonged to the community, it looked so right, it was natural: as natural to some degree as it was natural for Laban at Ascona to dance to the dawn and to fall into dance many times during the day - dances associated with meals, with work, with relationships, with play, with celebration, with need and finally, a dance to the Queen of the Night.

vii. On Movement Choirs

When Laban, and to a similar extent Lisa Ullmann, did their movement choirs, they included much spontaneity. You never really knew what was going to happen. A number of people would gather - twenty, fifty, a hundred, a thousand - and Laban would organise them a group here, a group there, a group somewhere else. He'd use pretty basic terms: one group to be very small and confined and grim-looking; another group expansive; another group very much looking for something. Each group would have a pretty clear understanding of what they were supposed to do to start with but then one never knew what was going to happen, and it was that uncertainty as to what would happen next that was to a great extent the attraction. It only remained an attraction of course if what happened next was exciting. There were some failures. Lisa Ullmann particularly would have off days, though I never knew Laban have an off day; he always seemed able to rise to the occasion and get people moving.

So he would have the searching group finding something, changing their looking to focusing on some particular direction. He would have the confined group becoming much more open and into discovery. And then he'd have the live group getting angry and thumping the ground. Having got change happening within the different factions in the group then he'd have them begin to inter-relate. The group that was becoming open would get to meet the group that was becoming firm and angry about something. So something would happen from that and Laban would see immediately

---

[5] Kurt Jooss (1901-1979) was a German dancer and choreographer. A student of Rudolf Laban, he is most famous for his 1932 ballet The Green Table. In 1933 he and his entire company escaped from Germany and found refuge in Dartington where he also continued his school. Lisa Ullmann was part of the company which explains why Laban was offered refuge in Dartington in 1938. Like Mary Wigman his dance was characterised as expressionist. When his school was re-established in Essen after the war, one his students was Pina Bausch.

and would start to structure it and get the group more spread out, or into an arrow formation, or a circle. Then the shape element would start coming into it: the arrow-group would start approaching the circle group. Then, of course, there would be the third group – there usually were three groups in Laban's movements choirs – and they would begin to have an influence. Then perhaps the groups would get mixed up. It was really exciting and you were doing real movement.

Laban was taking cues from his very acute observation of what was happening with the group. Other people trying this would create chaos very quickly with groups all running around not knowing where they were supposed to be and what to do. They began to get outside the momentum of the group, and giggle and have conversations – all of which was extraneous to the choir. That never happened in Laban's choirs. I think it came about because he very acutely observed what was happening at the moment that it began. He would fashion it in some way to be constructive within his overall structure, and structure itself was constantly changing. It's a good illustration of his sensitivity to both Effort and Shape. These were both coming from the group and he showed how he could shape them to create a composition.

Sylvia Bodmer's forte was movement choirs - getting large numbers of people together to move/dance for their own recreational pleasure rather than for any sort of performance. Sylvia was successful in promoting recreational dance and we students often found ourselves participating and, perhaps, trying to give a lead. Invariably there would be a point in the activity when everyone came together in a tight bunch, forming a knot prior to opening out and spreading in some way. This always seemed to me uncomfortable and redolent of a central European style often mistakenly associated with Laban. Mention Laban to many people and they picture strained earnest movement with a powerful earth connection. While there was some vestige of that heavy style, and Sylvia was the biggest offender, I felt it was unjustified to connect it to Laban. He adapted incredibly well to post-war British culture and his strength was to draw from whatever people were already doing and build on it, rather than to impose an external style or technique. Dance dates incredibly quickly as anyone who has studied contemporary dance over the past fifty years can confirm. Laban tended to be ahead of the times, influencing which new styles developed. He was not in favour of people performing established folk dances, but preferred to create a truly contemporary form of "folk" dance, appropriate to the times.

Today the people that I know who are doing movement choirs tend to even meet in advance and prepare it thus blurring the distinction between a movement choir and choreography. This may be interesting. It does seem to me that movement choirs have evolved in this direction of much more recreational dance. I always thought that spontaneity was the root of the movement choir experience. I have thus found it difficult to enjoy being in the movement choirs in which I've taken part over the past few years mainly because of this lack of spontaneity.

viii. Laban and Movement Education in England

There was a lot of interest in how Laban could offer influence in the education world, both in Physical Education and in Dance. Lisa was the person who got hold of the education idea and really followed it through, but Laban supported her. Of course, he did write a book called *Modern Educational Dance* (1948) in which he developed 16 movement themes for teaching children at different age ranges. What's interesting to me is that you'll find that the first eight or nine themes, more than half the themes, up to the age of eleven or twelve, are all Effort. It's only when children are approaching puberty that he begins to suggest that they should shape their movement. It's clear that he is aligning the teaching of Shape with dance, whereas prior to the age of puberty, the concentration on Effort seems to be that children want to do things rhythmically, initially perhaps in a primitive sense. There is an alignment of rhythm from the cradle to puberty and shape and dance from puberty onwards. Laban's idea was that a child's body should be educated fully, so that it got the fullest possible experience of movement harmonies, of Eukinetics and Choreutics at the appropriate age-stage so that eventually with this awareness of the whole world of movement the child could grow and mature into activities, of sports and work with a much better understanding of the body-mind connection. That has not happened. It is beginning to happen in the field of recreational dance.

It surprises me that Laban didn't think that teaching Shape to young children was appropriate. There's no doubt about his conviction and his desire to promote movement in education. But of course he was also promoting movement in industry. I don't like what he was doing being confined to industry. Since I'm associated with that aspect of his work it makes me feel that I should be wearing a boiler suit! I try to make the correction that it is really about management and work that Laban was interested in rather than just industry. Laban was very dedicated to a philosophy where movement was a common denominator to every activity whether you mention sports or work or playing chess – he would find that his approach through movement would have some relevance.

There is no doubt that Laban was totally sincere in all his initiatives to try and encourage the teaching of movement in schools. I recall conversations with him where he made it clear that Lisa was doing well. Laban was charming and gallant and really seduced all the schools inspectors. One of them, Myfanwy Dewey took a close interest in the

Studio. She lived nearby and attended everything that she could: end-of-term presentations, and that sort of thing. It was sometimes like Myfanwy was an adopted daughter of Laban. From the very, very revolutionary work that was being done in a lot of schools, especially those where people like Myfanwy Dewey and Ruth Foster (another of Her Majesty's Inspectors, or HMIs) had a direct connection, my expectation was that movement teaching would replace physical education. These were very powerful people in the field of education and they succeeded in creating a revolution.

A new syllabus was created in 1947 and two publications came out, one called *Moving and Growing* and the other called *Planning the Programme*. The first was for Elementary school-children and the second for Secondary children. They had some wonderful photographs of children doing really lively, adventurous movement. Everybody believed that this was how the teaching of physical recreation was to happen. But then it all got fouled with an argument between the physical education people and the dance or arts people as to whether this belonged to the arts department, or to physical education. Laban and Lisa didn't really care - from their point of view it belonged to both. People like me questioned why a distinction needed to be made in the first place – movement belongs to itself, and to life. But the boundaries between the two departments were hard and fast. That argument lasted for years.

One of the arguments of the PE people was that Laban was trying to replace Physical Education. That meant that we would no longer have Olympic-quality athletes coming out of these colleges. But Laban's principle was that, just as you came to the Art of Movement Studio to study movement for three years, and then consider whether you want to dance or teach or do therapy, similarly he believed that children should be educated in movement in their school years and when they got into their mid-teens they might begin to think about becoming a professional tennis player, or go in for athletics, or some other specialisation. But he was against specialisation at an earlier age. Of course if you want to develop somebody into a Wimbledon tennis champion you've probably got to get hold of them at the age of three. So this was an argument that weighed heavily with the physical education people.

I feel depressed that the categorisation of Physical Education from the arts or dance is as hard and fast as ever. While children might be taught a bit, given a few more opportunities for dance in a recreational setting, but it is still categorised as dance and physical education remains something very separate. Whether there is ever a prospect of movement education being embedded in the educational system according to Laban's dream, I don't know. All the current evidence is that there is a great emphasis on sports and that funding in this field goes to the sports, and to encouraging specialisation so as to develop sporting champions.

On a scale of being free or not free, there is a totalitarian tendency to inhibit people deliberately so as to conform. I think that there is a fear on the part of those in charge of education as to whether we can trust people to express themselves. I think that a lot of teachers don't want things to get out of their control. I think there is a lot of repression, actually. A lot of people on the streets don't know how to move their bodies. Just as I have a problem with new technology so one finds people who are unaware of how to make their bodies work and function. I would dearly love there to be a reintroduction of that revolution that happened in the late 1940s with a new syllabus. I may say that I am excited by sports, but I have also said that I can foresee in years to come people will be going to big stadiums to participate in movement choirs rather than go and watch a soccer match. This of course is very extreme, but it might happen!

I used to go to the Carnegie College of PE for Men in Loughborough, replacing Laban. I think Loughborough was very 'old school' but they had an enlightened principal who was very torn between a curriculum that would attract students to go with the trend – but he did invite Laban to do some teaching there. I used to go there twice a year for a visit of about a week over a period of about three years. I couldn't do some of the feats that the students were capable of doing, but I used to set the students simple movement sequences that I could demonstrate and which they were quite awkward at. I don't know that it is a good thing to make your students feel awkward, but I did this deliberately because I wanted to expose that, as rigorously trained as they were, nevertheless here was a simple coordination that they were having difficulty with. It provoked great argument which always divided the students about 50/50 - on one side there were those who said that this wasn't PE; they were athletes and had nothing to do with dance and such messy stuff. Whereas the other half were impressed with my course and would say that at the College they didn't learn flexibility, or how to move their bodies so as to adjust to life: the teaching just concentrated on the specialised PE regime. That was the sort of argument that was pursued.

This wide-ranging application of movement was something that interested me very much. Laban used to say that movement was the common denominator in many activities and this common element interested me. I tried to prove this by teaching at a boy's school for two years as well as working with actors, PE students, running my individual courses, and giving sessions in movement therapy at St Bernard's Hospital in Southall. I worked with the head of a department of medicine at University College who believed that doctors would benefit from having a training in movement. So long as you didn't try to assume abilities that you hadn't learned within your training as a movement professional you can contribute to a great number of different professions.

However, I would say that Laban's first love was the theatre. Originally his first entrée into theatre did come from studying art at a school of art and architecture. Dance came from that. Certainly his interest was in dance performance. But quite quickly he developed an interest in dance as recreation in the sense that everyone is a dancer. Everybody uses rhythm in movement; everybody structures their movement to some degree, so everyone is to some degree a dancer. Then of course, when he came to England he came more to theatre and to acting. But it was theatre as a whole that he maybe felt most attached to. Although in terms of his allocation of time in the twenty years he spent in England, I reckon about 95% of that time was spent in activities other than dance performance. But if we take into account his activity with theatre as a whole - he also liked to design theatres and quite often played around with such thoughts – maybe one should say it's more like 85% of his time. He did say to me that it was very convenient for him to have Lisa Ullman look after him and support him, and he wanted to help her to become established in the education world. But the way that he said it suggested that it was more of a duty than a desire.

ix.   The Therapeutic Dimension to Laban's work

Much of what Laban did was generalised, but his genius was to recognise the individual need within that. In Movement Pattern Analysis work we have learned to realise that we have to be very discriminating in every respect and that what may suit one person might not suit another. Everybody is different and we need to be discerning and specific about what those differences are. Whether this focus on the individual is politically acceptable today I don't know: the cult of the individual is often decried as being a bad thing. I would hate to think that I was putting people into slots.

The extent of Laban's influence in England and how it grew was astonishing, even accepting that he came with a reputation from Germany. He developed a link with a woman called Irene Champernown who had the Withymead Centre in Devon that specialised in Jungian therapy. In those few years during and immediately after the war there was such a breadth of interest that spread throughout England: in Education, Industry, in Theatre and in Therapy.

The Jungian approach to psychiatry really spread in that time – even though it was anathema to Freudians. One of the psychiatrists who became quite a close friend was Culver Barker[6]. He used to go to Switzerland to talk with Jung, and would come back

---

[6] Culver Barker was a Jungian psychoanalyst who practised in London in the 1950s and '60s and used to convene meetings where a wide variety of topics were discussed. Lamb and his then wife Joan Carrington were close friends of Barker. His most celebrated book is *Healing in Depth*.

and say how interested Jung was in Laban's ideas about movement. He was very much in favour of incorporating many of Laban's ideas into Jungian practice. I have a note in my archives that Joan Carrington, my first wife, who came to the Studio, gave a lecture with me to a group of at least 15 Jungians. I remember some of the questions. I did a lot of work with Dr Barker and another Jungian psychiatrist, Dr Lottie Rosenberg who became a friend of the family. As I've already said, Laban did have a reputation for being a healer.

Mary Wigman writes about Laban's healing hands and his touch. She tells the story of a woman who was crippled and confined to a wheelchair and he got her to move and so discover that she could rise out of the wheelchair and walk. Laban liked to think of himself as a healer; whether this was more from a mystique element, or because he used his intuition in movement, or both. Veronica Tyndale Biscoe (Sherborne) carried this work on and developed some students who continue it. I remember that recently somebody gave the Laban lecture for the Guild on her work.

Then there were other things like Bioenergetics: Alexander Lowen[7], is still alive and practising at the age of 93. This is rooted in the biochemistry of the body and different cycles of what goes on in the body. But it is rooted in an understanding of energy and owes something to Wilhelm Reich[8] who in turn was very influenced by Laban. Reich devised what he called an Orgone Box into which people would go to create energy. When I was in New York I went to visit Felicia Saxe at the behest of Laban: she was a partner of Reich at that time, 1953. Although I was there to take a message from Laban to this woman, I talked with Reich and it was obvious that he was very indebted to Laban. Basically his aim was to generate people's creative energy – whether his link with Laban movement comes from the Orgone box I'm not sure but there was a big sexual element; it was very much to do with dynamic energy. Of course Reich was judged to be insane and was incarcerated for the last couple of years of his life. In this field of therapy I am detecting quite a large amount of interest in Laban. This expansion is quite remarkable and quite desirable. Some contemporary dance therapists are publishing articles that are very rigorous in their research, some dealing with particular problems of children, autism for example. Janet Hamburg is working

---

[7] Alexander Lowen, a student of Wilhelm Reich's in the 1940s and early 1950s in New York, developed the mind-body psychotherapy known as bioenergetic analysis with his then colleague John Pierrakos. He is the founder and former executive director of the International Institute for Bioenergetic Analysis in New York City and is still practicing at the age of 93. [Based on an entry from www.Wikipedia]

[8] Wilhelm Reich (1897 –1957) was an Austrian-American psychiatrist and psychoanalyst, and a member of Sigmund Freud's inner circle. In the 1930s, Reich said he had discovered a physical energy, later called "orgone," which he believed was contained in the atmosphere and in all living matter. His views were not accepted by the mainstream scientific community. [Based on an entry from www.Wikipedia]

with people who have Parkinson's disease. Therapists have developed a particular application of movement study to specific needs.

I was talking earlier about the lack of interdisciplinary activity across the border between dance and physical education, but the somatic studies that are happening now are wholly good - and I hope that I have helped this to happen. Somatic Studies is becoming recognised as a field in its own right. It was initially developed in the University of Surrey, unfortunately in the performing arts department – I would have preferred it to have happened in another department. It is recognised at least as not belonging to dance. I am also associated with a course at a college in Chicago which deals mainly in somatics – but from a therapeutic angle. We still haven't escaped from the dance category completely, but some progress has been made and I think in the years to come, somatic studies (which includes Feldenkrais) will become much more a study in its own right.   The interest now into body-mind and the research into the brain can also be coordinated into the field of somatics, to a certain extent. I am hoping very much that somatics will grow in its own right and thus we can recognise Laban's contribution to this field.

x.   Two Therapists: Irmgard Bartenieff and Judith Kestenberg

You could say that through a proper movement education you avoid the need for any therapy. Irmgard Bartenieff was a pioneer who achieved a lot through movement, first working with people who suffered from polio. She escaped from Germany to New York just before World War II.   She couldn't find any work in dance, and that is what led her into therapy work, and she was successful. After doing a course with me she set up the Effort/Shape Department at the Dance Notation Bureau. Then she left the Bureau after a few years and set up The Laban Institute of Movement Studies.   Both Pamela Ramsden and I visited the Dance Notation Bureau. We did have some role in getting the Effort-Shape department started. She herself was a much-loved and very sharing person. She had been a dancer in Europe, but along with other Jews she had managed to escape Hitler's Germany and get herself established in New York. She must have been one of the first people to do movement therapy. Immediately after the Second World War there was a polio epidemic in New York and she worked a lot in movement with Polio patients and achieved quite a lot of success. I was there in 1952/53 and remember spending Christmas at her home and being taken to centres where polio sufferers were being treated and trying to observe her work.   She became a much appreciated person in the field of therapy: maybe she had healing hands. She had a very, very caring touch. When she formed the Laban Institute of Movement Studies there were about twelve people, mostly women, who were very devoted to Irmgard.

One thing that has happened at the Institute is that after having begun by offering courses in Effort-Shape, then Laban Movement Analysis; now they offer training in BESS: it includes "Bartenieff Fundamentals", a system of exercises which is looked upon in the same light as Feldenkrais or Alexander.

B is for Body
E is for Effort,
S is for Shape,
S stands for Space-harmony.

This doesn't add up to a coherent categorising for me. In any new theory there is always bound to be a proliferation of new terms but I don't want them to become fragmentary and lose contact with the core. When Laban taught, everything we did was done under the headings of either Eukinetics (Effort) or Choreutics (Shape). BESS muddles different categories: it is like putting together under a course entitled 'Gender Studies', Body, Masculinity, Femininity and Biochemistry.

I remember being with Irmgard Bartenieff and accompanying her to a mental hospital where there was a dance therapist working with an elderly patient who looked very subdued and depressed and was being exhorted to get up and be jolly. The poor woman tried to respond to this goading, but after half an hour I became dismayed to note that the woman was worse off at the end of that period than she had been at the beginning. It was so indiscriminate. The old idea used to be that it was good simply to get people dancing, and that this was good for them. Dance therapists have now become more discriminating with regard to movement factors that apply to different conditions.

Judith Kestenberg was recommended to me by Irmgard Bartenieff. She had approached Irmgard with regard to learning about movement. I don't know how she'd heard about it in the first place. She had heard a lot about movement and wanted to introduce it into her practice. She was particularly interested in child psychology. She had adult clients but was primarily researching into childhood growth – that was her special field. I was in London and she in Long Island, New York and we agreed to do a correspondence course which was remarkably successful. The correspondence course I think went very well and she referred to my method throughout the rest of her life. It obviously made a big impression on her, and she was a very, very good student and learned to observe true movement as opposed to fixed positions.

Then she formed a group in Sands Point[9] (see p.44), where she lived, and created what she called the Child Development Group. There were, I think, five psychiatrists and one psychoanalyst. They met with me one Friday and made observations of children, and they subsequently met every Friday to explore movement observation for the next fifteen years. I attended these Friday sessions on average seven times a year during this time. When we began observing babies in the early nineteen-sixties we would be looking at what we would then have called their shadow movements. Furrowing its brow, burping, being sick – all the things that babies do. But primarily its body seemed to be getting scrunched up or enlarged: it simply grew and shrank. Also it would get into a crying mode when it would become rigid and then it would seem to drop into softness. Kestenberg was really noting the flow of the baby's movement as a continuous pattern.

When I asked about what Efforts could be observed in the newly born baby you couldn't really detect anything in the nature of directing or indirecting; when a baby gets to about a year-old it can start directing movements. I came to the conclusion that Effort and Shape came to the child, layer upon layer, increasing as it got older until eventually you saw posture/gesture merging at the age of eleven or twelve. With young children the whole body is immersed in the Flow of Effort and the Flow of Shape, the whole body moves together. They may be doing a lot of movement, bouncing and bending down and jumping, but you don't see any gesture in the arm or leg, head or foot become merged into a whole. I assumed that the Posture Gesture Merging phenomenon was an indication of adulthood. This of course corresponds to the onset of puberty and to when Laban, in Modern Educational Dance, starts introducing shape into the child's curriculum. Of course this can change from one child, one culture to another – 12 isn't always the age at which these changes occur.

I found these sessions absorbing, I remember once going to an obstetric hospital to observe babies only minutes after they had been born. Then there was a group of children that we followed through their childhood up until the age of 22: they are mentioned in her book. A study of constant movement observation from birth to the age of 22 is I think a very important piece of research.

Kestenberg has linked MPA very closely to Sigmund Freud. She was very quick to see oral, anal and phallic drives. Her concept of drive comes from Freud. Frances La Barre in her book *On Moving and Being Moved* has noted Kestenberg's obsession with

---

[9] Sands Point Movement Study Group, 'began working with a vast array of movement specialists including Irmgard Bartenieff, Warren Lamb, Forrestine Paulau, Marion North, Jody Zacharias, Islene Pinder, among others. Their study focused on the work of Laban and Lamb and extended their applications into the realm of child development. Lamb, a student of Laban, not only enriched the group's knowledge of Laban's work, but also introduced them to his formulations of effort-shape correspondence, flow, and pressure. Originally, it was Lamb who identified the free hand tracings that Kestenberg drew as changes in muscle tension rather than changes in efforts as Kestenberg originally believed.' [*The Meaning of Movement*, p.6]

Freud. But I became increasingly disturbed with this concentration on Freud. I believe the way in which she used movement was tendentious. It seemed to me that she was making it appear that Laban's ideas all came out of Freud – that was her tendency to make it appear that when Laban talked about attention or intention that he really had in mind was Freud. I was very interested at the time in Jung: people in the arts have tended to be more interested in a Jungian rather than a Freudian approach. I tried to get her interested in Jungian principles and also in Abraham Maslow's work but Kestenberg rejected both Jung and Maslow. I think that was a pity. Maslow had the idea that people wanted to act according to their comfort zone but their first requirement was to get food and avoid starvation. Secondly they sought shelter until you gradually rose to the top of your needs which is self-actualisation. I tried to get Kestenberg interested in what was called this hierarchy of needs.

Whilst I was embarrassed and upset by this obsession and her refusal to go beyond Freud in any way, Kestenberg's work is now catching on; it is spreading amongst dance therapists in America and as a result is spreading to Europe. Also many cities in America have Jungian groups and quite a lot of them – some articles have been published on the subject – have become interested in Laban. So there is some renewal there. I gave a lecture to about 40 dance therapists a few weeks ago and it seems they, whilst becoming interested in the Kestenberg work, are not containing it simply within the Freudian doctrine. Now there are several Kestenberg Movement Profilers whom she has trained. This movement profile has some similarities to mine, except that it is rather complex because she creates nine profiles for each client. This profile is particularly used for difficult children and Mark Sossin who practises in New York is doing very good work in helping parents tackle the problems of having overactive children. Susan Loman does most of the training and she works at Antioch College in New Hampshire: she is head of the Dance Therapy department and teaches mostly the Kestenberg work. Just over the past year or so there has been a great boost in interest in the Kestenberg work: more students are enrolling, and it is now spreading to Europe. Although it might have seemed uncertain in the early days it is now becoming quite well established.

Extracts from Warren Lamb Diaries 1947 – 1949

October 1947　　Book 1

Laban　(Lecture at Art of Movement Studio)

The trend of our times is to indulge in larger movements, to imbue life with dynamic factor - in education, sport, art —Sadler's Wells and "Miracle in the Gorbals" etc.

The Studio is, as it were, the centre of this modem dynamic trend - a trend which is growing flexibly, is continually being adapted. Studio curriculum and our conception can never be a 'system' in any way. We must always have the greater philosophical view and application of the vast sphere of movement.

Contemporary movement based on Far Eastern movement a degradation

Education now goes along a straight line: Start* ——————————— *Finish; but it should first go straight, then broaden out, then there should be a gathering in. This applies to education as a whole on any particular subject.

History of Movement:

Relation of Space, Rhythm and Character to Body, Mind and Evolution. Different kinds of teachers in theatre and in education; one draws something from student for audience, other gives something to. But - similar application of space, rhythm, and effort principles. Principles or ideas and NOT a system. Will as non-existent or explained by attention, intention, decision and precision.

Importance of the diagonal scale to get the 'feel' of the movements as preliminary to choreographic composition.

History of Movement. Greek ideal of beauty, and analogy with contemporary P.T. - muscle tensions and relaxations, counter balance

Teaching Practice - The Meaning of Education. My definition - Education is the application of knowledge, experience and intuition to ourselves and others towards a greater understanding of the art of living. Many varied conceptions, all necessarily narrow. Most people have too narrow a conception. Example of individual or member of society, or compromise. Significance of the art of movement in teaching a proper balance between extremes (e.g. gathering and scattering) and a spontaneous yet well judged reaction to all stimuli.

Education as forming character - what is 'character' - and 'personality'?

Psychology and philosophy in education.

46

December 1947

The Studio party last night was spontaneously a success. Mr Laban's presence I think was responsible. Valerie and I think we might co-operate in our spare time earning money through industrial rhythm. Laban thinks so too and is going to help us. We await expectantly. I feel presumptuous because of my meagre experience but feel that I am being closely watched by Laban and Miss Ullmann and may confidently await developments.

Laban wasn't at all well and should have stayed in bed. Miss U. who looks after him very tenderly was very worried about him. But I think L likes nothing more than to be among people who idolise him, and the students couldn't do so more. But his reaction to the hero worship is very modest.

I was surprised to find the flat where he, Lisa and her mother live rather bleak and not very tastefully decorated. It would not appear to be like the home of a great man - yet what truly great man would surround himself with Twentieth Century conveniences and gadgets?

Biggest surprise at the party was the beautiful women. I am used to seeing my fellow students in the raw and little appreciate how attractive the girls can make themselves. So many women have so little idea how to make up but almost without exception these girls made up and dressed fully utilising their natural endowments and achieving a very satisfying effect. (Satisfying is perhaps not the word to describe the effect which it provokes.)

Said I before the party
  -   Let's welcome Mr Laban in a special way.

Replied Mary, characteristically,

We'll all lay down in the nude and let him walk over our naked bodies.

I wouldn't advise that for Mr Laban but you might arrange it for me
  -   Depends on what your reaction would be.
  -   I should stop where I was most attracted.

Mary to Hettie
  -   He knows all the right answers

Hettie:
  - I knew it. I could tell the first time I saw him. He hasn't been in the Navy for six years for nothing.

- No Hettie - I learnt a lot of seamanship.

..... and the subject was dropped.

Book 4   Around June 1948

Lisa Ullmann: ... that youth must be selfish. Theory that 'balance' is always to be aimed at, but that it need not be a harmony of everything all the time and it is good, for instance, for young people to throw themselves into something in which they become completely absorbed.

Laban: Rhythm - cohesive medium that brings together all the components of effort in their correct proportions. (It is) a cohesive medium giving beauty and shape.

Book 5

Laban; Plato's observations on proportional inter-relations (The Timaeus) due to laws of bodily movement. The order of the cosmos. Fundamental shape - the triangle - theory of proportion and has conditioned every concept of proportion - theory of proportion and space relations at the back of all structure and applicable to human anatomy.

The space element, the regularised mathematical shape, which absolutely expresses the harmonious correlation between all the possible movements of the head, limbs and torso is the ICOSAHEDRON.

Laban quoting the Law Giver of Athens: 'I wish them (the women) to perform the same exercises as men that they may equal man in strength, health, virtue, and generosity of soul, and that they may learn to despise the opinion of the vulgar.'

Laban: The dancer expresses the truth as he perceives it and does not express himself. Laban emphasises dynamism - "Anspannung and Abspannung" or the ebb and flow of muscular impulses or dynamism

Book 6   1948

Train journeys with Laban:

1. Movement in Education. Academic Action

2. Efforts in voice - need for using vowels; Englishmen emphasise consonants

3. Laban's personal accomplishments - influence of movement research upon some millions of people - need for travel - better to influence deeply and gradually, than advertise Studio etc.

4. New approach to drama through understanding of nervous system - need to give this approach to school teachers of drama - symbolical and realistic

5. Interview assessments - need for special observations. Industry through rehabilitation

6. Fundamentals of movement

Movement   Elements

Action process Operations

Given as introduction to Leeds (Carnegie College of Physical Education) survey.

(Laban's) criticisms of me: Take bigger steps when walking. In drama – audience: when they should be affected (are overwhelmed by sentiments) when they should understand. Need for more space observation along with effort observation.   Avoid 'Mephistopheles' voice when teaching.   Teaching must develop from what the student is able to do.

Book 9 1948
Teacher Group

Laban instructs NARROW-WIDE

Analogy of knot - how one can knot a scarf - ability to tie; knowledge is preserved by man alone - expression in dances of Red Indians and others. Narrow tension of walking holding pieces of paper under elbows and between knees, pushing forwards and backwards with thumbs.

Arm extended sideways, hand pressed back (middle finger leads)

Contrast - weak extension of whole body

Dance Circle

Theme: break away from group, conflict, reformed into group Start immediately - 'new world' whirling alone, partners, small groups, form big groups - 'Billowing' - becoming stronger - break away of small group - 'billowing' into large circle. Sssshhh...ing in group - choral speaking come 'back' rising to climax as close in on small group - fight - 'billowing' away - group choral speaking 'dark' and 'remember' - large group subsides small emerges - large 'billows' away into close group - small; rejoins - is closed in

28th Oct

Miss Bodmer on Expression

Danger of forming set rules, opinions, theories etc. (cf. masculine and feminine movement)

Sensitivity in men is NOT a feminine quality

Our experience of swaying in circle, hands lightly touching — different feel of different people - men's swaying quite a different quality to women's. Any movement can be performed by man or woman. Difference is in expression. Man can perform same shape as woman's movement with varying effort, or same effort with varying shape, and effort of flow comes into both. Is Flow the secret of difference between male and female?

Classical ballet is sexless - our need to preserve contrast male and female in our movement and dance - makes the whole spirit of dance.

Studying one's reflection in mirror is good so long as you know how to look, i.e. with expression.

Significance of composition of group - at the Studio vitally affects our work.

Must be aware of effort of changes in the group.

Wigman has developed womanly qualities in her style of dance.

Definition of Dance

Laban:

An actor will stamp his foot realistically

In dance drama the foot will be stamped rhythmically a number of times

In pure dance, the whole dance will be built upon the quality of stamping, yet the foot will not be stamped at all.

Symbolism of gestures

Laban on my observation

My need NOT to be so wrapped up in my own ideas as to affect my power of observation

Progress graphs of students should be in the form of sequences of characteristics showing habits of combining effort elements, certain favourite rhythms, and relation to mental efforts.

I never do a peripheral movement - could be employed especially in transitions in class

Relations with P & L [Paton Lawrence & Co.] Staff (Extract)

At present (November 1948) he [C.D. Ellis] demands that I make a kinetography time observation so that he can use it for his own, and what I consider quite unjustifiable, purpose. I can do in hours what would take him weeks, and this facility seems to him the whole aim and purpose of Laban's methods and of training me. I consider it a debasement of my capabilities and ideas, and foresee little hope of ever working satisfactorily with his co-operation.

Technique of Expression

Theme of condemned man in cell, friend who is really guilty visits cell – condemned man disdainful – friend pleads – man forcibly reproaches – friend frantically pleads, is repulsed – goes slowly away – man sorry for his outburst – is left alone again.

Performances varied between:

Dance (pure movement)

Dance-drama (enlarged and shadow movement)

Acting (shadow movement)

Expression of emotions:

Fear, Disdain, Contempt, Pride, Avarice, Sloth, Covetousness, Vanity, Expectation of Joy.

The Dance – The Kinneys

From the bible:

"Praise the lord … praise Him with Timbrel and the dance"

"…of the daughters of Shiloh come out to dance in dances, then come ye out of the vineyards, and catch you every man his wife … and the children of Benjamin did so, and took them wives according to their number, of them that danced, whom they caught" (Judges)

"Thou shalt again be adorned with thy tablets, and shalt go forth in the dances of them that merry" (Jeremiah)

"And David danced before the Lord with all his might" (2 Samuel)

"But when Herod's birthday was kept, the daughter of Herclius danced before them, and pleased Herod. (Matthew). Whereupon he promised with an oath to give her whatever she would ask."

The STARS conform to laws of co-ordinated movement.

Greek Gods:

Cybele taught dance to the corybantes

Apollo

Orpheus journeyed to Egypt to study dances

Sophocles danced around the trophies of the battle of Salamis

Aeschylus and Aristophanes danced in their own plays

Socrates danced among friends after dinner

Anaeneon declares, in his odes, he is always ready to dance

"Before logic, man knew emotion; before creed, ritual."

Moses bade the children of Israel dance.

Thursday 13th October 1949

Training went very well. I somehow adopted an attitude which encouraged the students really to work hard and enjoy it. I start with some vague intention and either develop it with my own invention or use some appropriate exercise I recall Lisa or Gerry has used – but I don't necessarily use it as it was taught to me. Today the class included examples of both – plus some statics[10]. The statics I sandwich in the middle and not at the beginning as Gerry does.

The development of yesterday's exercise I hadn't planned but in a moment of inspiration I incorporated it with an exciting rhythm and without losing sight of my original purpose. This is the sort of thing Lisa means by the art in training, and which she does habitually. I'm sure I couldn't have found such a rhythm had she been

---

[10] Exercises performed on the spot

watching, but I hope I may do in the future because it has taught me the sort of 'outlook' the trainer must have to facilitate the proper creativeness.

Dance Styles. Claire did some style – I know not which – but it was fun!

Observation. I taught very laboriously. I wasn't at all satisfied and must really try to think out some new ideas for my teaching.

Rehearsal of "The Crows", "The City" and a new dance for four men (how Hetty loves choreographing four men all at once!) from 2.30 to 6 during which time I was continuously dripping sweat – and enjoying myself immensely. The men's dance is purely an affair of showing off skill, agility and manliness, and why not? This was the function of much primitive dancing. The dance has no intensity – but much toil and sweat goes into the performing of it. I thought something like this might go down well with the PT experts at Leeds.

Leeds College of Physical Education. I discussed with Laban, immediately on his arrival home from Bradford. He was too tired to concentrate and asked me for all the ideas, either accepting or refusing them. I stressed a lecture giving a broad survey and stressing practical application of work and sessions starting with effort elements leading to basic efforts, the cube, effort rhythms and group work. He made notes of all my ideas - and will probably appear next week with completely new and superior ones of his own.

I told him how Dewey H.M.I. is going around telling people I'm not properly developed yet and teach only because there are no other men available. He agreed she is a lot of harm and remarked, "she's a cow".

Friday 14th October

Training, for once I was being trained, but not by Lisa, as I had hoped. Claire found a good exercise sweeping across and open, standing jump and down on one knee stretching arm and leg. Then she repeated an exercise Lisa once did – and didn't get on well. One can borrow ideas from other teachers but should never copy exactly.

Scottish Dancing was a substitute class taken by Ronnie. He danced brilliantly and continuously an Irish/Scots jig. We were stimulated but he taught nothing. As a class it was a waste of time.

Music History. Gerry lectured uninspiringly. Her technique of lecturing always the same and seems forced. I had to fight to avoid falling asleep.

Lisa's productions, started last week in my absence, in a sort of dance-mime to music for 5 groups; one representing 'personality' and the other 4 'power', 'envy', 'earthly love', and 'spiritual (something?)'. All have distinctive qualities of movement, influence each other and form varying patterns around the 'personality' idea. It will work out successfully, I think, and is the only exposition of dance mime which has really impressed me.

Lisa exercised the qualities of two of the groups and more or less made a training class out of those ideas. I often work in a similar way with drama people – only Lisa was able to carry the training much further. She has accepted – within her scheme – our own improvisations – which is exactly how a dance mime should be built up and what Gerry never does.

Personal relations at the Studio are being reduced to conflict between the dancers and the educationalists. This has always been so, especially when Hettie started doing things. Usually the educationalists give in to the 'theatre' attitude generated by the dancers. Not so an ex-training college teacher who finds Studio classes a come-down and Studio life degrading and refuses to give anything during classes and needs to be spoon fed. Our somewhat Bohemian existence offends greatly. Hettie's productions are called 'footling dances'.

This sort of thing has always been a danger with having public school teachers at the Studio & has existed before to a lesser degree. There is constantly a danger of the Studio changing its character to the extent that an art group will be unable to function. But we are determined not to give an inch.

Saturday 15th October

Industry from 9 to 11.30 I make observations from 7 interviews of candidates for job study technician position. I then went to the Studio for Rehearsal which was really a run through of several ballets for the benefit of a man from Leeds University. I have never danced so shabbily. I knew I would but could do nothing about it: perhaps if I'd had a moment to relax I could have composed myself, but everyone pounced on me, hurried me while I undressed and rushed me into my position for the Stravinsky. Just to make the change-over from industry to dance is exhausting and difficult. When industry has meant 2 hours terrific observation concentration and dance requires as intense but a much varied sort of concentration, one or the other must suffer unless I'm superhuman.

What depresses me is that always it is dance which suffers.

During the afternoon we rehearsed the Beethoven, with Sally taking over Molly's part. Poor Sally has a tough time taking over parts other people have created. This is an experience I've never had nor should I welcome it. It was wonderful to be doing the Beethoven again. Hettie's choreography is here at its most excellent. It is impossible to do the movements without becoming really 'in' the dance.

Quoting Laban

Need in teaching is to give both Practical Training (consciousness), Dance or movement experience (primal consciousness).

The teacher, therefore, needs both the movement experience and the bodily and verbal understanding of effort and shape to develop both in children.

Overdevelopment of the conscious means underdevelopment of the primal conscious & restriction of self expression.

Laban mentions that ballet without music performed in Balkans provoked spontaneous great applause (people have great tradition and richer primal consciousness).

In Berlin intellectual audience calmly applauded - talked about staging effects etc.

In Paris consciously emotional audience destructively criticised.

Further example:

Frenchman is disturbed by coughing in audience - ruins his pleasure. German notices, forces his mind to forget it. Balkan never hears the coughing - revels completely in performance.

Male and Female movement

Effeminate movement in men caused by contrast, e.g. arm stiff and hand light & flexible

Laban's lectures to Manchester University Students' Union

First lecture mentioned everything vaguely, confused everybody, but Laban's own personality was forcibly projected (he gave a brief life story – related many personal incidents). Students did not apply themselves nor did they learn anything. They enjoyed the lecture, went away thinking what a wonderful man Laban is (NOT what a wonderful thing the study of movement is).

Second lecture gave more detailed account of industrial application and some students were stimulated to perform efforts. They didn't enjoy it as much but learnt more.

Miss Bodmer - Individual approaches

Valerie takes class - asks for concentration on one out of the way part of the body. Pianist plays short theme - we improvise, trying to show part of the body we are concentrating on. Valerie guides composition.

This was NOT an exercise - Valerie gave imaginative stimulus - pianist helped composition. All performances were grotesque - the natural effect when one part of the body is exaggerated.

[Harmonious movement requires interplay of the whole body – concentration of the attention on one part is therefore grotesque. May be one way of deliberately creating grotesque character?]

I specialise (broadly) in primitive expression (!) and movement of the shoulders. Carolyn in sweeping leg gestures, attention upon hips, & 'swirling' inner content Valerie upon distaste for what everyone else is doing, 'stand offishness', originality. Meggie in detached interest in everything, showing off. Hettie upon dramatic intensity and sensuous feeling. Mary upon exotic, erotic temperament, twisted movement performed in direct way.

Laban - Primitive Rhythms

Walking - 2 or 3 steps, - towards centre of circle (fire), outside circle (forest).

Quickening of tempo, using voice.

With shaking of hands - whole body - knees, hips, shoulders

With leaping

With arm movement

Knees open and closed

'Making music', - slapping parts of the body

Solemn walking - leaning back 4 steps, leaning forward 4 steps - walking

kneeling

Arm, shoulder, head, hands, fingers, counter tensions.

Performances much improved when Laban gives clear rhythm

Laban on my effort deficiencies

3 manifestations of efforts
    functional
    dramatic
    dance

I have developed 'dramatic' well - always perform effort with accompanying mood. Dance expression begins. But I lack the functional or implemental because of the domination of mood.

Significance

When demonstrating, the mood can appear sentimental, and when teaching students other than actors, misleading. It also leads to distortions of the body which inhibits expression.

At any rate the functional or implemental manifestation is a necessary part of effort mastery, especially for men, and is lacking in my training because of the preponderance of women at the studio.

The action performed has an expression and significance independent of the mood in which it is performed.

E.g. If I push someone aside with a strong, direct and quick effort, functionally performed, he will be so influenced by the compelling force of the function as to move away spontaneously. The same effort, with same movements, will not have this effect if my mood predominates because it will invoke a counter reaction. This clearly has great psychological importance and must be related to my own life. Obviously I achieve an aim by the function of my actions, and not by the mood invoked by the aim or ideal.

Training

I could recognise the contrast when performing the basic Efforts and Laban stimulated the functional and subdued the mood. At first my tendency was to excuse myself - then I was able to eradicate feeling and perform the effort using my whole body as an implement. Using the mirror as a control is a great help. Speaking appropriate words & comparing contrasts is the best method.

Rhythm

I have a tendency to perform a movement i.e. leaping, which should be practised with the accent alternatively on the preparation & the leap. This can be partly explained that I do not realise a large enough range of bound and free flow.

Laban on my teaching deficiencies

Difference of mobility and stability of movement.

Basic efforts in diagonal scale dance - mobility

Working operations require stable application of efforts involving counter tensions.

I should not assume that everyone is keen to share my enthusiasm for movement - must approach students with their way of thinking.

Drama exercises - with P.T. students; movement character must be clearly and simply given to them and I should not aim that they find their own movement expression.

Demonstration of effort does not require exaggerated body performance - simple functional demonstration must be given.

Book 10 1948/49

First Day of Team Solos

Laban's general survey:

5 aspects of Dance:
    Content
    Composition
    Technique
    Music
    Presentation

No-one had a good presentation. Laban didn't say so but I think the tendency at the Studio is for us to be very conscious of our individual movements and to relate everything to ourselves. Every single solo showed a performer completely immersed in what she was doing and without any contact with the audience. They demonstrated many interesting things about the characters of the people concerned but were not the artistic expression of any idea. Content was usually good but it was not impressed upon the onlookers. We had nothing to give said Laban.

[WL] faults were:

    Too many ideas

    No unity in composition

    Everything performed within (audience were allowed to watch, not meant to watch)

Whole body took part all the time almost to capacity and allowed no build-up to climax
    Dramatic movement needed accompaniment by percussion or voice.

Music can be well chosen and used, content brilliant, composition as flawless as a Shakespeare play, and technique as perfect as years of training can achieve - but without 'presentation' it all doesn't convey a thing beyond the individual banalities of the performer. Valerie's solo was the most obvious example. Her movements were most charming - but they related so intimately to herself that all we saw was the crudity and immaturity of Valerie herself.   I'm persuaded to think that 'presentation' - how we present ourselves to others - is the aim and purpose of the study of the art of movement.

Tasks

Dance with Hettie to Scarlatti

    Laban Dance Drama - sorcerer

    Five rhythm sequence

    "Work and Play" solo

Hettie's ballet

Effort observation class for Group B

2, 8 and 5 study

Perform 'Saltabile'

Bass Dance

Technique of Expression (Dance)

Laban's method:

1. We show 'fear'

2. We show 'fear' as a character

3. We repeat 2. showing more attention to detail (significance of reacting with movement forward - opposite to usual 'fear' reaction)

4. We do 2 scenes with couples involving sudden changes of mood

5. We run through short scene consisting of:
    (a) pedlar selling pies
    (b) old woman buys pie, drops purse
    (c) loafer buys pie, slowly picks up purse
    (d) old woman returns frantic
    (e) pedlar saw theft, remonstrates and fights with loafer and his friend
    (f) old woman fetches policeman
    (g) policeman stops fight; loafer hands purse to woman; policeman takes away loafer
    (h) old woman overjoyed; thanks pedlar
    (i) pedlar arranges pies feeling conscious of his good deed.

Stages of rehearsal:
    Preliminary run through
    Finding movements and building characterisation
    Fitting movement with others
    Performing to percussion rhythm
    Repeat without the percussion but still with the rhythm
    Adapt movements so that audience's attention will not be distracted.

Bodily Technique

All concerns four types of movements:
    Walking (stretching points and muscles rhythmically)
    Running (stretching points and muscles rhythmically)
    Turning various parts of the body in the three planes of rotation

Polonaise

Practised for acquiring 'presentation'
Proud quality of dance - precision of steps.

Miss Bodmer's obsession with proper tension of hips & stomach & seat – relates to Life Force - analogy of plant growing straight upwards - no downward tendency

Floor Exercises

Legs beating
Legs circling open
Legs circling together
Legs apart (sitting) reaching forward, sweeping backwards
Legs touching floor behind head - swinging forward to stand up
On tummy, grasping ankles
On tummy, hands under shoulders, stretching

Laban on Teaching Technique (to Gerry & myself)

Women pupils accept explanation from men, demonstration from women - they are suspicious when a man does - psychological feel that man is always incapable of showing them how to do something (as though he demonstrates how to sew on a button) and suspicious when a woman tries to explain something they feel they understand intuitively.

Space planes:

Circles of	Adoration	-	Door plane	) Variation of
	Benediction	-	Table plane	) to or away
	Command	-	Wheel plane	) from centre

Gerry when teaching Strong and Light exhibited contrasting effort in her facial expression, particularly mouth

In teaching Direct and Flexible I was flexible with my head while body (except elbows!) was direct.

Habits especially exaggerated are often reaction to the lack of an effort quality. Laban has to discipline tendency for sudden brutal outburst which comes as a reaction to 'indulging in' quality.

Movement Expression in the Face

Suitable for Dance teaching:

Experiment expressing anger, contempt, disdain, fear, misery etc. mainly in face. Observe effect of movement of lip, eyebrow, nose etc. & find which feature is the key to the particular expression

Employ in short sequence with 2 or 3 characters

For me personally - acquiring expression first in the face helps expressiveness of whole body

Old people - movement character related to relative relaxation of stomach muscles? Tends to exaggerated L?

BOOK 11
Laban on "What is Dance"

Drawing the line between movement and dance.

Our attempts mostly just movement. In dance - overwhelming inner participation.

Laban's teaching technique;

1. We go up down et seq - jump and fall. Then jump with arms only - hand only - legs only etc. in various directions. Jumping around, eyes fixed on something - running to one place and another - becoming an animal etc. etc. Laban remains fairly still and gives stimulus and rhythm with his voice.

2. We run around in circle - are led or told or pushed to jump over objects on the floor in many different ways. We form couples, are each given movement - exchange places and do other couples' movements. More running about in formation. Laban runs all the time & says relatively little. Although we may not always be looking at him his continuous stepping of the rhythm infects us.

3. Laban tells us a story (Odysseus meeting the sirens). 2 are detailed as sailors in a boat, 2 as the sirens, and 2 as the waves. He stimulates our imagination with many suggestions. We repeat without help. There are three examples of teaching methods with children.

Question - where does dance come in? We consider dance as related to the following themes or stimuli! (are they themes?)

	(Emotion	-	fear
Preoccupation	(A happening	-	a story (see above)
with	(Satiation	-	exhilaration
self	(Mood or dream	-	space emphasis
	(Object	-	real or imagined
	(Other people	-	group feeling

We try individual dances built around one theme or nature (as above) Hettie (fear) and Valerie (dream) definitely approached dance. A 'happening' or 'object' did not seem to lead to dance within our strict definition of the term. 'Satiation' has still to be tried. 'Other people' can be tried in conjunction with other five but stress can be given to the 'flow' of relationships between groups.

This understanding of 'what is dance?" completely negates the conception of dance as an art form analogous to drama where the body is used as a medium of expression between an individual's idea and an audience's appreciation of it, and gives substance to Laban's declaration that all teachers of teachers should dance as well as stage dancers. What he didn't say, but probably believes, is that for stage dancers, including his own, never have.

The key to this conception of dance (which I am painfully trying to discover as I write) must lie in its *symbolic* expression.

"Man has an inner need to express himself symbolically" according to Laban. When one is able to do this in dance then one is, at least approaching the dance posed in the question.

Laban explained that a teacher of children did not need to have had this experience of dance but that a teacher of teachers should. Although children are always led towards dance it is palpably impossible for them to attain to such heights until after puberty and the teacher should think of movement and not dance.

In Germany teachers had attended a two year course, gone out to teach children for two years, then returned to the Studio for a further one or two years' course. Then they might be fit for teaching teachers.

Laban is tantalisingly vague yet this attitude probably provides a greater understanding than any spoken explanation. He's particularly vague about the relation of dance to industry but said something about dance being more obvious in this field than in any other. This, I think, follows from the conception of all XX century machine civilisation as a symbolic expression of man and an individual's symbolic relationship to his particular machine. In the expression of this relationship through movement there must evolve a spontaneous and subtle co-ordination of eukinetic, choreutic, and rhythmical elements without the harmony but nevertheless on a par with dance.

How fascinating becomes the industrial application of the art of movement and how galling that I should now, at this moment, be obliged to write out effort graphs and explanations for Messrs. Paton and Lawrence.

Next class - Past, Present, Future

4 variations -   Body (rhythmic)

Mind (dramatic)

Outside (spatial)

Sensation (Time)

Being oriented towards points & in directions.

Different aspects of music - abstract space better with percussion - player moving as he plays instrument in harmony with dancer

Weight as space time affair

Grotesque Movement

Chin forward, hollow back, chin resting on backs of hands. Wide shape, diamond floor pattern,

change to: Jumping on left leg, left arm high from shoulder, right knee high.

change to: Two small jumps, then high flinging, knees high.

Introduction to Part Two

> Movement in itself is a language in which man's highest and most fundamental inspirations are expressed. We have forgotten not only how to speak this language but also how to listen to it. [*Effort*, p. 65]

This section of the book is a sustained dialogue between Laban and Lamb about two fundamental aspects of movement – Effort and Shape, or, to use their Greek names, Eukinetics and Choreutics. Eukinetics is not listed in the Oxford English Dictionary as a single word: but you can search for its two parts separately. The prefix eu- means 'well' and kinetics is defined as 'The branch of dynamics which investigates the relations between the motions of bodies and the forces acting upon them'. In his book *Choreutics* Laban refers to the efforts as 'variations of natural dynamic activities' [30] and defines Choreutics as 'the practical study of the various forms of (more or less) harmonised movement' [viii]. Although *Choreutics* was published in 1966 it was a reworking of a manuscript written in 1935 and reflects his work as a choreographer and dancer in Germany in the 1920s and 1930s. *Effort* was published in 1947 and reflects his work in the factories with Frederick Lawrence – this book was very much about movement at work and in everyday life, while the other was about the aesthetic and spiritual dimension of movement. One of Lamb's major contributions to Laban-inspired movement studies was to bring Effort and Shape together.

Effort

To begin our consideration of Effort, here are three quotations from the preface which indicate the breadth of Laban's conception of Effort:

> Few people realise that their contentment in work and their happiness in life, as well as any personal or collective success, is conditioned by the perfect development and use of their individual efforts. We speak about 'industrial effort', 'war effort', 'cultural effort', without realising that each collective action is built up from mental and manual efforts of individual people. [*Effort* p. x]

> A person's efforts are visibly expressed in the rhythms of his bodily motion. It thus becomes necessary to study these rhythms, and to extract from them those elements which will help us to compile a systematic survey of the forms efforts can take in human action. [ibid p. xi]

The actor on the stage shows in his rhythmic movements a great variety of efforts which are characteristic for almost all shades of human personality. The actor studies the movements of all kinds of people in real life and what he observes are exactly those elements of bodily motion which are of vital interest to effort research. [...] In watching dancing, our interest is focused upon the visible efforts forming the rhythm in the efforts of any working person. Unconscious effort-reading is the explanation for our belief that we can see the thoughts and feelings shown in facial expression, in body carriage, and in the almost imperceptible expressive movements of hands, shoulders, and so on. [ibid p. xiv]

Lamb will pick up on several of these aspects. In the fourth part of this book, he demonstrates how an understanding of one's own unique movement 'signature' helps achieve greater freedom and joy in one's personal life and greater harmony and productivity in one's working relations with others. As regards the rhythmic aspect of movement, Lamb will insist that movements have to be understood as phrases, as processes of variation, and not as static snapshots. Finally, Lamb will develop upon Laban's statement that the movement analyst can understand the 'thoughts and feelings' of a person through 'almost imperceptible expressive movements of hands, shoulders, and so on'.

Here are two of Lamb's definitions of Effort that will be found in the text below:

Effort can be understood as movement which overcomes inertia.

We can look at Effort in quantitative terms – having to make a relatively large or small amount of Effort. This is very much in our language. We are always in the state of making relatively less, even imperceptible movements, or relatively more Effort. When we are making a lot of Effort we may become aware of the nature of the effort we are selecting.

So far we have only considered Effort in a very general way; now I shall consider how Laban analysed it. Laban proposed that any movement consists of four elements – **Weight, Space, Time** and **Flow** – which combine to create eight qualities of movement, or The Efforts.

Weight can be either Strong or Light

Space can be either Direct or Indirect (in Choreutics he uses the term 'roundabout')

Time can be either Quick or Sustained

Flow can be either Free or Bound

This is how the movement elements combine into the Efforts:

Effort	Weight	Space	Time	Changing
Gliding	Light	Direct	Sustained	
Pressing	Strong	Direct	Sustained	*Weight*
Wringing	Strong	Indirect	Sustained	*Space*
Floating	Light	Indirect	Sustained	*Weight*
Flick	Light	Indirect	Quick	*Time*
Whip	Strong	Indirect	Quick	*Weight*
Punch	Strong	Direct	Quick	*Space*
Dab	Light	Direct	Quick	*Weight*

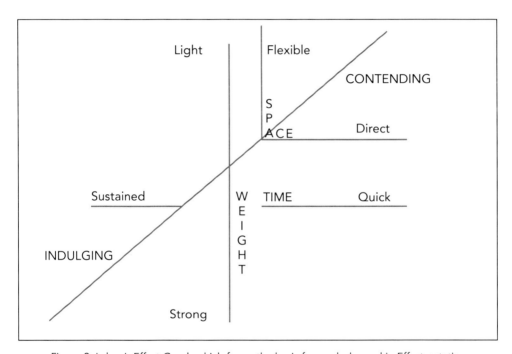

Figure 2: Laban's Effort Graph which forms the basis for symbols used in Effort notation

Laban made two other important observations about the nature of our movement: the first was that one could either contend with or indulge in any of the Effort elements, thus:

One can *indulge* in **Weight** and be *Light*, or *contend* with it and be *Strong*
One can *indulge* in **Space** and be *Indirect*, or *contend* with it and be *Direct*
One can *indulge* in **Time** and be *Sustained*, or *contend* with it and be *Quick*
One can *indulge* in **Flow** and be *Free*, or *contend* with it and be *Bound*

Laban goes on to study 'the attention, intention, decision and precision observable in the bodily attitude of the mental worker' [*Effort*, p. 60]. These 'mental efforts' corresponded to one's attitude towards the four movement elements:

Attention corresponds to **Space**
Intention corresponds to **Weight**
Decision corresponds to **Time**
Precision corresponds to **Flow**

We should commit these 'bodily attitudes' of the mental worker to memory for they are extremely important to how Lamb developed his decision-making model. As concerns the Effort elements they corresponded to, he made two significant changes. The first was to rename them: Space, Weight and Time became Focus, Pressure, and Timing. He explains his decision to change the original terms:

> Laban codified three components: Space, Force, Time. These terms are a little unfortunate because they invite philosophical speculation. [*Posture and Gesture*, p.61]

In *Management Behaviour* the authors display a similar concern when using words to describe movement: 'It is difficult to use words at all without implying an interpretation.' [p.71]

Flow as an Independent Element

The second and even more substantial change – or better, a realisation about the nature of movement - was to realise that Flow was a very different element to the other three. His work with the psychiatrist Janet Kestenberg helped him clarify his thoughts about Flow. Already in **Movement and Personality** Lamb realised that there was a developmental dimension to Flow: that a baby is born unable to frame their movement either in terms of Effort or Shape, but what they do can be understood in terms of Flow. Just as importantly, their development of Effort and Shape is at the expense of Flow: what he called the 'Gain/Expense of Flow against Effort'

> A new born baby is not able to compose any element except Flow. It may react quickly, but an observer will not find any composition or relative variations of quickness. It soon learns to make a strong gripping movement but is not able to compose relative variations of strength. [*Movement and Personality*, p.139]

But:

> He composes relative variations of Free Flow and Bound Flow with an enviable skill and he does it in a distinctively individual way. [Ibid., p.140]

Some have more, some less range in their Flow; that is, some babies are more alive or participative than others (this aspect will be developed later in his fully-developed framework where an adult's flow capacity is expressed as their ability to identify with others).

The sequence with which a child develops Efforts

> As a command over other scales of movement is obtained, and Functional Action is developed (which means a special development of Flow for this classification) it seems that the demands of the modern world - especially in the Functional Action classification - are such as to deprive the growing child of the most elementary, and perhaps the most perfect, skill with which he was born. [...] The preservation of this birthright is essential for a keen use of the kinaesthetic sense. [Ibid., p.142]

Lamb theorised that the baby learns Efforts in the following order: first Force (he will later use the less emotive word, 'pressure'), then Time, and finally Space.

> Observations show undoubtedly that a baby learns to compose positive and negative variations of Force Effort before Time, and of both Force and Time before Space. [Ibid., p.172]

He begins by noting how the baby develops his/her range of force.

> Acquiring a use of the effort element of Force means acquiring a sense of the resistance of one's body to the floor. It is impossible to get away from the pull of gravity (without artificial aid) and the only alternative to remaining inert is constantly to compose in the Body Attitude an effort of Force. [Ibid., p.145]

He returns to the question of Space which he defines in terms of Directing or Not Directing, and notes how the baby doesn't direct movements until the age of one.

> A broad range of Space means the capacity to compose a broad variety of communication relationships, to order and structure responses to other people and so structure one's own effort so as to bring about and maintain effective communication. [Ibid., p.174]

Finally, Lamb used the present participle to emphasise the process of a movement, and get away from a 'fixed-frame' approach. He explains this in *Posture and Gesture*:

> The terms used in the present scheme are quoted in the present participle - ending in ...ing - because this gives a better indication of the developing process of behaviour. *[Posture and Gesture, p.54]*

This is Lamb's revised scheme:

Focus ~ Directing/Indirecting
Pressure ~ Increasing/Decreasing
Timing ~ Acceleration/Deceleration
Flow ~ Binding/Freeing

It was precisely this emphasis on dynamic as opposed to static categories that led Lamb to reject the generalised categories of The Efforts where someone might be characterised a 'floater' or a 'flicker'. Throughout our interviews he has stressed the fact that there are no isolated Efforts; that a focused movement has, at some point, to lose its fixation and become less directing – in other words, it is one part of a larger phrase. I have already mentioned how Lamb insists upon using Laban's framework to liberate a person's full movement potential; this also means acknowledging that no-one is ever always and in every situation a 'floater' or a 'flicker' – this is to limit their potential; indeed it is little less than pigeon-holing them. There is a great humanity in Lamb's approach to movement analysis and it stems from this belief in their being more to people than they or others often give them credit for. Not surprisingly, he has created a form of movement analysis that doesn't stand in judgement over those being observed, but is a means of offering them a profile of what they are, *and what they could be.*

Choreutics

The term refers to the architectural element of movement. In the course of lecturing and writing throughout my career I have found that the one illustration which seems to make it clear is to imagine that little jet engines are fixed all around the body, and as we move they emit vapour trails, as aircraft do in the sky. After a few seconds a sculptural form will exist of all the vapour trails. This form can then be studied and its unique features noted. For example, one form may be elongated, another flattened, another composed of mainly twisted lines and another of short angular lines. They create a shape in terms of movement, a very different concept from the shape of the physique. To the extent that a building is shaped according to an architect's design, so the shapes of movement which we all create can be considered bodily "architecture".

Laban had done a vast amount of research in this field, variously called Choreutics, space harmony or the shaping of movement, (although a more advanced study gives each of these a more specific meaning). He loved to play around with polyhedral forms made from sticks and to catalogue the ways the body can move in space. The icosahedron was his favourite and such scales of movement derived from it were basic to the teaching at the Art of Movement Studio. Laban suggested we read Plato's "Timaeus" to appreciate the Ancient Greek contribution to this body of knowledge. While scales can be bodily performed as a discipline, with a teacher making correction when needed, a Choreutics class would usually be based on one particular form and require the student to create a study based on this form. I had some prior knowledge of all this and immediately found my first class fascinating.

Just as, for example, Chopin plays with a theme in one of his Etudes, so a choreutics theme could be performed with one sort of emphasis then another, introduced at a higher level, lead into jumping or to actual use of the floor - an unlimited range of possibilities. Such work requires a type of creativity which many people find comes easily once the basic concept is understood. Without necessarily having any thought of performance it can be interesting to experiment in creating a choreutic study. It can certainly be physically active, but it is not intended in any sense as a "work-out". Aerobic dancing is closer to gymnastics than to the creative experience which is a choreutics class. [*The Movement Man*]

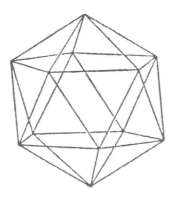

Figure 3: The Icosahedron

Planes of Movement

One way of thinking about the space that we move in is to think of the three planes of movement, Left-Right, Forward-Back and Up-Down. Think how you could cut an onion in half: taking the knife through the middle of the onion, separating the top half from the bottom you make a Horizontal section; or you could turn the knife at right angles and can cut the onion dividing the front half from the back, making a Vertical section; or you could take the knife down in front of you and make what is called in surgery a Sagittal section, dividing the left half from the right. All of Lamb's books contain a section when he or his co-authors try to represent three-dimensional space on a two-dimensional page. In Posture and Gesture he offers the following introduction:

> A simple breakdown of the components of Shape variation is into the three planes of Horizontal, Vertical, Forwards/Backwards (or Sagittal to use a medical term). Take three postcards and interleave them as follows:

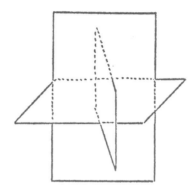

Figure 4: The Three Planes of Movement

> Place them (in the imagination) over the subject we are observing, and we have a framework which gives a rough guide for Shape observation. When he turns, the whole framework turns with him. If his 'vapour trails' of movement are more or less confined to one of these planes the amount of variation he is composing is limited. [*Posture and Gesture*, pp. 20 – 21]

Using these planes to read movement is one thing, but the authors of *Body Code* warn that of course just moving in the planes is quite robotic - you need to twist, to become more diagonal in order to achieve something sculptural or expressive.

> Symmetrical, dimensional movement anchors the centre of gravity, and restricts sculptural variation. [...] With sculptural movement, we are venturing into the kinesphere, which is the space between us and the inner surface of the imaginary globe. [...] Whereas a symmetrical lifting of the arms looks and feels robot-like, the sculpted, rising movement looks and feels as though you are drawing yourself up to your full height. [*Body Code*, p. 54]

Effort and Shape

One of Lamb's earliest and most major changes in Laban's approach to movement was bringing together Shape and Effort, Eukinetics and Choreutics. In his conversations he frequently returns to Laban's categorical separation of the two: Effort is for work, for the more primitive side of human nature while Choreutics – Shape and Space – appeal to the higher, more intellectual, more spiritual aspects of the human being. (Below he will describe this as the difference between the contrasting movement styles of Caliban and of Ariel.) He recalls:

> A great watershed for me was when I approached Laban a year or two before he died and asked whether there was any reason why I shouldn't observe how people shape their movements, and relate this to their efforts. He seemed rather surprised but agreed.

The division just didn't make practical sense to Lamb:

> A very simple example of how Effort is related to Shape is how you get out of bed in the morning. Some people find this task quite difficult, but once you've made the effort you still have to shape it if you want to avoid knocking over the bedside lamp.

No movement can just consist of Effort, it has to be shaped as well. But beyond this practical consideration I also detect another example of Lamb's more humanistic approach – all movements are human, whether they be specialised for work, for culture or for sport. Indeed, he rejects any training that limits a person's capacity for movement through overspecialisation – as we saw above, Lamb sees movement as being basic to the very stuff of human existence. While we live we move, only in death are we unmoving.

The Dimensional and the Diagonal Scales

The one area of Laban's training where Effort and Shape came together was the practice of the Dimensional and Diagonal Scales. Later we shall come to Laban's spatial concepts of the kinesphere and the icosahedron, but the Dimensional and Diagonal are predicated upon a cube. The dimensional scale is the simplest scale and corresponds to the cardinal directions – Up and Down, Left and Right, (in Laban's terminology, 'Across' and 'Outside'), Forward and Back. To each of these he attributed an Effort quality.

The Dimensional Scale and the Efforts

Up

A feeling of lightness, of losing strength, corresponds with the reaching upward to the point where the arm or the body prepares to relax and to fall back to the ground. Therefore, lightness is correlative with a tendency upward.

Down

A strong, firm movement always has at its source a vital connection with the stance. We can easily feel that every strong movement is correlated to a foothold downwards. Therefore, strength is correlative with a tendency downward.

Across

Movement across the body brings about a spatial restriction for the moving limb which makes for confined use of space. Therefore a straight, direct movement is correlative with one leading to the lateral direction opposite to the moving part of the body.

Outwards

Movement of the limb on its own side brings about a spatial freedom which makes for a roundabout and flexible use of space. Therefore, flexibility is correlative with an opening movement.

Back

A quick, sudden movement is connected with a certain contraction. The natural direction in the whole body tends to be backward as seen, for instance, in shock when jerks of fright cause the central area of the body to retract. Therefore quick, sudden tensions are correlative with movements in a backward direction.

Forwards

A slow movement seems to release into the opposite direction, namely into the area in front and, therefore, slowness and sustainment are correlative with reaching into a forward direction. [*Choreutics*, p.31]

In short, these correspond to the Effort Elements of Weight, Space and Time:

Up – Light (Weight)
Down – Strong (Weight)
Across – Direct (Space)
Outwards – Indirect or Flexible (Space)
Back – Quick (Time)
Forward – Sustained (Time)

Because every diagonal moves between three directions, each of the eight diagonal points corresponds to one of the Efforts. Take, for example, the diagonal point High Right Forward in a cube: to touch this point with your right hand you are going:

Up with your right hand (Light)
Opening Outwards (Indirect)
Forwards (Sustained)

And, as we saw above, a movement which is Light, Indirect and Sustained is called **Floating**. The Space/Effort correspondences for the Eight Diagonals are shown in Fig.2, Page 67.

In his autobiographical chapters, Lamb gives an account of how Laban would drill his students in the Diagonal Scale.

> Another aspect of his teaching was to instil the scales into the student's kinaesthetic awareness - we had to practice scales as assiduously as any pianist does. Often Laban would make it almost a form of drill. His teaching of the diagonal scale, for example, would require each movement to have the exact spatial orientation as well as the precise process of effort variation. If the movement required a combination of outwards, upwards and forwards spatial orientation, with an indirect, increasingly light and sustained effort, then all these six processes had to be accurate, no mean feat. Of course, accuracy in this context is relative - there is always scope for some sort of correction. If a student concentrated on getting more upwards orientation then more than likely he or she would lapse on the indirect effort. Laban would jump on this in a flash. Correction of the indirect effort would lead to some other process lapsing. I have known a class go on for more than three hours, students covered in sweat and desperately fatigued, but dredging their last ounces of energy to comply with the master.
>
> Laban believed that this form of drill helped to get the scales into the bodily instrument and make them second nature just as pianists' practice of scales becomes part of their musicality without need for conscious recall. Bad habits will always creep in, however, and therefore constant practice, and, desirably, a competent tutor are needed to maintain the standard Laban was setting. This drill aspect of the teaching which occupied most of the morning's training has been criticised, but it formed only a part of the experience, and was in contrast to the creative aspect of the studies. I loved it. It seemed to me then, and still does, as essential basic training. Once established in the body, movement scales are there for life. Even if bad habits should creep in the capability remains, just as once we have learnt to swim we never forget. [*The Movement Man*, Chapter 3, pp.8 – 9]

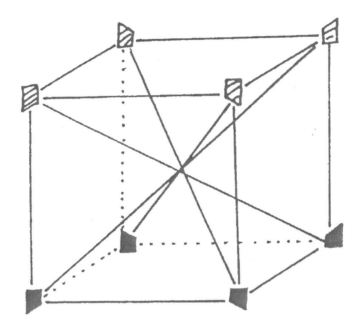

Diagonal directions are named by combining their three dimensional directions

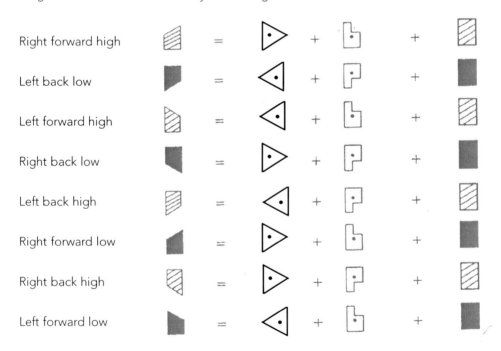

Right forward high							
Left back low							
Left forward high							
Right back low							
Left back high							
Right forward low							
Right back high							
Left forward low							

Figure 5: Directional directions are named by combining their three dimensional directions

Shape and the Flow of Shape

Although Warren Lamb teaches the Dimensional and Diagonal Scale with undiluted enthusiasm, his real revolution was in reconceiving Laban's spatial concepts of the kinesphere and the icosahedron. Very simply, these forms of space were much more closely modelled on the human form: the kinesphere being the imaginary bubble of space around you that you can touch; the icosahedron being a regular solid consisting of 20 sides that is almost round. Another way of thinking of the icosahedron is that it consists of the three basic planes of movement as described above. Every book that Warren Lamb has written, whether published or unpublished, has had a chapter with descriptions and diagrams of these three planes of movement. While Laban thought that an analysis of Effort was the way to understand human behaviour, Lamb believed that it was an analysis of both Effort and Shape, and in a much more subtle and complex way than we find in the simple schematic relations of the Diagonal Scale.

Lamb argues that we all have a very personal use of space: it may be that some people confine themselves to a very narrow corridor of space, but rise and fall a great deal, or that others take up a lot of space around them. Throughout his writings Lamb has used one particular image to help us understand an individual's unique occupation and use of space:

> The shapes of movement can be likened to the vapour trails left in the sky by jet aircraft. [*Movement and Personality*, P. 239]

Something similar is achieved in photography when small lights are attached to joints and a subject is recorded moving against a black background. Laban's book *A Vision of Dynamic Space* contains a wealth of drawings of movements in space, and his imaginary – or better, 'imagined' - traceforms in space look like the wavy lines left by these lights or imaginary vapour trails. Once again, we encounter the fundamental difficulty of trying to 'see' movement in space – a problem both of observation, but also conceptualisation. And, once again, we see Lamb struggling to avoid any limiting conception of movement – even the notion of a plane of movement suggests a flat rather than a three-dimensional shape. Throughout his writing he has sought for ways of accounting for the richness of human movement – its changes of pressure, speed, shape, and so on. Most of his refinements of Laban's terms are an attempt to get ever closer to the life of a movement.

We grow and shrink our kinespheres according to our emotional states and the situations we find ourselves in, but these always conform to a pattern, what a few pages above I called a 'movement signature'.

There is acceptance that we grow and shrink and everybody accepts that we move through our kinesphere and that we give it some kind of form through our movement – it may be flattened or elongated, there are all sorts of things that we can do to it through our movement. We may close and make the kinesphere smaller, or we open it and make it bigger. If you open your kinesphere you may be ready to receive somebody into your arms. Having arrived in your arms you may then close your arms around them.

Later in his thinking, Lamb will draw some searching conclusions from these observations. He realised that this shrinking and expanding could be understood as a Flow of Shape which is comparable with a Flow of Effort. In the passage that follows you can also detect the influence of the psychiatrist Judith Kestenberg who has already been mentioned above.

> The movement of growing and shrinking of the kinesphere is also a flow comparable to Effort Flow. Both flows (Effort freeing/binding and Shape growing/shrinking) can be observed to happen to a greater extent with young children than with adults and there is an actual loss of Flow variation as the other Effort and Shape components are gained during childhood growth. In *Posture and Gesture* I proposed the idea of calculating a 'Gain/Expense ratio' i.e. how much Flow (of both Effort and Shape) we have lost relative to how much we have gained in our repertoire of other Effort and Shape components.

Already in 1962 he accepts that Flow of Movement needs 'an amended technique for its recognition and assessment of degree' and be analysed 'from a different standpoint'.

> Flow is not an effort in the sense that any variation of Force, Time and Space represent an effort made on the part of the individual. Rather Flow happens as a result of absence of effort - an allowing or not of movement to happen relative to some condition or stimulus. [*Kinaesthetic Approach*, p. 75]

Another definition comes from his first published book, *Posture and Gesture*:

> Laban defined the process of Freeing/Binding as that of the 'Flow' of movement. His pupils differ to a great extent in their definition of Flow. Neither he nor any of his pupils have, so far as is known, associated Growing-Shrinking with 'Flow' although the process of variation, sometimes under the heading Narrow-Wide, is recognised and figures as a component in 'Space Harmonies'. To an observer simply wishing to describe what movement the body does, it seems that:

> 1. Shape processes 'flow' between relative growing and shrinking.

> 2. Effort processes 'flow' between relative freeing and binding. [*Posture and Gesture*, p. 56]

Effort affects movement:

All we can agree at present is that there is a distinct phenomenon to which we can give the name Flow, that it relates differently to Shape and Effort, and that it is particularly evident in tiny babies. If we look for any tendency towards the extremes of Abandoned and Rigid in adults we are most likely to find it in situations where the subject gives himself up to a situation, and then suddenly turns against it. [*Posture and Gesture*, p. 95]

In *Management Behaviour* the authors consider the question of flow from the perspective of control:

> We cannot see voluntary or involuntary control. We can, however, distinguish between movement which shows obvious exertion and movement which appears to happen of its own accord - movement which is made to happen and movement which is allowed to happen. [*Management Behaviour*, p. 73]

Polarities of Shape and Effort

Apart from Lamb's shift to the present participle when describing the action of a movement element – i.e. whether a Flow was binding or freeing – he was also interested in their polarities or absolute limits. Even in the 1950s he was already asking questions about what happens when you take a movement element to its extreme. He compares the Flow of Effort to a river, and compares the binding of Flow to a 'channelling' of the water:

> If this channelling is promoted to an extreme in the human body then a state of rigidity is reached; the river ceases to have any channel whatever along which it can flow and is completely dammed. [*Movement and Personality*, p. 131]

Or take the example of someone using Greater and Lesser Force:

> the distinction between the positive and negative maybe be seen in an orchestra conductor who exercises his authority over the strings in a light, fine touch manner, persuading them to play softly, then brings in the brass instruments by assuming a strong, thrusting manner, persuading them to play powerfully. [ibid, p. 149]

He argues that the conductor conveys equal authority in both. He is then led to describe the polarities of Force (what he will later call Pressure) as 'cramp' and 'flop'. Thus Lamb describes someone whose movement is characterised by the exercise of less Force as having a 'Fine Touch' [ibid, p. 152]. The concept of Polarities led him to representing them as the two ends of a see-saw, with the fulcrum point representing the neutral point. The see-saw allows Lamb to represent the range of a person's movement, in this case, how a movement can bind or flop. In other words, Lamb is reminding us of the defining feature of any aspect of movement – that it is a process of variation. But what he is adding is that this variation takes place between a range – and that range can be measured and represented. Thus the seesaws allow both for the representation of range and the processes of variation within that range.

What we see in Lamb's developments of Laban's terms and concepts, is an attempt to give a graphic account of all the processes of variation in any particular movement. Where Laban terms and forms of notation were more static and less integrated, Lamb's are both more dynamic and tend towards a more inclusive, holistic account of a person's movement.

Body Attitude, Functional Action and Shadow Movement

Laban considered that there were three basic types of movement: Body Attitudes, Functional Actions, and Shadow Movements. In Lamb's work of the 1950s he followed Laban's terms and in *Movement and Personality* (whose title, remember, he later revised to *Analysis for Personality Assessment*), he based his approach on them.

> Body Attitude movement involves a variation of the whole posture, from toe to head. An operation in this category has the aim of assuming a new attitude in relation to the situation. [...] The size of the movement is irrelevant; many people compose Body Attitude movement which is almost imperceptible except to the trained observer.' [*Movement and Personality*, p. 118]

The defining feature of a Body Attitude is that 'each completed operation expresses a new, renewed, or adjusted attitude to the situation' [Ibid., p.119]. A Functional Action is either an 'activity in relation to an object, or gestures where the aim is to give a functional communication' [Ibid., p. 119].

> More often the two classifications are inter-related - a Body Attitude operation takes up a posture for a Functional Action operation and will again adjust the posture as becomes necessary in order to apply the Functional Action. For example, the Functional Action of gripping the handle of a bucket with the hands is related to the Body Attitude movement which took up the posture by the bucket. [Ibid., p. 119]

He then turns to Shadow Movement:

> Shadow movement has the aim of making manifest all forms of mental effort. It is impossible to think consciously without there being accompanying Shadow Movement, although much of it may not be visible even to a trained observer. [Ibid., p. 120]

Shadow Movement operations (for they follow a similar action-operation process sequence to the other classifications) are often seen as responses to outside stimuli and may sometimes be revealing, as when an unexpected visitor interprets from his host's Shadow Movement response that he is not welcome. [Ibid., p. 121]

Shadow Movement can be distinguished from Functional Action in that the former 'fulfils no function'; it is expressive of an emotional state.

It can be said that Body Attitude *means* Appropriateness; Functional Action means Functional capacity; Shadow Movement *means* Discrimination and assessment can be made on a relative basis. [Ibid., p. 123]

We shall see later on that one of Lamb's major breakthroughs in thinking was to reject these three terms in favour of Posture and Gesture.

Notation

I thought Rudolf Laban a genius for having codified the elements of movement to the extent of making a disciplined study possible. [*The Movement Man,* Chapter 1, P. 17]

Throughout our conversations Lamb has always shown immense respect for the more objective, analytical aspect of Laban's thinking, and this is never more evident than in the two forms of notation that Laban developed. The first was what became known as Labanotation and was applied to choreography; the second was the Effort graphs which Laban explains as follows:

It has been found that the discussion and understanding of the various combinations of controlled or uncontrolled exertions and their importance for the economy of effort can be assisted by the use of effort graphs instead of, or in addition to, verbal description. [*Effort*, pages 12 - 13]

Lamb preferred graphic notation of movement because words tend to invite unwanted associations. For him, a graphic notation is a far more dispassionate and unambiguous account of a person's movement. When Lamb came to notate Shaping in movement, rather than using the Labanotation, he used an adaptation of Laban's scheme.

Observation

In Laban's book *Effort* he notes that much can be learned about a person simply from the observation of 'all his everyday movements': 'Many of the movements seen during conversation, in leisure time, play and games, or even in relative relaxation and rest, reveal much as to the general effort make-up of a man' therefore 'it will be most important ... to observe the everyday behaviour of aspirants as thoroughly as their skill in the performance of operations.' [*Effort*, p. 41] These 'private' efforts might appear 'with less intensity but not with less clarity' 'when one considers that a man being free to move as he wants will show off more of his personal habits and predilections than when using the more or less prescribed movements of an operation.' [Ibid, p. 41] Lamb agrees on this notion of what constitutes significant movement:

> Many people seem to have an arbitrary conception of what constitutes movement believing that someone who fidgets in an exaggerated way is moving much more than someone who sits composed and restrained. On the contrary, the restrained person is probably composing a much greater range or variety of movement in order to appear 'still' than the other who exaggeratedly fidgets in a repetitive manner. [*Movement and Personality*, p.256]

In my general introduction I stated my disbelief that Lamb could learn so much about me from observing simply my everyday movements: and it is clear that in this he was following Laban's line of research. I chose the title for this book because I am still amazed at how Laban and Lamb could actually see these movements. When Peter Hulton and I first looked at the video footage of my interview, we couldn't identify the movements that Lamb had notated – only when he pointed them out could we recognise them *as movements*.

Laban puts his finger on the major problem that most people have with the observation of movement – which is that they break it down into images. He warns that the observer 'has to follow the bodily mental line of the operator's action and is greatly hampered in his task when he applies preconceived academic or theoretical considerations in subdividing or breaking up the job' [*Effort*, p. 44]. Laban continues:

> This is one of the causes why the observation of working actions is so difficult and bewildering for the unskilled observer. It is almost like the endeavour to follow the tricks of a conjurer, in which one movement melts indiscernibly into the next, so that the eye and mind of the average spectator have no opportunity to reflect upon what has happened. [*Effort*, p.45]

Even in his earliest work, *Movement and Personality*, Lamb devotes some hundred pages to the problem of observation and points out how one of the pioneers of movement observations, the Frenchman François Delsarte[11], was limited by taking no 'account of the kinaesthetic sense' [*Movement and Personality*, p.113]. Delsarte[11] didn't see movement, he saw fixed gestures and postures: for example,

> The shoulder, in every man who is moved or agitated, rises sensibly, his will playing no part in the ascension; the successive developments of this involuntary act are in absolute proportion to the passional intensity whose numeric measure they form; the shoulder may, therefore, be fitly called the thermometer of the sensibility. [*Delsarte System of Oratory*, Edgar S.Werner, (New York, 1887), p.437]

Lamb is critical of Desmond Morris's writings, precisely because the movements discussed are illustrated by photographs – static images of a gesture at its point of arrival. To take a simple example, the gesture of 'touching the nose with the finger', can be captured in a still photograph, but this cannot account for the way that the finger travelled to the nose, in other words, the movement as a process of variation, as a rhythmic phrase. This is why both Laban and Lamb stress the importance of an approach to observation that is as free from theoretical prejudices and prior assumptions as possible. It is important to distinguish between stages in Movement Analysis: first there is observation, then notation and only then evaluation. So the first job is simply to describe what you see as accurately as possible.

Lamb is unambiguous about the degree of skill that is involved in movement analysis:

> The trained movement observer and analyst is a highly specialised practitioner. He is very much a child of the times, thrown up, as it were, by the rate of modern industrial and scientific progress. He cannot claim to have created a new science but there exists already the beginnings of a new profession. [*Movement and Personality*, p.476]

He adds that to train to be a 'skilled observer' may take 'as long as five years' [p.258]. In *Kinaesthetic Approach* he suggests that 'It takes at least three years to train an observer and analyst of movement and longer to acquire the techniques for design and execution of individual courses.' [p.64.] Elsewhere in his earlier study he points out that every operation consists of a number of constituent actions all of which have to be recorded.

---

[11] François Delsarte (1811-1871) was probably one of the very first researchers into movement studies. He was also a voice teacher of some renown. His ideas were championed in America by James Steel MacKaye (1842 – 1894) and then choreographer and teacher Ted Shawn, himself a pioneer of Modern Dance in America.

The observer has to be very quick therefore and cannot hope to observe all the actions that happen. But he must observe all the actions in each operation that he records. He must seize upon one operation, memorise it, and speedily write it down without allowing himself to be distracted. It is from observations taken in this highly specialised, highly skilled way that conclusions about their meaning are being made here. [*Movement and Personality*, p.135]

Later on he notes how to observe when looking at groups of people in public places:

The students should not observe casually, as is the general tendency, but fix their concentration definitely upon one particular person and transfer to another only after they have clearly observed something, and, if possible, written it down. [Ibid., p.459]

He also points out that the observer needs to participate in the movement of the observed: 'When the term Body Attitude is understood it can be explained that the observer mirrors in his own attitudes the movement he is observing' [463]. This is echoed in his later book, *Kinaesthetic Approach* where he writes about the necessary kinaesthetic sympathy between observer and observed.

to determine the effort of the movement ... he follows a technique of participating in the movement of which he has observed the shape, simulating it in a very restrained way, and with a disciplined, detached concentration which enables him to judge the degree of variation in the Force, Time and Space elements. [*Kinaesthetic Approach*, p.30]

Some fifty years later Lamb still holds to the same approach to movement observation:

My reply still today is that body movement study does not attempt to attribute meaning to any one gesture. It embraces a vast concept of components and harmonies and forms, analogous with music, and the search for behavioural or psychological meaning is only one small aspect of this total concept. The study of movement is betrayed if a fixed image is used for the purpose of interpretation, as is the case with Body Language. [*The Movement Man*, Chapter 1, p.13]

This focus upon movement as flux (according to Lamb one of Laban's favourite words), as a process of variation, is central to understanding Lamb's philosophy and practice of movement analysis. In our conversations he offers several memorable anecdotes to illustrate how we habitually think of movement in terms of static images, or freeze frames. The meaning isn't in the destination but in the journeying towards it, the pattern of changes that we make along this journey.

Although Laban and Lamb insist that observation be as objective and comprehensive as possible, there are certain things that they hope to identify from these observations: for Lamb in the 1950s it was the 'constant patterns of composition of effort' [*Movement and Personality*, p.259]. Later, he would add to this 'and shape'. But in the final evaluation it is not simply the movements themselves that are significant: it is also the context in which they take place.

> Clearly there can be no objective assessment until it can be made relative to the situation. In other words, the meaning cannot be understood without reference to the appropriateness of the movement. [*Movement and Personality*, p.117]

Once again we come back to Lamb's holistic approach to movement which judges its meaning in relation to the living situation of the person being observed.

Let me summarise the developments and main concepts that are covered in Part II where we deal with some of Laban's concepts that Lamb was to adapt and develop. We began by considering Laban's concept of the Efforts. We then moved on to a consideration of Laban's rich concepts of Shape and Space – the Dimensional and Diagonal movement scales in Cubic space, then his concepts of the Kinesphere and the Icosahedron. Although Laban brought together Effort and Shape in the Dimensional and Diagonal scales in movement practice, it was Lamb who realised that **you cannot consider Effort in isolation from Shape** in movement analysis. This led to a second development of Laban's approach: to adapt the Effort Graphs so that they could also serve to notate patterns of variation of Shape. Lamb also changed the names of the effort elements, so that as categories they lend themselves to a more dynamic analysis. Thus with Pressure (what was formerly Weight) we have increasing and decreasing, rather than Strong and Light. The use of the present participle suggests a movement that is in the process of happening. Equally, if not more important, was Lamb's use of see-saws to represent the **Polarities of Effort and Shape** elements. We saw that Lamb had kept with Laban's triple typology of Body Attitude, Functional Movement and Shadow Movement. Finally, we examined Laban and Lamb's approach to observation, and noted the difficulty both men had in confronting our ingrained habit of seeing movement in terms of fixed frames rather than processes of variation.

xi.   Effort (Eukinetics)

Laban's Definition of Effort

Laban developed a great philosophy of man's effort and how it should be recognised and enriched. He had a very special understanding of the role of effort in human life - people didn't live unless they had a richer vocabulary and awareness of Effort. He used to give highly generalised talks about the development of human beings right from the days of primitive man, and it was this man who was always depicted as doing things with a lot of effort. These movements were badly formed and primitive man looked crude and all over the place. The most civilised aspect of man was when we had really become at one with space, with the kinesphere, with the space beyond his kinesphere, which could be extrapolated right to the cosmos. This is evident from his recommendation that in the context of teaching children, they can only comprehend this when they reach adolescence.

On the other hand, Laban argued that Man's effort had not been recognised, or at least not in modern times, and since the Industrial Revolution the expression of effort had been abused and degraded by the experience of how work was conducted. He argued that people were being made into robots because their individual effort, the distinctive rhythm of effort which each person has, and which is different from that of everyone else, is being suppressed by modern conditions. Very often Laban would use the term that people were being 'mechanised'. He believed, firstly, that human dignity depended upon people being able to apply effort in a rich, full and rhythmic way; and secondly, they had to apply rhythm in their own individual, unique way of moving - people were not expressing the Effort that was there in them to be expressed.

This is why Laban constantly referred to Effort in terms of rhythm. Rhythm, for him, was doing different Efforts within a sequence, within a phrasing, and he taught Effort particularly making use of rhythm ideas – the Greek rhythms, for example: the iambic, anapaestus, trochaic, dactylus, peon, etc. Those rhythms could be used to stimulate movement in a particular effort-ful way. That's why I think in his work in industry he referred to Industrial Rhythm. I always think that it is remarkable that during World War II he was able to go into factories and encourage the management and the workers to participate in industrial rhythm. He was introducing rhythm to factory workers during the war – a remarkable achievement! It is interesting that industrial rhythm for Laban meant exclusively, Effort. All his work in factories at this time was concentrated on Effort, without much reference to shape, or space harmonies. He was teaching space harmony to dancers and teachers, but it seemed that he had made an inseparable connection of work with effort.

His emphasis upon Industrial Rhythm explains why we were looking at movement phrases and yet he continued to talk about Effort in what seemed to me to be a very generalised way. For example, I have never been able to classify people according to Laban's basic Efforts - Floating, Punching, Gliding, Slashing, Wringing, Dabbing, Flicking and Pressing. I feel that they offer a generalisation and a summary, perhaps, of what he has seen in somebody. He would describe a person as 'Floater', a 'Glider' a 'Puncher' or a 'Flicker'. I felt that this was oversimplified and not accurate in that what I think he had actually observed were phrases of a sequence of movement. When he described somebody as a 'Floater' he had seen a diminishing pressure of movement, he had seen more of sustainment and deceleration occurring, he had seen more indirecting happen. Having actually seen those movements he brought them together by saying that they were 'Floating'. Laban would go from a generalised view of whatever basic Effort was closest to what a person was doing to a more definitive explanation.

I've never been able to do it that way. It would certainly be limiting to me, though it was Laban's starting point. Someone was just described to me a few days ago as 'bubbly' – I can just picture the movement quality of someone described as bubbly. Other people might be similarly described, but they'd all be different, but at least it could be the starting point. All people who tend to be described as 'bubbly' have this, that and the other in common. Laban would probably say that all bubbly people are 'flickers'. Somebody else might be described as 'stolid' which might mean more weight, they might be more 'pressers'. This has never been a good starting point from my point of view.

Notoriously, people can appear differently in interviews to how they will behave when they get into the job. With someone described as 'bubbly', is she always bubbly? This is always a good question to ask when someone is described in this general way. When might they be different, indeed very contrastingly different? When might the person be very down in the mouth? Obviously, it may depend on circumstances. If a disaster happens then you would expect that they would behave differently. That was an important question to ask when attempting to give advice. You can then get the distinction between what might be temporary and what might be relied upon as more constant.

Effort in Dance and Theatre

A similar philosophy was applied to his work on Effort in dance and theatre. Although *Effort* was only published in 1947 following his work with Lawrence, he had explored Efforts with dancers and movement choirs in Austria and Germany. In his pageants with different craft-workers he had already explored the particular types of movement each of them had. Laban developed this idea that Effort was an indication of the character, the personality of the person.

It seemed that he aligned the Efforts with work and Shape exclusively with art, dance and the spirit. One was material and the other ethereal. Primitive witch-craft dances are predominantly concerned with Effort: Wigman in her dance on witches was concerned with the idea of it being effortful. This was a very popular and successful piece, whereas any sort of religious expression of dance would emphasise more the Space-Harmony. I never accepted this, believing that you could be civilised and effortful, and even primitive and have fairly complex shapes. One could say this was the difference between Ariel and Caliban.

Laban would refer to what he contributed to dance as, 'Making dances more effort-ful'. All the choreography of Hettie Loman (one of the students at the Art of Movement Studio) was effortful: it exhausted audiences. She did a choreography called *Song of the Earth* to Bach's toccata and fugue in D minor for organ. Her three dancers began on the floor and started doing the seven rings which got bigger and bigger. I thought it used Choreutics beautifully, even though Hettie was so effortful. Nevertheless the inspiration was the seven rings. Unfortunately none of our presentations was very finished. I remember someone saying that what we were doing was remarkable but we were all doing it with dirty fingernails – the costumes were pretty awful; the staging was mostly poor. Her ideas fell over each other.

Just as we can have Choreutic studies so we can also have Eukinetic studies – and this is, in fact, what we used to do in the Art of Movement Studio. In connection with Eukinetic studies maybe harmony was not so much the right word as 'expressive' or 'consistent' which could be more useful terms. Nevertheless, it is similar to an understanding of harmony or beauty. It was notable to me that a composer called Dino Castro who worked in Paris in the late 40s and 50s was interested in this field. I used to give him some effort phrases lasting up to a minute, maybe ninety seconds, which I would record and he would then transpose it into music. The result, he claimed, was a theme which could be possibly built on to create a major work of music. I do have some of these compositions that he created. Many composers since that time have incorporated efforts into their works, but Castro was saying that this was a way in which you could bring together movement and music with an understanding of the matching effort and shape processes.

Just as Castro would claim that he was making music which was effortful, so Laban in the early 1930s made the same claim for Kurt Jooss[12] and his ground-breaking ballet *The Green Table*. This ballet, which dominated the dance world for so long, really incorporated effort – it was effort-ful. Choreographer Kurt Jooss had been very influenced by Laban's early ideas about Efforts. He and other dancers saw this as being something new to dance. Laban must have felt that he was the man who was introducing this whole new concept to dance, and I suppose the first fruit of it must have been *The Green Table*. Jooss continued to work with Effort and to claim how important it was for him.

I think the Efforts were also helpful to many of the actors that Laban taught at the Northern School of Theatre[13] in Bradford. I met Bernard Hepton who had been taught there and he remembered the Effort terms and maintained that they had been helpful to him in his acting career. But I would repeat my warning that in order to understand some meaning in movement from a point of view of personality, or some aspect of personality, we have to be very, very careful not to summarise somebody as a 'Floater or Flicker' or whatever.

Warren Lamb's Critique and Development of Laban's Efforts

Much of what I am saying now gives an idea of the impact that Laban's thought had upon me when I began working with him in the late 1940s: that Effort was a neglected study; that Laban had discovered a great deal about Effort and its relation to work and that this was important because we all have to work in some form or other. I was also exploring the distinction between work and play: how differently do we move when we work and play? How do we make different Efforts? Do we simply slump when we play and strain when we work? Maybe we shouldn't make a distinction between when we are working and when we are playing: there is an overlap between the two. The aesthetic question and the question of harmony was part of all that I got from Laban, around this time.

---

[12] Kurt Jooss (1901-1979) was a German dancer and choreographer. A student of Rudolf Laban, he is most famous for his 1932 ballet The Green Table. In 1933 he and his entire company escaped from Germany and found refuge in Dartington where he also continued his school. Lisa Ullmann was part of the company which explains why Laban was offered refuge in Dartington in 1938. Like Mary Wigman his dance was characterised as expressionist. When his school was re-established in Essen after the war, one of his students was Pina Bausch.

[13] Northern School of Theatre was created by Esmee Church in the early 1940s and was part of Bradford Civic Theatre. Laban was invited to teach there, where he was assisted by Geraldine Stephenson. Notable pupils include educationalist Dorothy Heathcote and actor Bernard Hepton.

Laban felt that I had understood his theory - one could almost call it a philosophy - of Effort and how effort needed to be understood. My own interest in and recognition of the importance of the Efforts certainly impressed Laban. At the Studio I was always characterised as the Eukinetics man while Valerie Preston-Dunlop was the Choreutics person. I think that Laban correlated Effort with work and space harmony and shape more with art and philosophy: things away from work. I was designated by Laban to teach movement observation at the Studio and I still have some notes from my teaching. There was one report that I made of twelve or fifteen classes given over a term and Laban came to two of them. Everything that Laban got me to do in my visits to factories and my observations was to do with Effort. I used to take groups in parks and railways stations and asked them to observe people's Efforts. Everything was conceived in terms of Effort observation.

It was not until much later that I realised that one didn't have to concentrate on Effort alone and that there is another world of movement. This was an indication of the significance of Laban's belief with regard to how people express themselves, particularly at work. All of his work was isolated, concentrated upon the Effort field. The work was called Personal Effort Assessment; Laban-Lawrence Industrial Rhythm meant Effort rhythm. I have more recently come to the conclusion that although there was never any mention of Choreutics or Space Harmonies or shaping in anything that's been written about the work in industry that Laban did take that into account in some respects.

Effort has been defined by others as the inner impulse which originates movement. I think that this is inadequate and that it creates problems concerning what is inner and what is outer; in any case movement is going on all the time. There are a number of ways in which we can understand the initiation of a movement, and how they can have purpose or intention. I have come across quite a lot of psychology where 'intention' seems not to mean 'intention' as I would define it and is much more like an 'impulse' – something which is unconsciously causing some sort of expression or performance. We can look at effort in quantitative terms – having to make a relatively large or small amount of effort. This is very much in our language. We are always in the state of making relatively less, even imperceptible movements, or relatively more effort. When we are making a lot of effort we may become aware of the nature of the effort we are selecting.

The difficulty in making a definition of Effort is that one is trying to define something that is going on all the time one is alive. We are alive because we move: we stop moving and then we're not alive any more. Effort can be understood as movement which overcomes inertia. People die because they stop making an effort: they get depressed because they are old and they just give up on life and eventually they die. So we have to keep overcoming inertia. However we can overcome inertia by exerting a lot or a little effort. The fact that we are creating an effort and a shape is another way of saying we are making an effort not to fall down on the floor. What we describe as muscle tone needs an effort.

A definition of Effort must refer to three components: focus, pressure, and timing. Any definition of effort, I would claim, has to take these three components into account and to recognise the concept of more or less effort relative to getting closer to a form of extreme. One could think of Effort in the same way as one talks about muscle tone: someone has 'Effort tone' when they maintain a balance: that balance can be with relative inertia, that can mean very, very little effort being applied to maintain the tone, or it can be applied with a lot of effort in respect to a form of balance, of the variations of effort in the components I've mentioned.

Focus (directing/indirecting)

If we accept that Effort is going on all the time, and we can make a lot or a little of it, the next stage is to define the component parts. Laban defined them as Space, Weight and Time. With regard to Space effort it seemed there was confusion with Space Harmony and I prefer Focus. We can direct our focus of attention (through space, obviously) or we can make an effort to be indirect.

If you are inert in regard to this component of Effort then you neither have a particular focus nor a lack of one. You have a non-descript energy with regard to any aspect of focusing. On the other hand, a person engaged in a conversation may be said to focus on the other person very directly. Or there may be occasions when you deliberately avoid focus and you want to maintain a spread of your focus. There are extremes here, where, if you focus so directly that you can't get any more so, you then get paralysed in what could be called a fixed stare. Whereas at the other extreme, you have made so great an effort to become unfocused, you almost tie yourself in a knot. You can see this sometimes when people are embarrassed. As distinct from those forms of analysis evident when you go to an extreme, there is still that neutral mid-point where you can remain poised between being neither too pointedly focused, nor too flexible and unfocused.

Pressure (increasing/decreasing)

Laban defined this component as Weight but I found that people often used its opposite polarities of strong and light to describe fixed states and not movement. For

Movement Pattern Analysis it is essential to see movement as a process of variation. So it helps to use the present participles of verbs. Whatever Effort we make, it must have a limit: if I make an effort of increasing pressure, if I begin to get stronger then there must be a limit beyond which that effort cannot go. I usually refer to that as a 'cramp' because it's visible as a shaking on the part of the person. At the other extreme, if we diminish the pressure then there's a limit beyond which we can't get any lighter - that is manifest by a flop. The more there is inertia the more we avoid extremes. We can define one of the components of an Effort as the process of movement between one extreme and another: if you like, the extremes of cramp and flop. The more there is inertia the more we avoid extremes. Effort very often is referred to as a struggle, it is regarded as forcefulness: a dictionary includes the terms 'force' in its definition.

Timing (acceleration/deceleration)

Similarly with the third component, it requires an effort in order to speed up or slow down, to set the pace. We can avoid time-effort, i.e. we can have a high degree of inertia in respect to time, which means that we basically get through life trying not to vary the pace very much. The definition in this case is between being so fast that you really can't get any faster and being so slow that having decelerated, you reach a point at which you can't get any slower. Basically, you have come to a dead stop. As with focus and pressure, so with the time value, the extremes are always indicative of a paralysis of movement. Paralysis is a very different thing from inertia, that point between the opposite poles at which one is just poised, as if sitting on a see-saw. You don't allow yourself to move either side because this would make the see-saw go down. You are trying to keep your effort in a very poised way; you are consciously avoiding going to either of the extremes. The more you go to an extreme then the more effort you are actually exerting.

Flow

Another need that arose for me was to deal with the concept of flow. It always seemed to me that Flow had been stuck on at the end: it wasn't really integral with the three others. This was confirmed when I did a lot of work with the psychiatrist Dr Judith Kestenberg. We made a lot of observations from new-born babies through to later ages and it seemed evident that young babies flow a lot: their whole movement is flowing and they certainly don't do any integrated efforts of Space, Weight or Time. If we are born with a lot of Effort-Flow and then we develop Space, Weight and Time, then I think we have to consider Flow as being quite different from the other Effort components. There is still opposition to this idea, although I think it has been gradually accepted over the years. Probably there are some people who would still talk about Space, Weight, Time and Flow.

The need for Flow to be looked upon differently is important. It helps when talking about Effort to consider that there is some degree of Flow going on, and the Effort may be said to arise out of the Flow. Now if we regard Effort-Flow as relative, if you free the flow then some sort of falling is going to occur, and if that goes to an extreme then you abandon yourself and fall down. On the other hand, if you bind or control the flow then you reach an extreme when you can't go any further and you become rigid and paralysed. You see this quite a lot in babies who can be by turns abandoned and rigid. We should recognise that there is this form of flow going on. Most breathing consists of a freeing as you breathe out – relatively speaking - and to a degree you become more bound as you breathe in. Out of this Flow may arise the Directing, or the Increasing Pressure, or the Acceleration – or at least these may be *in relation* to the Flow. This is something that I have researched a lot. There is a lot to be achieved, there is a lot of research to be done on the *rhythmic* relationship between Flow and the other Effort components: how adjustment in our Flow-rhythms may be helpful to the other Effort-rhythms.

The definition somehow has to contain the question of selection. Both Effort and Shape are on a bi-polar scale of being alive and we neutralise the movement relatively for much of the time. It is there, it is always happening. So effort is always there, it is part of life, it is there before we are born. The nature of the effort, whether it be a space-force-time, or whether it is a flow-effort can vary. So we have a conscious option of whether to choose one or the other.

xii. Shape (Choreutics): Laban's Conception of the Aesthetic Dimension of Movement

Laban's dream was to revolutionise the world through a greater appreciation of the aesthetic dimension of movement. Although Laban didn't begin his life in the dance-world (he started off by studying architecture and went to an art school in Paris) it dominated his years in Europe between the world wars. And if you look at the history of dance from early ballet to Isadora Duncan, it has always been understood in terms of Shape. Laban began by codifying Choreutics and it was only later that he began to analyse Effort. Whenever Laban was talking about Choreutics he was in a dance mode and then he would get into a mysterious, metaphysical realm and start talking about the cosmos, trying to convey that this really was such a vast subject that none of us could get to understand it. Laban certainly was provocative in his statements about cosmology and movement. Space harmonies took us up into the cosmos and into dreams and the occult (of course, he was interested in the occult). The Egyptians understood space harmony, and the Greeks understood it even more and this influenced Laban himself in developing the polyhedral forms, giving him a mathematical base for defining space harmonies. Choreutics has to do with Platonic space, but people will always interpret whatever Laban offers according to where they are coming from.

When harmony is ever mentioned in connection with Laban then it is always Space-harmony that is referred to. That is understandable in respect to the world of art and dance: for Laban, Space-harmony was a very important part of choreography. As I've said when talking about Laban and Education, he advised teachers that Space-harmonies should be taught to children only when they were teenagers. Choreutics was primarily linked with the spiritual, whereas Efforts was much more linked to the world, to the material, with the practical and down-to-earth. He regarded it as a phase of development within civilisation to which we have advanced. In the primitive and relatively more barbaric state we wouldn't have any sense of space harmony.

I think that Laban has set the groundwork for a field of research that is to come. Certainly a lot of people who are highly qualified are coming to recognise the potential in recognising some of Laban's ideas. I think the future will be with these researchers rather than with some of the originals like Geraldine Stephenson and me. Carol-Lynne Moore has spent more than two years trying to work out what Laban had discovered in terms of the mathematical proportions of movement, and concepts of harmony and dis-harmony and linking it with music. She has, I think, discovered some important principles and her book will be quite significant in this field. I think, possibly in the academic field, that musicologists may come together with choreologists, and there will be a matching of music harmony with movement harmony. Movement and music harmonies will be developed in kindred terms. Then of course it would become taken for granted that if people wanted to become dancers then they would really have to become educated in the basic harmonies. It is disappointing that much that Laban opened up in this field has not been followed up and only now is this beginning to be done.

The Icosahedron and the Kinesphere

Of the four polyhedrons designated by Plato as fundamental to life - the tetrahedron, cube, icosahedron and dodecahedron – it is the icosahedron which was found by Laban to be most appropriate as a basis of reference for studying space harmony in terms of movement. The twenty points of the icosahedron divide the kinesphere into twenty equilateral triangles and three planes. Connecting the points together in a certain way establishes harmonious 'trace paths'. If the points at which these paths intersect are joined the shape of the cube is created. The tetrahedron is more restricted, the dodecahedron more extended. All this provides a model for specifying different ways of moving within a kinesphere recognised as potentially having these forms and their many variants. The icosahedron alone provides scope for a vast number of movement scales and derivatives, facilitating an understanding of space harmony analogous with music harmony.

Laban never talked about specific points in the icosahedron. He thought more in terms of planes or lines which divided the sphere, for example into what is called 'above' from what you'd call 'below'. Most religions divide space according to the high/low axis with all that is evil being in the lower part. That is the first step in appreciating that the bubble can have some form. But we can also create an imaginary wall or door that divides everything that is in front of you from what is behind you. This is in our language: 'putting things behind you', 'turning your back on things'. This is also clear in what faces you, what you have in front of you. Since we're dealing with planes we can also make a distinction between all that is on the left and all that is on the right – a division that enters into politics. It is more of a differentiation between what you can do with you right and left hands.

The 'kinesphere' is usually described as a bubble of space which we carry around with us. It roughly corresponds to your physical reach, so if you stretch your arm and draw a circle to the maximum of your reach around you, then you've drawn a spheroid and this is a kinesphere, which by the way is not just a movement concept, it also is used in psychology. Laban talked a lot about Narrow and Wide, Pin, Ball and Wall – different images that he gave in order to give some form to the kinesphere.

What we are doing when talking about Horizontal is seeing a kinesphere which is oriented so that it is primarily flattened out; by Vertical we mean a kinesphere where front and back come towards you; and there is a Kinesphere which comes in from each side and is elongated forwards and backwards. A better way of describing all these, is to think of a horizontally-oriented movement as a way of dividing what is shaping upwards from what is shaping downwards. This may be in some people's psychology where they see everything which is upwards as good because it leads to Heaven and downwards as bad because it leads to Hell. Then the Door or Vertical Plane divides all that is in front from all that is behind and if you make that distinction then you tend to be very clear as to what you turn your back on as distinct from what you are confronting. Finally, if the kinesphere is squashed in from the sides then you are really aware that you are in a sort of channel or tunnel in which you either advance or retreat.

The movement of growing and shrinking of the kinesphere is also a flow comparable to Effort Flow. Both Flows (Effort freeing/binding and Shape growing/shrinking) can be observed to happen to a greater extent with young children than with adults and there is an actual loss of Flow variation as the other Effort and Shape components are gained during childhood growth. In *Posture and Gesture* I proposed the idea of calculating a 'Gain/Expense ratio' i.e. how much Flow (of both Effort and Shape) we have lost relative to how much we have gained in our repertoire of other Effort and Shape components.

But what can be learned from observing children is that they grow or shrink their kinesphere as well as free and bind it. There is a Flow of Shape which is analogous to the Flow of Effort. Again, this was my attempt to organise Laban's creative ideas and there was a lot of opposition amongst those who had been trained by him, and there is still opposition. I come across some very odd misinterpretations of what the Flow of Shape is. All we're trying to explain at present is that this is a form that you can give to the bubble. This is the first elementary form of understanding a structure of the spheroid.

However, if we look at the body-spheroid in terms of movement, it doesn't always stay the same. We can go on to make many different structures and ways of going around the sphere. Growing and Shrinking are my terms but there is nothing particularly creative about them – they just seem to be more accurate than using the architectural terms that Laban had used. There is acceptance that we grow and shrink and everybody accepts that we move through our kinesphere and that we give it some kind of form through our movement – it may be flattened or elongated, there are all sorts of things that we can do to it through our movement. We may close and make the kinesphere smaller, or we open it and make it bigger. If you open your kinesphere you may be ready to receive somebody into your arms. Having arrived in your arms you may then close your arms around them. One has to ask whether a closing movement is a drawing away from people while an opening is a welcoming of them.

In interpersonal relationships you see a lot of this going on. When sitting in airports I enjoy watching people arriving from somewhere and being met by friends or relatives – there are all sorts of greetings, with different types of opening, and then both will close their body-spheroids together. The extent of the movement in the opening and closing of the kinesphere can be looked at in a more specific sense, in terms of when they do their closing. Are they doing this more in a sidewards way? Are they rising up when they do it? Are they actually going forward? The answer could be any of these things or in any combination. Not only do we open and close the kinesphere but also we grow and shrink the kinesphere. An actor may project from the stage so that all the audience feels that they are within that actor's kinesphere, or he might close his kinesphere, so that he is remote and on his own. Taking into account the way in which the opening and closing happens then we can see that there are variations of the dimension or the shaping of the kinesphere: so if the emphasis is put on the side-to-side, it is as though the kinesphere is squashed – it becomes elongated like a rocket on its side. Whether it's an open rocket, or a closed rocket it is squashed. On the other hand, if you rise particularly in your opening and closing with a descending movement then your rocket is elongated up and down. Similarly, in a forwards and backwards way.

On the theme of opening and closing (convex and concave are synonymous terms used in the framework) this is often linked with breathing. We do have the opportunity to make the Kinesphere grow and shrink, and we should remember that when we breathe in we grow, and when we breathe out we tend to shrink. But you can do it the other way round as in the Martial Arts - I would like to learn more about the connection between breathing and body movement.

All of these will be variations of relative opening and closing: whether we use those words or concave and convex – the words I've chosen to use – they do correspond to much of what Laban preached as being 'Gathering' and 'Scattering'. The Gathering was of course a closing movement and the Scattering was an opening movement. He regarded this as psychologically very significant: significant for what we gain from it. Lots of people assign great significance to this. It may extend to people believing that you gather energy into yourself. The opposite movement, the scattering, is about getting more in touch with what is beyond you. Gathering is getting in touch with the inner being and Scattering is getting in touch with the outer being. I never like to refer to inner being, though a lot of people do,   simply because I base everything I do on an attempt to observe objectively. You can't observe what is inner, but you can observe someone who is gathering; whether you then interpret it as having significance for a person psychologically, in one way or another is something else. You can of course gather and scatter as a gesture – you can gather in one part of the body and scatter in another.

The practice of Laban's Spatial Scales

Laban thought that the practice of the Scales was a civilised thing to do as opposed to the primitive or barbaric ways of moving that we considered above. In our advanced civilisation we could aspire to ways of moving that were in harmony with the cosmos to a degree that earlier civilisations had not succeeded in doing – with the possible exception of the Greek civilisation where there was some understanding of harmony and beauty. The scales were devised according to rules of mathematical proportion, proposing ways in which we could move around the kinesphere, looking at the kinesphere as having a polyhedral form. Laban talked a lot about the tetrahedron being an appropriate form for the Egyptian civilisation because they had a more limited understanding of the space around them. In our advanced civilised age, the Icosahedron is more appropriate to the way that we move.

But looking ahead into the long-distant future, the dodecahedron was advanced as being more appropriate. I always understood Laban's talk about the dodecahedron as being a projection of the universe. It is interesting that recent research does seem to offer some substantiation of the view that the universe has a dodecahedral shape, however quite how to relate doing your scales to the shape of the universe is a big jump, and I'm not sure that there is a relationship, or even that doing the scales is going to make us more harmonious people. I think there may be something in it, and certainly Laban believed that when children reach an age of perception it was good for them to practice the scales, and that this might induce a more harmonic relationship with the environment.

I understand that Laban held the idea that if we practice these scales we will achieve a harmony with the cosmic structure of all matter; however I am not sure that I personally can follow up on it. I like to do the scales and have a sense that I am keeping my body tuned, rather like keeping up with language by working on vocabulary. If you stop reading or having any stimulating conversation I suppose that you would start to lose your vocabulary and you would no longer have such a facility for writing and talking. Maybe it's the same with the scales: only I would add that it not only applies to space-harmony scales, but also to our Effort and Shape scales and in that way we would keep in touch with our repertoire and would be more likely to use that repertoire and therefore have a greater range of movement.

The scales are simply a technical basis. When you play musical scales you are reminded of certain intervals: you are not creating anything, but perhaps you are reminding yourself of the basis of harmony. The same goes for movement: if we go through certain Effort-Shape scales or some Effort-rhythms that remind us of the range available to us of effort, then we do keep in touch with the relatively larger repertoire. It doesn't mean that we are going to use the entire Effort-Shape repertoire because we have our own individual selectivity, our own individual patterns that we prefer. But that is a matter of proportion: we will still have a bigger repertoire that we can call upon in one way or another. The recommendation that I give to people for development purposes is not just to do with scales but rather to understanding the relationship between extending their movement-vocabulary through recognising what movements come most easily to them. I have already made the connection between language and movement vocabulary: say we have a stroke which leaves us with a very small vocabulary, then we have lost our full range of linguistic expression.

When I trained at the Art of Movement Studio we quite often had to do a study based, for example, on a particular ring. There are two rings which divide the icosahedron into two: there are three rings which are triangles that are oriented at different levels. The four rings aren't particularly interesting – they simply come in and out of a plane. The five rings are the more peripheral aspects of the icosahedron. But when we get to the seven rings they are fascinating: there are scores, indeed there could be hundreds, of them. Around each dimension you can build a seven ring. They have certain characteristics of joining steeples which have angular transitions with volutes where the angle is obtuse. They all have different forms of expression and different qualities and I've always seen them as directly analogous to say a Chopin étude. I've often wondered why no-one in the dance world has wanted to develop this. As far as I know, there is no school that has encouraged the choreographing of studies based upon Laban's space harmonies: it is a vast potential that I think could one day be realised. Many of these scales, or rings, as Laban called them, can be made the subject of a choreography, of a creative work. Just as in music we have forms like studies and etudes and preludes in certain keys, I think there is the equivalent in dance.

Laban's Diagonal Scale

My conclusions about Shape/Effort affinity originated with Laban's propositions about the affinities between Effort and Shape that can be seen in the Diagonal Scale but he took it no further than that. It was only the Diagonal Scale where he brought together the Effort and Shape into any sort of relationship. He would teach the Diagonal Scale as primarily to do with Effort, demanding at one moment more pressure, more punching, slashing or whatever, and in another movement insisting that we went down lower, for example. But he would always correct people if they weren't doing the appropriate Shape - he was aligning both Effort and Shape. In his teaching of the Icosahedron Scales, all the rings, Effort was never referred to in my recollection. The two fields were kept distinct.

The first movement of a Diagonal Scale which he considered was Floating: the first element of this consists of an open movement, which goes together with an indirecting movement, but this also includes a rising, and therefore a progressively lighter movement. It also includes some forwardness and therefore a sustained movement. The combination of the indirect, with the light, with the sustained he described as floating, and the shape appropriate to that would be open, forward and rising. He would always refer to basic Efforts and I always think in terms of basic Effort/Shapes. Still I am almost alone within the Laban fraternity in considering the basic Efforts as being in fact basic Effort/Shapes.

The Diagonal Scale is not just three Effort processes as in the example I've just given, but six processes: flexible, light, sustained as well as open, rising and the forward. Take into account also that there are two 'flow' processes as well and that these will most certainly be involved in the six Effort/Shape processes in ways that can be both fascinating and meaningful. So in the first movement of the diagonal scale there are eight movement processes happening. To get them all going together is an impossibility but you can work at trying to align them and get them into relationship with each other. When you reverse the first movement, then get into a punch, this can be quite an immense transition from one extreme to another: the contrast between a float and a punch is truly extreme.

When I have seen students performing the Diagonal Scale I have never seen them manage to get the six different movement elements happening together in one of the movements. Somebody will have got the indirecting process but then the sustainment process might become so arrested that it looks like the movement is being performed in slow motion. In the sense of movement being a process of variation, to see six processes of variation – or eight if you take into account flow – happening together is virtually impossible. The extreme of one component very often will be reached before another – what we actually see is not so much a floating into a punching movement but one that consists of a phrase, a sequence of graduated actions. This is why I regarded the idea of basic Efforts as a generalisation.

Another form of harmony can be regarded in not just the matching but in the consistency of the processes going together. An example is, if you are going to rise and you want to increase the element of lightness, the diminishing of pressure, in order to have delicate, fine sort of expression. For this to happen consistently you have to avoid the tendency for these processes to happen one after the other rather than together. The cohesion of a movement lies in the consistency of the linking of its different component elements.

Bringing Effort and Shape Together

A great watershed for me was when I approached Laban a year or two before he died and asked whether there was any reason why I shouldn't observe how people shape their movements, and relate this to their efforts. He seemed rather surprised but agreed. I don't think that there was ever any dichotomy between Laban's understanding of Effort and Shape, or Eukinetics and Choreutics.

Now I have got so wedded to the relation between Effort and Shape and look upon movement as a combination of them, and that nobody makes an Effort that isn't Shape, nor do they ever Shape their movement without an Effort. I think it helps if we look upon all movement as comprising both Effort and Shape – you can't do an Effort without it being Shaped, if only to a small degree, and you can't achieve a variation in your Shape unless you make an Effort, however slight. I'm constantly thinking of how Effort is being shaped and what effort is being put into the Shaping. The two are so interrelated.

My attempts to interpret the movement process in terms of the decision-making model was worked out very much in terms of the togetherness, the coming together, the relationships, the links between both the Effort and the Shape. I think that this was the case with Laban too. Recollecting how he taught me, although he was concentrating his questions on what I had observed in terms of efforts, nevertheless he was taking shaping into account because I don't think that he himself could segregate the two. He was an extremely perceptive and penetrating observer. I came to the conclusion eventually that this is what he'd been doing all the time – he'd been teaching me just to observe Effort but he himself had been observing Effort and Shape. I'm sure he didn't do it deliberately and maybe wouldn't have admitted it to himself, but who knows, he might have done. He did have the character of reserving to himself some element of his method. Although Space-harmony was at the heart of Choreutics, if ever he got angry, he would say that your knowledge was very elementary and he conveyed that he understood far, far more than you were ever going to understand. He might have not admitted to himself that Effort and Shape went together but might have still been aware that he had chosen to isolate industrial work to Effort.

In my own movement pattern I use more Effort (what I call Assertion) than Shape (Perspective), just the same as Dick McCaw does – we are both effortful characters. I think the relationship between the two is so rich: I would never accept an invitation to teach Effort by itself. In actual fact, all movement contains elements of Effort and Shape. We have to look upon movement as a kind of continuum, as a bi-polar process, because we are never completely still. We are always breathing and making involuntary twitches and reactions to the world around us. Even when asleep we continue to move. It is a fiction to segregate Effort from the Shaping that goes with it. We can never make an Effort without changing the Shape and we can sense this with our balance. To be able to have good balance means that you are probably making Efforts which are well-shaped. You cannot talk about Effort without Shape.

A very simple example of how Effort is related to Shape is how you get out of bed in the morning. Some people find this task quite difficult, but once you've made the effort you still have to shape it if you want to avoid knocking over the bedside lamp. The inter-relationship between the Effort and the Shape is always present, even though you might emphasise one more than the other. Somehow the definition has to include the fact that you are making a selection. You have noticed that the alarm clock hasn't gone off and you elect to jump out of bed with a massive thrust and in so doing knock over the bedside lamp and then slip on the floor. On the other hand, you might in different circumstances get out of bed rather carefully and take care how you step, and put an emphasis on the shaping. However, in both cases the potential for the Effort is already there, already alive.

The framework consists of the three Effort components and the Flow of Effort, and the three planes of Shape - which I refer to as Spreading and Enclosing, Rising and Descending, and Advancing and Retreating - and the Flow of Shape. These planes of Shape are also known as Horizontal, Vertical and Saggital, but I should emphasise that they refer to movement which is oriented towards one or other of the planes and, of course, in a diagonal movement the orientation is equally towards all three. It still upsets me to hear of people talking about Shaping in the Planes as if we were looking at a two-dimensional movement. We are not, we are looking at three-dimensional movement but it can have the different effects that I have just tried to explain. When you make this framework of three Shape orientations in the kinesphere combined with Flow many links or relationships become possible to be researched: for example, one polarity of Effort with one polarity of Shape, there are so many possible linkages. Some of these do seem to suggest that they are more harmonious than others: some may indicate whether we want to be sociable or not, whether we want to interact with other people or be private. There is a very fertile scope of understanding that can be gained or at least can be researched from a framework that defines Effort in relation to Shape or vice versa.

Polarities of Effort and Shape

One understanding which I have gained is that the polarity of our range of movement can change so that on a range of directing or indirecting, for example, the polarity tendency may indicate that a person uses more directing: a few years later a new profile may reveal that the relative extent of the directing/indirecting to the other components may have remained the same, but the polarity has changed. This may have significance in their interaction. In terms of movement a person can move from being very sharing to very private or vice-versa. That sort of change can happen in some patterns of behaviour more than in others. People can be more or less locked into their movement patterns.

What happens when you go to an extreme has interested me recently. I have given names to the different bi-polarities. If you increase pressure to the point where you can't do it any more, then you develop a cramp. If you decrease the pressure through the neutral area to a lightness you will reach a flop: this is a result of a positive decreasing of pressure. If you try to direct a movement so that you can't go any further you reach the point of a fixed stare, they become fixated. If someone starts pointing at you with their finger there will be an extreme beyond which they can't increase the pointing any more. If you indirect the movement positively then you get into twist, where people basically tie themselves in knots. If you accelerate so that you can't accelerate any more you reach a state of oscillation. Quite often people feel that if they've darted back it is because they've been afraid of falling, and they've accelerated to such an extent that they get into this oscillation as I call it. Whereas if you decelerate then you come to a standstill. I think it is often helpful to have an idea of these extremes so that it is between these extremes that we are observing the variations. Coming back to opening and closing, you can become so open that you reach an extreme. I remember seeing a pop singer who so wanted to open to his audience that he was liable to injure himself. I see the tendency to get close to an extreme in any movement as being in danger of approaching a pathological state. In terms of the kinesphere if you do a sideways enclosing then you look as if you have straitjacketed yourself. If you do a descending movement you can't fall any further than the floor, just as in rising the next step after the extreme would be to levitate above the floor.

On the Shape side if you enclose to an extreme you become completely enwrapped as in a strait-jacket. If you can't spread any more you become spread-eagled. Over the years I have been interested in people who are getting close to an extreme. I think this is where movement-development training can help them to avoid these extremes. An extreme is always a state of paralysis of movement - be it a cramp or a flop, or fixated, or whatever – unless you retrace the movement that got you there in the first place. If you are in a knot there is no point in trying to make quick movements to get yourself out of it: you can only untie yourself. And if you are in a fixated state there is no point in applying pressure, you can only indirect in order to get out of this state. If in any movement whether it is Effort or Shape you get to an extreme, you can only overcome the paralysis that it induces by returning along the same route. If you've got into a cramp because of increasing pressure you can't shake yourself out of it, you've got to diminish the pressure. That can and is being used in a therapeutic context. Quite a lot of therapies make the mistake of trying to help overcome the states that people have got themselves into through some sort of influence which is foreign to the way that they got themselves into that situation in the first place.

Another aspect of future development is the question of gender. I do believe that I have discovered the difference between male and female in terms of movement. Not quite! But there seems to be a tendency which is universal that men and women make different associations of flow with Effort and Shape. This leads me to say that women can do everything a man can do and vice-versa, it is just that they both do them differently. Women behave differently when in authority, for example. Whether this is a refinement or not, this has been an area of interest for me. However, I have failed miserably to get anyone other than Eden Davies, author of *Beyond Dance*, interested in this. She is working on this now.

Warren Lamb's Development of the Concept of Harmony

As I've said already, harmony was always being linked to Choreutics. I would like to emphasise that this isn't the only form of harmony that we can look upon in movement. We can also consider whether Effort Rhythms are harmonious or not. If you exert Effort in an inharmonious way what are you doing differently to when you exert it in a harmonious way? Laban did suggest that there were good rhythms and bad rhythms; that the combination of weight, space, time and flow all combined to make it a really positive rhythm as distinct from rhythms which were broken and discordant. You could make the same analogy with music, I suppose. The question becomes immensely richer, when aesthetics are introduced into a consideration of Efforts. Laban too got into that question but not to the extent that he could have.

Certainly with regard to the industrial work that I did we were trying to help workers achieve a more harmonious way of doing the job that they had to do. This could be perhaps by incorporating some additional movement; replacing a movement that they had got into the habit of doing with something that was better related to the nature of the job. This intervention, of course, was also to help them succeed in relating their own individual rhythms and patterns of movement to the job: then they would achieve a more harmonious relationship. It was never really referred to as 'harmonious', Laban talked about their movement achieving rhythm as distinct from having no rhythm. A better way of looking at it was that there was always some form of rhythm but you could have either a good or a bad, an appropriate or an inappropriate rhythm. Some rhythms could be harmonious whilst others could be relatively grotesque. The same could be said in respect to space harmonies: by going against the rules of mathematical proportion which Laban built into all his scales, you would get into various degrees of disharmony, or even extremes of grotesqueness. Similarly, the same phenomenon could apply within the field of the efforts.

It is difficult to observe, to analyse or prove whether there is any harmony or not in a movement without looking at all the parts of the body that are involved. It may be that a form of disharmony is created because one part of the body is contradicting what another part does. A one-man-band where the player has drumsticks tied to his elbows, cymbals to his knees, whilst he blows a harmonica, an act of immense concentration, can create some music - possibly not pleasant to listen to - but at least something that can be achieved.   I think it would be extremely unlikely for any person seeing someone playing all these instruments to think that the movement was beautiful.   On the other hand someone playing a violin or harp, even a conductor conducting the orchestra is much more likely to convey harmony. Whether a conductor of an orchestra actually assumes some element of disharmony in his or her own movement to accompany passages where there is dissonance in the music is unlikely but interesting to speculate upon.

The example of the one-man-band was to illustrate the point that we have to look at parts of the body in relation to each other if we are going to try to understand harmony in movement. It would be useless to regard just whirling an arm around as being a harmonious movement, unless we look at it in relation to the body. I don't know whether we can relate harmony to beauty but beauty as well as being in the eye of the beholder, has often been attributed by poets to how a person moves rather than in a subject's fixed presentation. I was fascinated by Goethe's description of how Lady Hamilton moves:

> She effects changes of postures, moods, gestures, mien and appearance that make one really feel as if one were in some dream. Here is visible, complete and bodied forth in movements of surprising variety, all that so many artists have sought in vain to fix and render.   Successively standing, kneeling, seated, reclining, grave, sad, sportive, teasing, abandoned, penitent, alluring, threatening, agonised. One follows the other and grows out of it. [Quoted in *Posture and Gesture*, p.28]

Plutarch wrote that Cleopatra wasn't really anything to look at – in today's terms she wouldn't be a pin-up - but that she was beautiful in her movement because it was so fascinating and compelling. Today models very often conform to our Western cultural notions of beauty. This is of course something that is culturally specific; canons of beauty in this country have changed over the ages. But they let themselves down when they gesture, smile or walk. After seeing their photographic images, their movements are disappointing.

There are Space harmonies and there are also Effort harmonies and we have to look at how one part of the body is functioning in relation to another. Then there is a whole other aspect of harmony which I think is better referred to as affinity or disaffinity when we look at the relationship between the Effort and the Shape and there seem to be certain relationships that are more concordant than discordant.

To give a couple of examples: if you are going to wield a hammer then it seems that you do a more appropriate Shaping to the Effort by hammering in a downward direction. Maybe you have to hammer a nail into the ceiling, and it can be done; but there is an argument for saying that it is not so appropriate to do an increasing pressure movement upwards. It is much more 'natural'; it seems to be much more appropriate to do a strong movement in a downwards direction. Similarly, if you are really focusing on something, say you are repairing a watch, then you don't do it at arm's length, you want to bring it into a more concave-shaped kinesphere, so that you can get the effort of directing and perform the very delicate movements required. On the other hand, if you are brushing things away, say flies that are swarming around you, then it would be more appropriate to have a more convex shaping of the kinesphere and bring together a spreading shape of movement with the more indirect effort. One could say that our muscles are so arranged that we are physically preconditioned to move forward in a more sustained way and then to accelerate more in a backwards direction. I think this is related to our 'fight or flight' protection response. We dart back from danger quickly whereas we advance more cautiously towards what may be ahead of us. In these ways, although we can move in a contrary way to what I am defining as having affinity, from a point of view of efficiency at work it seems to be sensible to try and get as much affinity as you can between the effort and the shape in the working movement.

But it has another significance which I have found does seem to be remarkably cross-cultural. If we want to interact with somebody, say to share an activity with a person, then we tend to produce movement where the Effort and Shape are in affinity. Whereas if someone approaches you and you do not want to interact with him or her then what we do in order to discourage any interaction is to generate a form of disaffinity between Effort and Shape. This is remarkably cross-cultural. You do find this when looking at people who are known to be loners and who have a reclusive tendency that there is a considerable disaffinity between Shape and Effort; whereas people who are more sociable, who like to be with people, constantly produce movement where the Effort and Shape are in affinity.

The understanding that people may or may not want to share their activity, and the tendency that we have to introduce disharmonies in our movement if we don't want to interact is a very important factor in team relationships. Somebody without necessarily being uncooperative, may nevertheless feel that he or she just can't contribute something at that moment and wants to withdraw and so will introduce a disharmonious movement. Other people will sense this in the group and therefore conclude that the person is anti what the rest of the group wants to do.

I find that misinterpretations are made when people are working together on the basis of how they move. Sometimes the interpretations can be correct but very often they are misinterpretations. I have found that on the part of the person who is thought to be uncooperative that there is often no intention whatsoever to be so. The movement creates a misunderstanding. This can often be recognised and dealt with in a way that avoids misinterpretation and which rather draws upon a knowledge of how and when a person does want to interact, as distinct from an attempt to compel someone to do so because this is expected from a good member of the team. I think exhortations to work well as a team have very little merit, whereas understanding how people are motivated to interact can have a significant effect on how people can work together better as a team. Of course, teamwork doesn't always consist of just being physically together. Even when people are on the other side of the world your perception of them, built upon previous encounters where that person's movement has had an influence on you, will influence how you interact with each other, even though you aren't in their physical presence.

On the Grotesque and the Ugly

Laban did seem to have an interest in the grotesque and in his choreographic work of the 1920s he used to like satyrs and witches and that sort of thing. I think he needed to develop ideas about what was grotesque in movement because of his interest in what is harmonious: that way you get the one in relation to the other. I feel that if you get an inconsistency or a contradiction in a movement that very often tends to create grotesqueness, and comedy too. You get the unexpected: a comedian moves in a certain way and then collapses the pattern of movements I remember studying Charlie Chaplin who maintained a posture and then often did gestures that were contradictory to that posture and the comedy very often is created in this way. Sometimes grotesque movement might be created through this kind of contradiction. I don't know whether Laban would say that comedy is related to the grotesque; I don't know it is necessarily so. But this is a vast subject and I feel that it is a bit crass to generalise.

There is much to be said about the aesthetic dimension of movement. You see people doing ugly gestures; it often seems to me that it would be much more pleasant for the people that they're in contact with, as well as for themselves, if they could not do such grotesque movements. I think I see more everyday grotesqueness in the United States than I do in England: the way that people walk very often, in supermarkets, getting in and out of their cars, very often the way that a mother will handle her child   lots of things of this sort. What makes them grotesque is firstly that the gesture is very often inconsistent with the movement that is going on in the rest of the body; secondly there is an inappropriateness of the Effort in relation to the Shape: this is inefficient. They don't necessarily have to be aware that they have hunched their shoulders in this way or that, or that they have gesture idiosyncrasies, but one has the sense that they don't have much spatial awareness – this much is clear from the way that they move around you. They don't really know how they move about in space. It seems as though there is something mechanical in people's movements. I can even recognise this tendency in myself despite all my work in movement. One can very easily get into habits which I think are ugly or potentially so. Children need to be educated so that they can grow up to be confident that they can move harmoniously. The feedback from someone who moves aesthetically makes them feel better about themselves.

I begin to wonder about my own movement since we all seem to be able to relapse into such forms of grotesque behaviour. It can happen if you are worried about something, or are having to give attention to practical things whilst your mind is trained upon some bigger issue. Very often when we are torn in this way our movement reflects it in some form of ugliness. Whether learning about movement harmonies is going to help us to avoid slipping into these movement uglinesses in adult life remains to be proved, but it is a possibility. I think that it's worth paying attention to Laban's grotesque in relation to the harmonious: I think it could be a very valuable form of study to be incorporated in general education.

We can relapse into bad habits in many aspects of life, and we can allow it to continue. Take the example of food. If we eat too much then we get fat, but if you continue then you suffer worse. We can get into a bad habit of movement because we might feel tortured about something – this is human nature: we get distressed and express this distress in various ways. But I think a movement education can make you perceptive enough so that eventually you can correct it. You do begin to apply the corrections. This does require a discipline, just as one has to monitor one's diet. It may come more easily to some than to others and there are obviously many factors involved. But the process of applying corrections seems to me to be what is mostly going on. We have to expect to relapse but we can have some sort of moderating power or control over the extent to which we relapse; and by constantly applying corrections we will be able to keep more on the side of harmony than grotesqueness in the long term. You go a little off balance so you make a corrective movement so as to restore that balance.

xiii. Movement Categories: From Body Attitude, Functional Action and Shadow Movement

Laban varied quite a lot in the categories he used to describe movement – however he mostly categorised movement in the factory under three headings:

Body Attitudes
Functional Actions
Shadow Movements

This is what he taught. I struggled for years to define the limits to these categories. What was a Shadow Movement? It could be a flicker of an eyebrow – that would always be agreed upon. But if you did a startled movement of the head – was that a Shadow Movement, a Functional Action or something else? Body attitude seemed to me to be referred to by others in a static sense, in terms of a physique posture. It could be sloppy, dreamy, militaristic. Laban's imagination was very fertile when it came to giving names to Body Attitudes. But it seemed to me that this wasn't something that moved or changed but was general.

Body Attitude has been very much misunderstood and was considered as a fixed thing rather than a movement term. It was like someone having a hangdog expression or a military bearing.

Functional Actions were considered as being different to expressive actions. Functional actions one observed in industry: you moved your arm in order to pick up a cup. But if you move your arm to accompany a speech then it is expressive. Functional actions were to be observed at work. I could never succeed in making a satisfactory distinction between functional and expressive but they were all part of the same category. I spent quite a lot of time thinking about Body Attitude and came to the conclusion that it was movement that I wanted to observe and not attitude.

Shadow Movements he would define as ones that flit across the surface of the body. He probably described Shadow Movements in other ways too. What is a movement that flits across the body as distinct from movements that use body parts but don't flit across the surface? He gave the flicker of the eyebrow as an example of a Shadow Movement. That can be very meaningful depending on the context. I remember a performance where a slight flicker of an actor's eyebrow was the cue to start a revolution. Shadow Movements can be very useful in television and film acting especially with the greater interest in close-up shots where you can see the very pores of the actor's skin. Some people say that Shadow Movements are very revealing and show people's feelings. Jack Nicholson's more recent performances on film have consisted almost entirely of Shadow Movements – smirks, grins and rolls of the eye.

What do doodles mean? They could be described as Shadow Movements. I can see that this is a useful rough idea to encourage the actor to be aware as to what might be expressive for an audience. I find it difficult to know where to draw the line between Shadow Movements and other movements. I have grouped all Shadow Movements under the category of Gestures. If you're observing and you want to be precise in your observations, they may be too small, too slight to be observable. If you want to make an actor aware of how the twitching of his lips is either impairing or adding to his performance, then that's fine. By definition, they will always be isolated gestures, though a flicker of an eyebrow might develop into a movement in the rest of the body, it can lead into a fuller Body Attitude. Very often you see this happen in a conversation: very often a Shadow Movement can develop into a bigger movement phrasing.

You couldn't really observe Body Attitudes as movement. It was difficult to distinguish between a large Shadow Movement and an expressive movement.   Surely Shadow Movements can be very expressive and meaningful. I just felt that these were not tenable divisions and that Shadow and Expressive movement came together.   But where did Body Attitude come into it? I remember Laban being asked the question, 'Do Functional Actions always mean that you have to be dealing with an object, for example touching something?' He replied that no, a Functional Action could be expressive. It may be as simple as the expression, 'Put it over here please', and you make an indication of where that should be. That is functional.   The definitions I've just given of functional and shadow movement were not always adhered to.

When Laban was advising on people he was recognised as having a very deep perception into people's personality, women in particular, felt that he could penetrate into their innermost being. In order to gain that understanding I don't think that Laban just remained with the concept of the person being a flicker or a slasher - he saw much more than that. During the late 40s and early 50s when I started observing and trying to work out what it was that I was observing, I was meeting with Laban. He would add to the definitions in some way, during which I would say, 'Yes, yes'.   But when I subsequently sat down to think what it was that he had told me, and how I could systematise it, then it was very difficult to do so. As I've already mentioned, if you came to him to say that you were having problems trying to systematise his thinking he would say, 'My work is not a system, I am not interested in a system'. So I didn't really get much help.

Thus, I was left with the problem of trying to distinguish between these three types of movement. Was an actor's movement Functional or Shadow? It became very difficult for me to differentiate between the two. The only differentiation that I could make was trying to clarify different types of Effort Rhythms. This is something that I really did learn from Laban. Whereas other people latched onto a generalised, and in my opinion an often very static, concept of what he meant by Body Attitude, Functional Actions and Shadow Movements, with me he was always talking about Effort Rhythm. In the industrial work this is how movement was described. I was always presenting Laban with phrases of movement, and very often you could see how the rhythm was used. I wanted to see some sort of progress, some sort of rhythm in any movement I was observing. You just can't see that in the Shadow Movements - it may be happening, but it is too small to observe. So I slowly came to the conclusion that there is only one category of movement and that is movement that you can see, as opposed to movement that is so small that you can't see - so as to determine whether it is slow, quick, strong, light, direct or indirect. That was the first step towards getting some sort of categorisation.

xiv.   *Movement as a process of variation*

In terms of movement we can never say that we are making just one movement because we are making a phrase, in which something changes, in which there is an increasing of one Effort component and a decreasing of another, or the combining of some elements. If I make an effort of pointing I can stay like a statue but obviously something eventually has to follow; it can be a withdrawal or a directing which goes on to something else. We have to think of process when thinking of Effort; process is an essential element when looking for a definition of Effort or Shape. It is something that advances or retreats, that accelerates or decelerates. Any process of Effort, for example, can only go so far. If I am getting more and more direct I must reach a point at which I can't get any more direct. Usually that registers as a fixed stare, so if I want to make a direct effort, if I want to point something out to you, to focus on that thing, I have to keep renewing it. So a definition of Effort has somehow to include the fact that for an effort to be effective it has to be renewed.

I find myself constantly exhorting people to look upon movement as a process of variation. I am really surprised that I have to do this because you would think that it was obvious, but I can understand how easily movement terms can be used to described a static position. I have heard of somebody being described as 'direct' – a New Yorker, for instance – because they assume a 'direct' attitude and maintain it. A maintained, 'frozen' movement ceases to be a movement: there is no process of variation. When I meet 'direct' New Yorkers, one might say that they have this frozen attitude of being direct, but not in the sense of having relative qualities of direct and indirect. For the movement to be alive, any directing, as we discussed earlier, will either go to a limit where it will become paralysed or it will be reversed. It may often be reversed in order to be renewed. Then one can say that the quality is direct, or I prefer to use the present participle, 'directing' to get away from the idea of there being a fixed 'direct' but a movement that is going somewhere, something is happening to it.

With that understanding, when a person does a gesture then it can belong to and join in with another process. It is like when you are jumping off a bus which is going at a particular speed and, as long as it is going slowly enough, and you jump off in the direction of travel then you join in the bus's movement and you don't fall: but if you jump in the opposite direction then there is no joining – you are going against the bus's direction. Similarly, when you are trying to integrate gestures into the body you want to do so with the process of movement in the rest of the body rather than to impact against it. We need to recognise both the movement - let's say the gesture of the arm – then we have to recognise the process of the movement as it leads into the body: it may become a movement within the process of variation within the body. Or it can be the other way round: the body as a whole may move and then that leads into an arm, and then the phrase is finished.

xv.   Observation

I don't think that I'm unique in having an eye for movement, a sense of movement, or being able to observe movement. I often quote an engineer whom I met many years ago who just seemed to be able to observe movement very easily but wasn't particularly interested to do so. He was an engineer and was quite fulfilled in his work, so he didn't regard observation as something that he wanted to develop. I quote that as an example of those people who do have a kinaesthetic sense which predisposes them to observe other people's movement.   Where that sense exists it can be developed. If you are teaching courses in observation the first thing is to find someone who has that predisposition for a kinaesthetic sense. As in all things, you need to find this initial potential.   Then it is a question of time and practice, even if this is based upon a certain body of knowledge. Laban has provided that body of knowledge.

I think I was interested in observing movement during the War. I recall the movement of some of my shipmates, for example. Although during actual battles I was too distracted, I do remember the movement of a Petty Officer who panicked under attack and I observed him rushing around. I still have a picture of that in my mind.   I think I was already primed when Laban came on the scene and I recognised that here was a man who had developed a body of knowledge that was really going to be interesting for me on the basis of what I'd already established to some degree.

Laban taught me by throwing me in at the deep end. I've already described how I used to have to stand in factories taking masses of observations, he spent very little time actually with me. His contribution was during the hours when he would examine my records and question me as to whether it was this or that, did this happen, and was I sure about it all? These were quite penetrating questions which revealed Laban's own ability to recreate the situation and understand what was going on. His observations were, as I've frequently said, highly generalised. He had the observatory capacity to look at somebody and sum up the main features of their movement very quickly. Although I have always tried to go into as much detail as possible, there is a need for some selection. You can't observe all that goes on in a person's movement – there's too much happening. While you're still using the human eye to make observations, and making notes on paper, Laban was quite right to say that you have to select something that you can see, and then record – and you don't worry about what you can't see. I have followed that very strictly, and taught that to other people. You look and then you look away. One thing that I've added is that if you've once found yourself struggling as to whether a movement, for example, was directing or indirecting, and you begin hesitating, then it's too late. You need to be able to see something and record it in the next instant. You do have to be quick. As I say, 'If you hesitate, then don't notate!' Speed of response is an important factor, and something I am increasingly concerned about because as you get older your speed of reaction is slower. I do still manage to take observations adequately quickly, but I wouldn't recommend that anyone takes up the study of movement observation too late in life.

The ways of teaching movement observation are, I suppose, the same as teaching anything. You can teach using the 'Standing Next to Nelly' approach. In other words you ask the student to come along with you and do what you are doing, and afterwards you can both discuss what happened. In that way gradually the student can learn, through seeing the teacher at work. That's how I taught Pamela Ramsden. Although she is a bit scathing about it, I taught her rather effectively – she became a very good observer. We had an office in Regent Street near Piccadilly Circus and there was one café where it was convenient to sit and watch people walking by. People are rightly critical of the 'Standing Next to Nelly' approach where you are using highly technical equipment and there's a lot of technology involved. But this is a situation where you are using the human eye and making a record of what you see. This doesn't apply to any technology other than your own capacity. What has since developed is looking at video tapes of people moving. I have always been critical of this. It can be helpful so long as it is accompanied by a lot of live observation because the video distorts movement. Pamela went her own way and she disregarded this and has tried teaching using only video-tape, but eventually admitted that it could not and should not be done. I think there is now a general consensus that you do need to supplement or complement video footage with live observation.

Another distinction has been whether you just note down the PGMs or whether you record the phrase in which the PGM appears. This is what I developed as a method and what I always practiced, but Pamela developed the Recording Sheet on which all the various Efforts and Shapes were recorded by putting a tick when you saw it happen. For example they may see an increase of pressure and then tick the appropriate box: but it may have been a fixed state and not a movement that they were observing. I think that was the first step, or mis-step, that led to the problem of people not observing movement as a process. Secondly, this takes away from an understanding about how the PGM arose. That is, that a particular gesture became merged into the posture and then came out of the posture into another gesture, perhaps. I've always found this understanding of movement to be helpful, particularly when, having made a record, I can go back to a phrase and just reconstruct what happened at the time. That's really a bonus – it should not be necessary to do that in order to make the profile, but, as I say, it is helpful to recreate for yourself something of the situation in which the PGM appeared.

Thirdly there is the question of the participation of the observer. You can, I'm sure observe movement from behind a one-way screen, but I would find that difficult. I've been working recently on the nature of that participation. I think it is that we associate our own flow of movement, our own breathing, for example; even if this is unobservable as a movement, there will be some freeing of the flow as we breathe out, and binding of the Flow as we breathe in; there might be some growing Shape-flow as we breathe in and some shrinking as we breathe out. It may be very slight but there will be some harmonising – and breathing might be one illustration of what I think happens when an observer associates his or her flow of movement with that of the interviewee. Carol-Lynne Moore advocates this and she is a very good teacher of observation. She has done an immense amount of work to clarify what she is doing, in order to improve it. She always recommends that the observer spend twenty minutes attuning herself to the other person before attempting to observe.

These are all points that I would advocate for teaching movement observation. There could be 'Next to Nelly' along with class-room teaching, as well as video, as long as there is sufficient live observation. I used to take my students into railways stations and into parks, just where people were milling around. I don't think that most of Pamela and Carol-Lynne's students do that. Perhaps I should try to sell them the idea that this is worthwhile. If we just take the opportunity when waiting in an airport lounge to observe all the people around us. I have advocated this repeatedly, but no-one ever tells me that they do it very much! It may be a little bit too much like work. But observation can be fun! Sometimes in my leisure moments I do take out a pad and take notes of an interesting movement – maybe I should do this more frequently. But I do think it is good to keep in practice by observing and knowing what it is you are observing. Whether it happens in my lifetime I don't know but hopefully observations will eventually be taken electronically and then we can really become more scientific in the whole process. It does need to have this kind of precision if it is going to make a worthwhile contribution to the field of brain research.

Laban talked a lot about Effort without always being specific about how we see it. In the evening after standing all day in a factory, I brought him pages of observations which I had made. He would then spend all evening – two or three hours maybe – questioning me on how I had seen the movement.   But he never taught me how to see the movement, so I suppose this was throwing me in at the deep end and that this was his belief as to the best way of teaching. I was designated by him to go into factories and observe people's efforts without really being taught how or where to look.   If you are going to observe Effort then you must see it somewhere and somehow, so there must be a part of the body in which you are seeing an effort. It seemed to be essential to note the part of the body where the Effort appeared, then of course the appearing: let's say you saw somebody increasing the pressure of his hand, perhaps becoming a fist, then something follows on from that: having started with an increasing pressure it then becomes perhaps more directed, more focused on a particular aim, or point. In the process of aiming, in order to get more momentum there may be an acceleration: so we see the increasing pressure get into a directing and an increasing pressure, but then with the actual impact there is a rebound and perhaps you see an indirecting occur and that maybe with a lessening of the pressure, or even a retention of the pressure. I am trying to give a word picture of the effort actually happening.

I think the problem which Laban protégés have in trying to get his work understood and recognised lies in the fact that it is about process of variation, flux. It is difficult getting this over to people who want to pin things down. Quite often people who studied with Laban never quite overcame the problem of trying to render kinetic phenomena statically – for others that distinction is very easily understood, it is just part of their nature. We are still primarily in a static world. Laban was so absorbed by movement. The world consisted in movement. Stillness for him was something that he abhorred. He would often refer to everything as being in a state of flux. 'Flux' was a word he often used. We have to recognise that most people are trying to pin down flux and yet there is so much to be gained if we can only rejoice in the flux of the process, if we are to understand movement.

To explain the concept of movement as a process of variation I used to take students to railway stations and construction sites and so on because you could stand and observe without your subject of observation becoming too self-conscious. I took this girl to a railway station and asked her to observe someone who was getting really quite agitated because they wouldn't let him on to the platform although the train was still there. After having tried to observe him she then exclaimed, 'If he'd only stand still I could see something'. Observing movement requires immense concentration and discipline. It is so much easier to observe something that is still and therefore if it isn't still and is moving we try to convert it to being fixed so as to render it more amenable for observation. I think a great deal of misunderstanding arises because a lot of people who think they are studying movement are not. It's not movement that they are looking at.

I remember a woman who worked in New York, in some ways a very capable person. She took observations of a patient and a therapist and her study was headed 'Observations of Movement'. She listed about twenty or thirty static positions even though she was trained in movement. One said – I remember it exactly – 'Hands held still by the side for long periods'. That was given as a movement observation. It is quite a legitimate observation to make and record, but not under the heading of movement observations. Movement is sometimes considered as ephemeral and therefore unimportant. By extension, one can say the same thing about dance and ballet as art forms. It is a perennial problem one has to face. It is almost like those times when if you wanted to study animal behaviour you killed the animal and then laid it out. Only recently have biologists studied them alive: and the fact still remains that the observation of animal movement is immensely complex – even though animals don't have the same range of movements that humans do.

I remember talking to Henry Moore about movement and he said, 'Everything I do is movement'. Whether he understood that movement can be studied I don't know but Laban used to talk about how with certain painters you could see the movement of the brush through how the paint had been applied to the canvas. Everybody moves and yet the extent of understanding is pitiful and I just wonder whether one day there will be a breakthrough when the scope and possibility of studying movement will become recognised. It certainly doesn't show any signs of happening now.

With regard to Movement Pattern Analysis we need to record, say, two hundred phrases of movement so as to be able to analyse an adequate sample for making an individual profile. As long as you have two hours in which to observe someone, then it can be undertaken in any situation - a cocktail party, a reception, or whatever. With all the distractions of a cocktail party it would be difficult, but it could be done. This will offer a representative sample, a true picture of the person's movement. You can, as I am doing now, observe people on video tape as they give speeches on official platforms, and suchlike. But in order to make as rigorous a profile as you can, you need to see a person continuously for two hours. If you saw them in eight fifteen minute periods they might contrive their movements and sustain them for each of those periods, so one does need a continuous two hour observation period. Their pattern of movement will be revealed in this time. Very often you see that pattern emerging early on in those two hours, but you still need the rest of the time just to confirm the precise nature of that pattern.

xvi. Notation

When I came across Laban I was impressed by the discovery that a form of movement notation existed. Of course, that only revealed my ignorance since forms of dance notation had existed for centuries – going back to Greek and Egyptian times. I did think that it was obvious that since there was music notation then there should also be movement notation. Laban's notation seemed to be analogous with music notation. As I got to learn about Laban, his standing in Germany, his contribution to theatre (especially Theatre Workshop), I understood the background to his notation and also came to the conclusion that of all the other notations around in the 1940s his was the most comprehensive. Although it was primarily used and known as dance notation – it was controlled in the U.S. by a Dance Notation Bureau – I maintained that it could be used to observe workers' movements or everyday movement.

Of course Laban's system is still used for notating or teaching dance. The reason why I concluded that it had become so superior to other systems was because of Laban's codification of the components of movement. There was much more research and creativity behind it than was the case in other forms of notation. He was constantly adding to and developing his notation. He had such a creative mind that if you tried to refer to something that he had thought yesterday, he would already have moved on to something else and have some alternative ideas or solutions. If he had been still alive the system would have kept changing and never could have been used as a historical record of dances. Without the work of Albrecht Knust in Germany and Ann Hutchinson Guest in the US and the UK, nothing fixed would ever have been written down. They were responsible for getting it into a strictly defined form: unfortunately the two schools have followed separate paths. The notation enables us to be disciplined, we can make a record. While I have never claimed to be scientific I have always been disciplined and practical, to be able to know and demonstrate what I have seen. If there has been some interpretation I have been able to show how I have interpreted it and how it could be interpreted in different ways.

Then Laban came up with what he called Effort graphs - which weren't really graphs at all – which is a separate notation. It is possible to have the dance notation and the effort notation side by side, just as in a musical score dynamic there are indications of forte, piano and so forth. Just as in music these indicate how a piece should be performed, so the Effort graphs show how a dance should be performed. I started off using the Effort notation, and when I included shape in my observations I simply adapted the Effort graphs to include Shape. Laban was constantly experimenting with notation, even when he was working with me. I have never looked upon the notation we've used for analysis purposes as comparable with a notation whose function is to record a choreography. Effort graphs had been developed before I came on the scene, he was still flexible in how it could be used and was open to developing something else should it prove more convenient.

The graphs that I subsequently developed are not so much notations of movement but the representation of the framework of movement. For observation purposes I use the Effort 'graph' originated by Laban with a single addition so that it also works for recording Shape. Labanotation (or Kinetography as the version derived from Albrecht Knust is known) is designed to make a complete record of a choreography so that it can be used to reconstruct a performance be it a dance, work operation, or gymnastic display. My requirement is to make a sampling of a person's movement. We cannot possibly observe every movement a person does.   I present it in this form to demonstrate that movement is a process and that one should not use movement terms in order to describe something which is fixed. The framework has been crystallised in the way it has to keep movement understood as a process of variation.

PART THREE ~ THE DEVELOPMENT OF A METHOD (1950 – 2000)

Introduction to Part Three

This short section of the book follows Lamb's development after leaving the Art of Movement Studio and how he set up in business. Although in our conversations Lamb gives the impression that after leaving the Studio he worked solely in factories, a sentence from *The Movement Man* indicates that in 1950 he was still as committed to dance as to the industrial work:

> My personal priority at that time was still to dance with the British Dance Theatre, and only secondly when we had no engagements to work for Laban and Lawrence. [Chapter 9, pp.9 - 10]

The British Dance Theatre was run by Hettie Loman, who was mentioned above in Parts I and II, and in his diaries from the late 1940s. It is important to recall that Lamb is not simply a theorist of movement, but someone who started off with a practical engagement in movement, and who in his teaching remains an enthusiastic mover even in his early 80s. He admits to being incapable of lecturing unless he can give his vivid demonstrations (echoing what he said about Laban as a teacher in Part I).

Part III begins with an overview of the different phases of Laban's and Lamb's work in the factories. At first it took the form of training sessions in which workers were taken from their posts to perform a series of movements which would 'compensate' for the repetitive movements at the machines. Another kind of intervention was to teach workers how to achieve certain tasks more easily – for example, women in the Tyresoles Factory[14], swinging heavy outer tyres onto hooks, rather than lifting them as dead weight, as men would do. Laban described this approach as 'Lilt in Labour'. Very soon both Laban and Lamb began to use their movement analysis less to train people how to do a job, and more to assess whether they were suitable for that particular job. Lamb describes two massive programmes he undertook at Faithful Overalls and in Glaxo. From selection of workers on the factory floor it was a short step for Lamb to start considering the recruitment of new staff for a position. Finally, we see Lamb graduating from the factory floor to the board room where he has been operating ever since.

Warren Lamb's method will be discussed in much greater detail in Part IV; in the meantime I shall offer a chronology of his major conceptual developments over the

---

[14] Tyresoles – see a full description of it in Eden Davies' *Beyond Dance*, p.39

past fifty years. We have already described how Lamb's first breakthrough which occurred in 1957/8 was to realise that Effort and Shape did not need to be considered separately. The next was to develop Laban's four mental efforts of 'attention, intention, decision and precision observable in the bodily attitude of the mental worker' [*Effort*, p.60]. Lamb realised that Attention, Intention and Decision could be considered as a sequence, indeed as the necessary sequence, for a decision-making process. He describes his discovery in one of our conversations:

> The decision-making process became much clearer as a sequence. Laban never considered it as a sequence: I claimed it began with Attention, which develops into Intention and the Decision reaches a point of no return. This was a stage when the nature of the decision-making process was clarified in my thinking.

This breakthrough must have happened in the mid-1950s because we already find it in *Movement and Personality*:

> This order, i.e. Attention - Intention -Decision, is unalterable without breaking the composition of mental concentration. It is obviously impracticable to form intentions about something which has not yet been brought to the attention and ineffective to make a decision where no intention exists. These are stages in a process which must conform to the prescribed sequence and they are measurable states in themselves - the state of attention, or being attentive; the state of intention, or determining or resolving; the state of decision, or of committing oneself. [*Movement and Personality*, p.223]

Attention Intention Decision

Lamb also asserts that the necessary order in decision-making echoes the development sequence in which children learn to move, and in which they play. (Possibly this gives us some indication of the possible contents of his unpublished manuscript about work and play.)

> When children are left to themselves, at play for example, it is noticeable that all new demands are first approached with a physical manner of attentiveness – observing, exploring, investigating the new situation involving predominantly variation of Horizontal-Space. Then there is an actual physical adjustment suggesting - or of some intention being formed – an expression of resolve of determination (Vertical-Force). Finally the child commits itself to action - makes its decision and accepts the finality of it (Saggital – Time) [*Posture and Gesture*, pp. 98 – 99]

Later, he will go on to assert that this sequence of Attention, Intention, Commitment refers equally to our Shaping as to our Effort initiatives. Again, we see him using the example of the observed movements of children at play.

> The sequence as shown is deliberate. We tend, for example, to spread-enclose, or indirect-direct, before we rise-descend or diminish-increase pressure, even if variation in the latter case is greater. The logicality of the sequence is shown from studies of children, in whom it is very obvious, or from adults in a learning situation. It is fascinating, for example, to watch young children suddenly faced by something new or in a new situation. They go through a stage where they clearly give attention to what is going on, while staying close to a parent or just standing still. Then there is a stage when they begin to look as though they are going to do something - the intention stage. Suddenly, without further warning, they are off, acting on some decision which in a moment they may think better of, but meanwhile has a definiteness to it. [*Management Behaviour*, pp.70 - 71]

Later in *Management Behaviour* he states that 'movement in the spreading and enclosing planes precedes the rising-descending, which precedes the advancing-retiring' [Ibid., p.86]. Lamb now uses 'Retreating' rather than Retiring. I hope these quotations are sufficient to make it clear that Lamb considers that Attention, Intention, Commitment is a 'logical sequence' and not arbitrary.

Once again we see Lamb applying a methodological rigour to Laban's inspired but unsystematic ideas. By establishing a logical sequence of Shape and Effort initiatives Lamb could explain in an objective way how a person's movement pattern corresponds to their favoured approach to the sequence of decision-making. It is disarmingly simple: before you make a decision about something you have to notice it, so at first you take it in, you give it your full Attention. Then you need to ponder and deliberate what action you can take in relation to what you've seen. Interestingly the first meanings for the verb 'Ponder' listed in the OED are all to do with weight and weighing. Very literally, the second stage of decision-making is about weighing up the pros and cons of the situation. Finally, you have to take the plunge; you have to Commit to action. Lamb changed Laban's word 'decision' to Commitment, simply because the word 'decision' is vague: the whole process is about decision-making, and he needs to distinguish the particular function of this third, time-based stage of the process. We should also note that Lamb leaves out of consideration the correspondence between 'precision' and Flow. As always, he is after greater precision and clarity in his method.

COMMITTING THROUGH
THE POINT OF
NO RETURN

INTENDING

ATTENDING

Figure 6. The Decision Making Process

This clear and deceptively simple approach to decision-making is what would now be called an example of embodied thinking (George Lakoff and Mark Johnson have written extensively on the subject in *Metaphors We Live By* and *Philosophy in the Flesh*). Lakoff and Johnson would begin by demonstrating how fundamental are the three focuses in this sequence: firstly, the physical experience of looking around at, of searching for (the first actions that a baby takes, even before it moves); secondly, the kinaesthetic and haptic sense of weighing something in your hands, or feeling the weight of something bearing upon you; finally, the sense of time, which is a feature of our later, more social development. With no support from other researchers, and decades in advance of what has become a massive field of research, Lamb arrived at the startling conclusion that our primary movement experiences are what determine (and what allow us to have) our process of decision-making. Because his theory is so elegant and presented with so little theoretical flummery and ornament it is easy to overlook its importance within the field of embodied psychology.

Before we move on to the next major breakthrough – Posture-Gesture Merging - we should go back a few steps and remind ourselves about the underlying purpose for all these terms and categories – it is to describe and understand how someone moves the way that they do. One of the underpinning assumptions behind the work of both Laban and Lamb, is that each of us has our own peculiar pattern of movement.

> The discovery that there is a constant pattern of movement running throughout a person's behaviour irrespective of the situation which is open to an analysis is of far reaching importance. [*Movement and Personality*, pp.192 - 3]

> Nearly everyone can recognise a friend by his walk, even though he may be sprightly one day and sluggish the next - there is still something constant in the way he walks. [Ibid., p.193]

As Lamb suggests, in order get at that 'constant pattern of movement' we need something more than figurative adverbs like 'sluggish' and 'sprightly'. In *Movement and Personality* Lamb uses Laban's terminology of Body Attitude, Functional Movement and Shadow Movement to describe three different categories of movement. In this early work Lamb is already interested in how these types of movement merge into each other:

> Shadow Movement can, as it were, grow into Body Attitude, as may be observed when a yawning operation of the mouth grows into a yawn involving the whole body. Similarly, Functional Action can grow into Body Attitude, as when a hammering movement of the arms grows into a hitting movement of the whole posture. [Ibid., p.214]

The corollary is that the only link between Functional Action and Shadow Movement is through Body Attitude. Already Lamb is interested in the dynamic aspect of these movement categories: when and under what conditions does one merge into another?

In order to demonstrate how ineradicable is our movement pattern, Lamb takes the example of an actor, who though unrecognisable to his friends when in character, to a trained analyst he would still be moving with the same underlying pattern: 'observations taken whilst he is on stage will be analysed to reveal the same ratios' [Ibid., p.194]. He goes on to argue that in some ways the personality assessor is working in the same territory as the actor.

> The illustrations in relation to acting can be usefully continued in examining the constant patterns in the composition of effort because an actor is simply working the other way round to the personality assessor. The former is concerned to compose the movement which will express the personality and the latter to explain the movement which the personality is creating. [Ibid., pp. 194 - 5]

Lamb continues his exploration of movement theatre by pointing out those mimes who confine themselves to the reproduction of the 'conventional alphabet of mime', which, he argues, 'is as tedious for the audience as it is meaningless from the point of view of expressing the author's work (excepting when the alphabet has been stylised and become a highly specialised technique, as in the Chinese theatre, for example). [Ibid.,p.195] This distinction between the creative and the conventional, leads onto a broader argument about movement in everyday life.

> Somehow modern conditions have encouraged this easy, unthinking taking for granted of thousands of conventional movements and the effect is to make people like puppets. It is as though they are moved by some outside agent rather than that they compose their individual movement. [Ibid., p.203]

Throughout his later writings Lamb will use the expression 'puppet-like' movement to describe 'unthinking' movement. In *Kinaesthetic Approach* he notes how some teaching methods result in students acquiring movement habits which are 'meaningless'.

> These people appear to a sensitive observer to be forcing themselves unnaturally at their studies and their movement appears to be more like that of a puppet than a living human being. [p.39]

This bring us back to Lamb's belief that all of us, whether professional dancers or actors, or office-workers, can live much more fulfilled and creative lives if only we explore the movements that we are all capable of. While he may talk of movement-patterns, these aren't in any way a limitation – they are simply a set of possibilities which are unique to each individual.   Movement re-education worth its name will help develop our kinaesthetic awareness and liberate our full movement potential.

Lamb used Laban's terms Body Attitude, Functional Movement and Shadow Movement to create what he called a 'ladder of expressiveness in movement' [Ibid., p. 457].

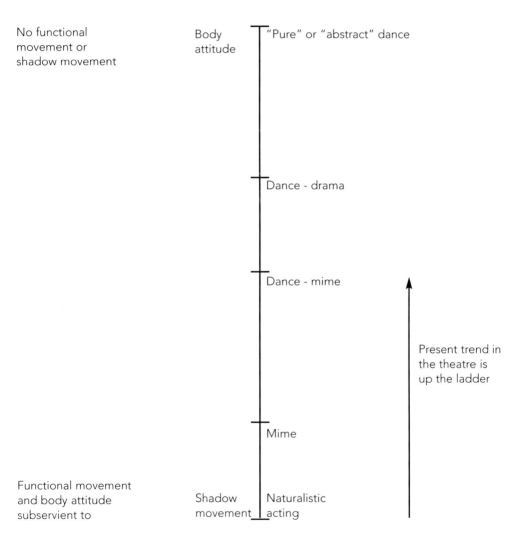

Figure 7. Warren Lamb's Ladder of Expressiveness

His observation that 'The present trend in the theatre is up the ladder' [Ibid., p.458] very accurately points to the Physical Theatre Movement of the 1960s and 1970s and to the work of Jerzy Grotowski[15] in particular. Indeed, some of Lamb's comments about what one might call the ethics of movement (how we allow ourselves to get trapped in conventional movement habits) could have been spoken by his Polish contemporary. Both men are concerned to help people discover their own identity and freedom in and through movement.

Movement and Personality was, as I've already noted, written between 1954 – 56. By 1962 Lamb had made another ground-breaking discovery – in the place of Body Attitude, Functional and Shadow Movement he proposed just two terms Gesture and Posture. If we recall Lamb's definition of Body Attitude, this will provide a bridge with his concept of Posture:

> Body Attitude movement involves a variation of the whole posture, from toe to head. An operation in this category has the aim of assuming a new attitude in relation to the situation. [*Movement and Personality*, p.118]

In his later work he will define a change of Posture as 'when it affects the balance' [*Kinaesthetic Approach*, p. 20]. This is simply a more concrete, a more accurate way of saying that the pianist assumes 'a new attitude in relation to the situation'.

> Any deviation away from a position of balance necessitates an adjustment in every part of the body; this is not to say in every muscle but certainly in every limb, the upper and lower parts of the trunk and the head. These movements may be likened to those of a tightrope walker who sensitively adjusts his balance with arms outstretched to improve his kinaesthetic 'feel'. [*Kinaesthetic Approach*, p.20]

By using the notion of balance Lamb introduces a much more dynamic sense of postural movement. Later in the book he notes that 'posture movement ... is concerned with establishing appropriateness'. He describes the kinaesthetic sensation when making a 'postural adjustment' 'as though we are taking up a new stance or posture, and therefore making ourselves more appropriate' [Ibid., p.32]. Once again, we should remember that this echoes his earlier definition that 'Body Attitude means Appropriateness' [*Movement and Personality*, p. 123]. Elsewhere he stated that 'the

---

[15] Jerzy Grotowski (1933 - 1999) graduated from the Theatre School in Kraków with a degree in acting and then studied directing at the Lunacharsky Institute of Theatre Arts (GITIS) in Moscow. In 1959 he joined Ludwig Flazsen at the Theatre of the Thirteen Rows in Opole, South Poland, where he created some of his greatest productions including *Doctor Faustus, Akropolis* and *The Constant Prince* (said to be his masterpiece). In 1969 he turned his back on a theatre of production and engaged in a series of research and training initiatives. He was the author of *Towards a Poor Theatre* (1968).

meaning cannot be understood without reference to the appropriateness of the movement.' [Ibid., p.117]. Clearly, Posture developed from Body Attitude, and it is in these fully-bodied changes of position that we find the meaning of a person's movement.

Gesture, on the other hand, resembles the more conventional movements that were described above: his first definition in *Kinaesthetic Approach* still has echoes of both Functional and Shadow Movement.

> A gesture may be defined as an effort which alters the shape of only part of the body – it could be the entire upper part of the body or just of an eyebrow. Two types of gesture can be differentiated:
>
> 1. A movement of part of the body which carries out a voluntarily composed definable function, for example hitting with the arm, nodding the head, lifting the eyebrow as a signal, so long as these movements are confined to the parts mentioned.
>
> 2. A movement which appears to cross the surface of the body, is involuntary, and whose function is contained within the body, for example, licking the lips, fidgeting with the fingers, furrowing the brow.
>
> Both types of gesture movement are discriminatory in contrast to posture movement which is concerned with establishing appropriateness. [*Kinaesthetic Approach*, p.32]

We have already picked up the echo from *Movement and Personality* with regard to Posture and Body Attitude and here we see that Shadow Movement and Gesture are both concerned with discrimination ('Shadow Movement means Discrimination' [*Movement and Personality*, p.123]). Later, in *Posture and Gesture*, Lamb will be much simpler in his definitions: postures are whole body movements while gestures are 'confined to part of the body' [p.14].

Quite as important as the distinction between postural and gestural movement is the notion of Posture-Gesture Merging. In our conversations Lamb would give the example of someone waving goodbye with just their arm (which really does look like a gesture that isn't heartfelt) and then demonstrate how, once the movement involves the whole body, it becomes clear that the person is saying goodbye to a loved one (a full-bodied movement carries an immeasurably greater emotional charge). Lamb has already used the word 'meaning' in terms of movements, and I'd argue that when a gesture (which can be acquired) merges into a posture, it is at that moment that the movement takes on a personal significance: it is not being 'put on' any more, but is fully intentioned and 'comes straight from the heart'. In *Kinaesthetic Approach* we see his first articulation of this incredibly original and subtle observation about human movement:

> It is the associations which the gesture has within the posture which feel meaningful and represent the difference between the purely physical movement (fixed associations) and movement expressive of personality (varying associations). [*Kinaesthetic Approach*, p.33]

This is made clearer later when he states 'it is the kinaesthetic sense which tells us whether or not we "feel right"' [Ibid., p. 35]. He returns to the specific case of the pianist and points out how no two play in the same way.

> It is significant for each individual how he composes the great many actions involved and how he relates the different gesture movement with posture movement. For example, a certain effort and shape of hands 'feels right' when coinciding with a certain effort and shape of the posture. The movement of most intense 'feeling right' is the recognition kinaesthetically of an integration between the two processes of movement (posture and gesture). These points of contact are individually extremely important and significant. Psychologically it can be hypothesised that they are points of contact between afferent discriminatory sensing by way of response to environment or stimuli and efferent appropriate sensing by way of adjustment. [Ibid, p.34]

The final sentence is an observation of incredible suggestiveness: the gestural movements register a person's reaction to what is happening in the world, and the resulting postural adjustment is the personal response. It is such touches which characterise his early writings when he was still a student of movement.

This introduction serves simply as an overview of his development: I shall study in greater detail the nature of Posture-Gesture Merging in the introduction to Part IV. For the meantime we should note that this merging is a moment when the movement 'gets personal', it becomes included in a person's unique pattern of movement. It is for that reason that 'it feels right'. Lamb's work as a movement educator was to help people identify for themselves their core sense of movement, that place from which the whole person can resonate.

We have already seen Lamb split from Laban and Lawrence in 1952 when they introduced a Test rather than an Assessment. The same thing happened forty years later when Lamb left his own company, and had to give up the elegantly titled Action Profiling precisely because his former protégé Pamela Ramsden had begun to introduce an element of testing into her profiles. He recalled the split in one of our conversations. 'It seemed to me that this approach risked destroying a form of assessment built on movement.' Everything is given in the last sentence: Lamb insists that assessments have to build on movement categories and not static categories. I believe that it is for precisely this reason that he spent the 1950s and 1960s searching for terms and categories that would get him ever closer to the heart, to the art of movement. As we shall see in Part IV, there is a formal elegance to his approach which has less to do with mathematics (Laban was fascinated with crystal forms and mathematical permutations) and more to being true to the movements that he was observing.

Somewhat dismissively Lamb states that his later books were simply attempts to reach a wider audience. In fact each book includes incremental subtleties in his approach. *Management Behaviour* builds upon *Posture and Behaviour*, and *Body Code* introduces a sociological perspective that isn't so pronounced in earlier books. He breaks new territory with his unfinished *Movement Man*, examining how men and women move in different ways. Lamb embodies the principles that he espouses: life is movement, and his approach is always on the move.

THE INTERVIEWS

xvii.   An overview of the development of Action Profiling 1946 - 1965

During the war years the work that Laban, assisted by Lisa Ullmann, Sylvia Bodmer and Jean Newlove[16], did in the factories involved giving the workers a class in movement. During two fifteen-minute spells they would let the workers experience movement which they could then incorporate into their working rhythm. When I came onto the scene, the emphasis was much more on selection and then training for that particular job. This was when there was a choice of jobs for which workers could be recruited: it wasn't a question of firing people but of finding the best match of job to worker. Whereas before Laban's work had been called 'Industrial Rhythm' now it became known as 'Laban/Lawrence Selection and Training'.   People were assembled into groups as before, but they were being prepared for particular jobs for which a movement job specification existed. We were matching workers for jobs and training them to do them. This matching process was new and was initially an extension of the

---

[16]   Jean Newlove joined Laban in Dartington in 1942 and along with Betty Meredith Jones was one of his first assistants. In the 1950s she joined Joan Littlewood's Theatre Workshop where she created their Laban-based actor training. She also helped to create a Laban-based actor training in East 15 Drama School. She is author of *Laban for Actors and Dancers*.

kind of work that he had done during World War II - helping individuals through movement awareness to adapt to the job to better effect.

In this next step in my development I began to use movement terms in the specification of the job. I started by really trying to understand how effective a worker was at a job and to help that person specifically and individually. I remember standing in weaving sheds and in engineering factories looking at workers and then taking pages and pages of Effort observations to Laban. He would look at these observations and then say, 'this worker needed to do such and such'. Laban would occasionally be with me, drawing my attention to somebody's movement being very sustained or more floating, or what I came to regard as pretty generalised. But, because of his genius, Laban made these generalised assessments with a very deep perception of how it really related to the situation. The circumstances played so much into his guru-like hands that he had to portray that manner.

In a simple repetitive job like packing, the essential Effort would be assessed - a light touch would be required perhaps. If the objects were to be fitted together then some Directing would be required. There might be Lightness followed by Directness followed by a quick movement in putting a box back onto the belt. This is what Laban taught me. We would look at the operation itself and assess what were the essential Efforts that had to be performed for the job to be accomplished. A placing of something in a particular groove, or something that had to be handled lightly because pressure would break it – that sort of thing. The essentials were specified. Then I would observe the individual's Efforts and match the one with the other. From this and as I began to work more and more away from Laban it began to happen that I was rating the matching process in terms of a person's strengths and their weakness. I think Laban was involved in this to a certain degree.

There was an overall factory called Faithfuls – described by Eden Davies in *Beyond Dance* - where I observed about 300 women. The workers had all been doing very isolated operations – one sewing on pockets, another buttons, etc. What we did was divide them into groups of ten workers, with every worker specialising in between two and four of the operations, and this group working as a team would make the full garment between them. This worked very successfully. That was 1951. Nobody else in the world had done this and it was well ahead of the Japanese who came out with 'quality circles' a few years later.

However, soon my work became about the selection of new recruits and their suitability for which job. If there was a shortlist of candidates I was influential as to who was to be selected and who rejected. On the basis of my findings a training programme would be developed. I remember working with someone to develop some equipment that would be designed for the training of recruits. This process of selection and training eventually got into the management field and I did quite a lot of advising on new recruitments but always the work on team-building continued.

Then the question arose, 'How do we observe new recruits?' Independently of Laban (though I was still working closely with him), I experimented with a manager of a bra factory by making wooden contraptions with which we could measure the movements of some of the women workers. I began to observe prospective workers when they were being interviewed.   As before, I would then discuss my observations with Laban. I was still looking for Shadow Movements, Functional Action, and Body Attitude. Laban would often claim that he could tell if someone was unhappy from their Shadow Movements, and therefore was unsuited to that work.   This approach of matching existing workers to more appropriate jobs seemed to be successful. Of course there are other factors: a worker was happier with their former workmates - but although there were certain disruptions, the workers did eventually testify that they were happier in their new jobs.

Then Laban was increasingly asked by the managers about their own problems, or problems with supervisors. I think he was very often advising as a healer as much as anything else. It was from that sort of status that Laban gave advice.   Laban said you had to think of mental Efforts more when you were advising managers rather than the machine-workers – however I never quite managed to draw a line between them. It goes in steps as one progresses from being a machine-hand to a supervisor to being a manager. When Laban wasn't there they would ask me and I had to figure out how to adapt the direct matching of a worker's movement to the requirements of a particular manual job or a particular managerial or supervisory sphere. When people came to me on my own, then I had to think what on earth I could say. On what basis was I giving advice?   I was trying to work out how to find a way of offering such advice in a disciplined way and this led to the development of what used to be called Action Profiling and what is now called Movement Pattern Analysis. It took me fifteen years to develop this way of analysing managers. I only achieved this in the early 1960s. With Lawrence and Laban nothing had been crystallised, partly because Laban never wanted to formalise anything. He always said, 'I have not created a system'. Whatever he created one day he would have new ideas about the next. He truly followed the principle that everything is in a state of flux.

The sense that I have round the 40s, '50s and '60s was of a considerable interest from a wide range of people in what Laban could offer the world, and in movement. I met people in industry, and then in management, then in the world of therapy – particularly Jungian psychiatrists. I was in with quite a group of artists and have already spoken of how Henry Moore had said that everything he did was movement. Quite a number of people – not Moore himself – did individual courses with me which were dedicated to extending their range of movement and getting them to become aware of their own personal movement. Outside the dance world and in the theatre I worked individually with actors. I also directed a few plays, including one for the Religious Drama Society. There was enthusiasm for Laban's ideas, and in movement itself, across a wide range of activities. I don't find this to be the case now. There is much academic interest in the universities rather than in practical work. Someone recently remarked that the success of my ideas in the 1960s might have had something to do with the 'swinging sixties' and the generation of that time. But this had started much earlier and was a post World War II phenomenon.

xviii. Attention, Intention, Decision

I decided to adapt Laban's idea of Attention, Intention, Decision. There were two distinct developments:

1. Laban aligned Space Effort with the expression of Attention; Weight Effort with the expression of Intention; Time Effort with the expression of Decision; and Flow (somewhat dubiously) with the expression of Precision. He never spoke or wrote of this being a sequence.

2. Shortly before Laban's death in 1958 I began to observe people going through stages of Attention (Space), Intention (Weight) and Decision (Time) as a sequence. At the same time I understood Flow as a related but a separate process. I also realised that there was a shape component to all the stages.

Laban first associated Weight Effort with Intention probably in the early 1930's before making the other associations. He found that some commedia dell'arte characters fitted one or other of these descriptions. For example, the Captain was Intention-oriented and Pulchinella, Attention-oriented. Laban's main use of this development was in teaching actors.

The Framework I developed shows the Effort/Shape components of Attenion. Intention and Commitment to action (as the whole sequence was a decision-making process the final stage needed a new name), with 'Precision' eliminated and Flow an underlying separate component. This simple model of the decision-making process can be applied over a wide range of situations, not so as to analyse each decision, but, when matched with movement, to discover a person's preferences in respect to all decision-making. While circumstances obviously have an influence a person's preferences remain and it is significant to what extent they are or are not applied.

Attention

If we are going to make a decision we have to give attention to what we are going to make this decision about. By way of illustration, if I maintain a high level of attention as I walk along the street, suppose I recognise someone I know. Many variables will dictate whether I just continue or whether I call to attract their attention. We begin a decision the moment we give attention to something. If I give attention to a thief stealing a woman's handbag this attention will result in the intention of calling the police or something.

Intention

The next stage is to form an intention of what we want to do as a result of what we have given our attention to. If the person has obviously heard my call but is pretending not to I will probably get to making an effort at the Intention stage. What do I want? Do I want to insist on speaking with them? They are getting further away all the time. If I then run to catch them up I have gone to the next stage (see below) of Commitment to action. If the person continues to snub me then I will likely revert to the Intention stage. What do I want to do now? Protest? Or perhaps inertia takes over and nothing more happens.

Commitment to action

Then there has to be a third stage of the implementation, the commitment to action. I changed the word 'decision' to 'commitment to action' because the whole thing is a decision-making process.

This concept of a decision-making sequence began to be developed in the 50's as I became more challenged to offer advice to managers. In each case of the supervisor or manager that I was observing I asked myself to what did he need to give Attention in his job? In what respect did he need to apply Intention? In what respect did he need to take decisions? I sometimes would come up with as many as sixty items (sometimes only twenty to forty) that they needed to give attention to in a particular job. If I couldn't find these items by asking those people who knew what they needed to give attention to, whether it required discipline or control, then I would find this out through observation.

As before I would sit in on the interview as an observer, but not conducting the interview, I would make observations of Shadow movements, Body Attitude and Functional Actions which somehow I matched against the specifications. This was when the difference between Functional Action and Shadow Movement didn't really seem to apply. It was difficult to assess. I began to look at Body Attitude as the movement of Body Attitude. It was the beginning of my looking for two types of movement – what I would later call Posture and Gesture. So when I was observing a person I'd look to see whether they were direct or indirect, or strong or light, or quick or slow, or free or bound. If there was more Space-Effort than Weight-Effort then I thought that this person acts more to express Attention than Intention. I began to base how I was responding to these people in that way.

I remember using the word 'weakness' with regard to a client and he said that he didn't like the word because it sounded a bit cruel, so after this discussion with him I changed the word to 'limitation'. This didn't come from Laban but from a client. When discussing with Laban we discovered an in-between stage which was 'latent' – latent capacities. I remember discussing this question with Lawrence and he didn't like the word 'limitations', he liked the word 'inert'. In my archives there are series of Laban-Lawrence Tests which list the features as follows:

a group of strengths
a group of latent capacities
a group of inert capacities.

I like the term 'inert' because it has a movement, or rather, an absence of movement element.

The features themselves which were being put in one of these three categories did come from the matching process. If one of the job requirements was focusing on the essential elements in the work in hand and if that person did show a lot of directing then that would be rated as a strength. If the person had a lot of timing then that would be rated as a strength if that was also a requirement. If the person didn't have much directing then that would be rated as inert (or a limitation or weakness). I did worry and puzzle over this as to whether it should be called this. When we said that something was a limitation or inert I came increasingly to believe that we weren't saying that the person could never do it. Quite early in this process, and I believe this to be quite significant, I felt that if the incentive was enough, people could make themselves do anything. But what we were concerned with was that people were not only doing a job but also doing a job within a satisfactory career growth.

I was asked quite a lot to advise on people who had been shortlisted for a new appointment. I always gave myself the discipline that if somebody I felt was unsuited for the job, and this was on the basis of a very time-consuming Effort study on my part to assess what were the requirements of the job and then my observations of the candidate, that if I was rejecting the candidate, then I had to convince myself of what that person was suitable for. If I was saying, 'You're no good for this job', then I must be able to say what job he was good for. That brought in a career guidance interest and I did run a career guidance service for quite some time.

I did try to bring in the Flow element. If there was Flow associated with this particular feature then even though it was low relatively in the person's movement, maybe it did have the potential for development. It was very unscientific and there was some basis – I was struggling for some basis. That went on for years.

There are three stages of the decision-making process and each stage breaks down into two further stages because of the Effort and the Shape aspect of attention. So that gives us six initiatives in the decision-making sequence. A person's pattern of initiative may be equally divided, more or less, between those six. This applies to very few people but it does happen that some people have a fairly even distribution. They may be understood as not having so much character as being 'overall': taking everything into account they are often respected in a team as being coordinators, or good all-rounders, to use a cricket analogy. Now managers do tend to be good batsmen, good bowlers or wicket-keepers – something that has individuality. It varies but different business cultures tend to want one more than another. You tend to find managers who will perhaps give emphasis to one or two of the six initiatives but nevertheless have a good backing up of the other four. But then you get others who are at the opposite extreme. It's almost like saying that we have somebody who is an all-round character, and then we have somebody who is so extreme as to be an eccentric. For example, someone who has a lot of attention wants to avoid taking action, wants to be able to function in a complete research environment. The meetings that they enjoy most are those where there isn't much likelihood of their having to agree to taking any action.

In any of the three stages in decision-making we can be proactive or reactive. Some people just follow their leader and take as little initiative on their own account as they can. Other people like to take a lot of pro-active initiative. Pamela Ramsden's claim (which I agree with) is that we are more motivated to take initiative according to our movement pattern, than one which is incompatible with it. It is often said that people have a high motivation for their job. A job advertisement might be worded, 'Only people who are motivated should apply'. We thought that this concept of motivation to take initiative which is compatible with your movement pattern really explained how people will do some things and not others. I then related that particularly to top management decision making. The more responsibility a person has the more scope he or she has to take initiative that they want to do. It is not a question of whether they are motivated or not. When you're lower down the scale you don't have so much scope. It depends on whether you want to keep your job, whether you are aiming for some specific promotion which would require a particular form of behaviour.

It is usually when you are in the top job that you are more free and you have more scope to act according to your motivation. Therefore, and this goes for CEOs and Prime Ministers, if you are motivated primarily to give Attention – this is a crude example for purposes of illustration – then you like taking such initiatives, to having surveys carried out, to employing consultants. But if you are more motivated to take the initiative of Intention, then that motivation expresses itself as soon as you wake up in the morning saying, 'Right, what do I intend doing today?' This can effect what can be done because the strategy which a person with big responsibility will follow in the two cases I've illustrated would lead to them both taking different decisions, even though the situation might be similar. The first person might spread, might go into new things, might diversify. The strategy of the second person might be to stick with what they've got.

Overall, the whole management field fashion might dictate how you'll act. There was a fashion twenty years ago when every company wanted to become a conglomerate. In more recent years things have changed and people like to stick with their core business. You can say that there are big trends overall which tend toward the reactive rather than the proactive element of how responsible CEOs will react; but within the overall trend, each will apply their individual motivation. And these trends are of course created by people in the first place!

Harmony, perhaps, or proportion, can be applied to the decision-making process because if most of your initiative is in the intention stage but none in the attention stage then you're going to be very vulnerable to working in a structure where all the signals are given to you by cooperative and loyal people to ensure that you don't do something disastrous. I worked with a Chief Executive for over twelve years and he was really out of proportion because he had an almost complete lack of the intention stage. He would give a lot attention to investigating and exploring, he was very ready to take decisions and get things going, but he was never clear on what his intention was with the result that he got into all sorts of difficulties and had to be protected by good people working with him. He was a brilliant technologist and had fantastic ideas and strategies - he was a great visionary. He was greatly admired, but anyone could take advantage of him because of his lack of intention. Without loyal people working for him and supporting him he was pretty useless.

I am just quoting the example of this manager because he was someone of whom it could be said that he was so out of proportion in his decision-making process for it almost to be disharmonious. He would not grade issues as to whether they were important or unimportant, with the result that he would often be distracted away by all sorts of irrelevant matters. In fact he was never at all clear what issue he was dealing with at any particular time. In meetings someone might think they were dealing with a particular matter, but he would handle it in such a way that it didn't seem to exist as an issue; it just created a great fog. He was also very weak because anyone could persuade him. He would leave things in the air a lot. I am just asking the question whether a decision-making process which is so much out of proportion could be regarded as disharmonious. He failed to recognise the relative importance of issues. On the other hand, perfect harmony or balance in the sense of equal emphasis to all three stages seems to tend towards a conventional, unadventurous decision-making type, usually interpreted as not having 'character'.

xix. The 1950s

A few years before Laban died when I introduced the matching of Effort and Shape I became more convinced that Laban's association of Attention with Space, Intention with Weight, Decision with Time had merit *as a decision-making process*. Laban never referred to it as a decision-making process, but called it the **Laban-Lawrence Personal Assessment**. I was developing this in the early 1950s and was still working closely with Laban, but not so closely as I had been in the late 1940s. I was more on my own. But my work seemed to be appreciated; it had some degree of accuracy. It divided the degrees of matching, into the three categories of 'good', 'poor' and 'capable of development'. I shudder now at the lack of rigour in the method I was applying. I must have added my own perceptions in a subjective way.

The assessments do contain maybe twenty to sixty aspects of the management or supervisory job, and these were divided into those in which the person matched well, poorly, or had development possibility. That was successful enough for Laban and Lawrence to want to train other people. I have already mentioned that when I first came along Laban and Lawrence had pounced on me for this very reason. There just weren't people available, they weren't coming forward. Those who did were PE teachers and other teachers interested in incorporating movement into their teaching. There were two or three people who followed me and we seemed to be quite successful in the Laban-Lawrence Personal Assessment. There was a teacher called John Armitstead, and another person called Frank Culver who were going to be trained, but they soon dropped out because they couldn't stand the pace. Eventually there was only me left and I disagreed with Laban and Lawrence when they changed, without any consultation with me, the title of Laban-Lawrence Personal Assessment, which I was personally happy to work under, to the Laban-Lawrence Test. It was quite telling that here you had a guru and a consultant who had only one person to carry out their particular method and they renamed it and redesigned the whole procedure without even consulting me! That is typical of Laban. I don't know whether it is part of his Teutonic nature or not.

I felt that the matching activity wasn't a test and that we shouldn't align ourselves with personality tests like the '16 PF' or the paper and pencil tests, intelligence tests that existed. I pointed out that we did not do a test, and that the principle that we were working under was to advise people as to what were their unique individual strengths and then match these with a particular job. We weren't testing them for anything, but rather matching them. I didn't like the idea that we were testing people: we were trying to find the right fit in terms of their job. So in 1953 I went independent. There was a bit of a rift but we soon got back into some sort of working relationship and even though we didn't see each other so often I did still keep in touch with Laban. We kept up quite a correspondence.

The next stage – and this came before the Posture and Gesture, or Posture-Gesture Merging arose – was to consider the question of Shape and Effort merging. This was in 1956, two years before Laban died. I started developing the framework of Effort-Shape that is still in use now. That was the stage in which the decision-making process became understood as being influenced by both Effort and Shape. It was also at this stage that I thought it important to look at Flow. Laban had often referred to Flow, but as a fourth Effort element. In our discussions of my observations his comments on Flow seem very generalised: some people did and some didn't have Flow. From this moment I began to consider that it should be considered differently to Space, Weight and Time. I had done some observations of children and was beginning to have the idea that flow diminished during childhood growth, whereas the other elements of weight, space and time developed in this period. Then, with the linking of Shape and Effort in my observations, there was obviously a flow of Shape that could be related to the flow of Effort.

The decision-making process became much clearer as a sequence. Laban never considered it as a sequence: I claimed it began with Attention, which develops into Intention and the Decision reaches a point of no return. This was a stage when the nature of the decision-making process was clarified in my thinking. Laban died around this time and a number of people had courses with me, and I was under pressure to justify what and how I was observing.

xx.   After Laban's Death (1958)

The first thing that happened after his death was that a number of his distinguished pupils wanted to get from me what they thought were Laban's latest developments in his thinking. What were the last fruits of his genius? What was this Effort work about? I had the reputation of being the Effort man and so they came to me for enlightenment about what he had been working on and what I had learned from him about Effort.

These include Irmgard Bartenieff and Laban's daughter Juanna, and Betty Meredith Jones, one of the earliest of his English disciples and a few more people. Having to teach these people what I had learned from Laban was a good discipline for me: I tried to get it into some kind of order. I don't think that they contributed any component part, but having to work out what I had to teach them, was a very good incentive for me to get it done. Through this process I identified gaps and possible contradictions in his thinking. During Laban's life he was always there in background so if anything went wrong he would always be there to solve everything. But once he's dead ...

After his death I was very often being asked to prove things, to offer validation for his ideas. How reliable were his theories? Quite rightly, those issues began to arise at that time. Someone must have questioned the reliability before his death, but afterwards it became much more of a challenge to me during those years in the early sixties.

xxi. *Aptitude Assessment – Action Profiling – Movement Pattern Analysis*

Aptitude Assessment continued with the basis of the decision-making model. I think that the terms Strengths, Potentials and Inert were to some degree modified but it was in the middle '60s after *Posture and Gesture* had been published that I started talking about the decision-making process, and that I was advising people on their aptitude for going through that process. Pamela Ramsden joined me in 1969. She was a psychologist and she poo-pooed the whole idea of aptitude, given her understanding of the term when used in psychology. She didn't think we were reporting on aptitude at all; she thought we were reporting on motivation. So we started talking about Action Motivation, a person's motivation to act, and that a person had a motivation to go through a decision-making process in a particular way. That fitted in with my own thinking: I mentioned earlier that somebody could force themselves to do something which was contrary to their decision-making pattern, but by doing so they would not feel any motivation for what they were doing. Thus we came to the conclusion - and I still maintain this - that if we do act in a way that is contrary to our movement pattern then we experience stress, our decision-making is not so good, and personal relationships suffer. There are all sorts of negative implications when by force of circumstances you are obliged to accept a job which is incompatible with your way of working - there will be stress. Knowing where to draw the line comes from being aware that if you find yourself having to do something that is contrary to your movement pattern, then you must recognise this and keep it within some sort of check.

That is when she came up with the name **Action Profile** (1972). It has been a very good name in the sense that it has stuck. Since my split with Pamela I now refer to Movement

Pattern Analysis rather than Action Profile; far more people know of Action Profiling than they do of Movement Pattern Analysis. It was a good title from the commercial point of view. On the other hand, Movement Pattern Analysis enables people to get some idea of what it is about.

xxii. Developments and Refinements to Movement Pattern Analysis After 1965

By 1969 I had developed the concept of a decision-making sequence; the concept of someone's true preference for a certain kind of movement, and concluded that this came from posture-gesture merging. The observation that there are affinities between Effort and Shape also dates from this period. After that I and others added certain refinements to my theory, especially in the Effort-Shape affinities. Maybe more refinements will come since a number of people are working in this area. People working in the field of counselling have told me that the notions of Attention, Intention, Commitment have much application therapeutically. There may be a lack of affinity between the decision-making processes of two partners, and my concept of Attention, Intention, Commitment might help them understand each other better. As concerns the two types of flow - Flow of Effort and Flow of Shape – they are much more evident in children and actually the extent of movement flow which occurs in children diminishes as they get older - I feel that this is an important discovery. Much of what is currently done today is still pretty close to what we were doing in the 1970s.

Pamela Ramsden has developed some of my ideas and coined the term 'Action Profiling'. I used to use the terms Communicative, Presentational or Operational in respect to the motivation to interact and she added a sub-division to this which is helpful. We worked together very closely in the early days and she contributed quite significantly especially in respect of the training materials. She wrote a very worthwhile book called *Top Team Planning*. She and I worked together from 1970 to 1992. We were a partnership until 1982, when she left to set up her own organisation but we continued to meet a lot in connection with Action Profilers International. I suppose it was after 1982 when she went independent that she started to develop some independent ideas to which I was, at the start, sympathetic. However, it eventually emerged that these ideas were developing along the lines of making the profile into a score of attributes and she divided each of the six initiatives into two polarities and gave each of them a different name so, for example, the indulging/investigating had a name as did the contending/investigating. Both the convex and concave explorings had different names: people were being rated, given scores for each of those attributes. Although she had expanded the six to twelve initiatives, the main objection that I had was that she had segregated the polarities: I consider them as a process of variations between two extremes. There is a renewal process in this variation: if one becomes too focused it becomes a fixed stare and you have to renew the process. I also have found, and this has been corroborated, that the range of variation in any one of the components may vary between any of the polarities during our lifetime. For example, someone with a big range of Timing who puts more emphasis on accelerating and maintains a fast pace might gradually put more emphasis on decelerating and begin to work at a slower pace.

It seemed to me that Pamela was creating a laundry-list of attributes that you ticked off; in fact making the action profile into the sort of test where people are scored on each polarity independent of the other polarity. I believe they can not be treated independently because this destroyed the movement basis of what we were doing and encouraged a type of assessment that did not belong anymore to movement. I did invent a questionnaire based on this type of categorisation just to see if it worked and found that it can be understood by people who have no idea of the movement basis of the analysis but find it an interesting exercise. They know of people who are 'investigators' or others who are 'determiners': they pair these types off with well-known figures. It is very easy to get a consensus in pretty crude terms as to whether people are relatively more determining or investigating. It seemed to me that this approach risked destroying a form of assessment built on movement.

Pamela was Director of Training and so she was in charge of conveying and teaching to our students what I believed to be a flawed concept. That was very troubling. We had a council of eight of whom Pamela was one and I thought that they would understand what I was trying to say and vote accordingly. At a conference in 1992 I put this to the test, suspecting that perhaps the vote might go against me. Even though they accepted the main thrust of my argument they still wanted to support Pamela. Maybe there were personal reasons underlying this. I had no alternative but to resign, besides which I now felt that in my eyes Action Profiling was tainted. A lot of faulty work was being done.

It was a pity that I had to leave; normally in these situations it is the founder who stays and the others who leave. I think it's good that it happened because although we have fewer people, they are people who I believe are following a correct theory and doing much more professional and valuable work. There may have been subsidiary factors in this split. I felt that Pamela had been encouraging work that really belonged to the heading of New Age mystical activity – maybe Laban would have approved of that! They were trying to get executives to do Indian Dance and the Sweat House rituals, for example. These can be very valuable and are interesting from an anthropological point of view. But they have nothing to do with Action Profiling. The professionalism of some of the people had to be questioned: Pamela allowed someone to qualify within three months and with practically no training. She claimed that it came naturally to her.

This does remind me of Laban and Lawrence turning their aptitude assessments into a test. I still can't see how they could call it a test: it is so contrary to what Laban was teaching. They may have been persuaded by some marketing person, I don't know. It was a sort of split. I angered them by continuing to call them assessments rather than tests, but it was only for a month or two that we had no communication. It was a very similar situation to that with Pamela Ramsden. With Lawrence and Laban I did their tests and my own aptitude assessments in parallel. This was early days, 1952, but I reacted immediately to this idea of a test because it contradicted all the principles that I had understood to apply to Laban's work. I still do. I would hate to have presented you with your profile and state that you have scored so many points in such and such a category, that you are good at this and not so good at that. Instinctively people look at the scores and start thinking how they can improve it. I have a different approach: I go out of my way to say that there is nothing good or bad about a profile, you are who you are and let us rejoice in who you are. Let us simply try and understand how you are different from other people. I believe this is very characteristic of Laban.

A Summary of my development from 1946 to 1969

1. Firstly, generalised movement with individual instruction to help workers adapt to the job they were doing.

2. Trying to understand individual workers' movements to help in that process of adapting to the job.

3. Trying to select from a pool of recruits to allocate them in jobs for which their movement showed them to be most suited.

4. Training workers through classes or individual training that would help them specifically to align their own movement rhythm with the essentials of the job they were doing: for example, to get the right degree of lightness, strength or precision that was required. This was selection and training based on a more specific observation and analysis of movement.

5. The supervisory aspect came next. Whereas previously we had said, 'this job needs directing at this point, strength at that', now we were saying, 'This supervisor or

manager because of the circumstances in which he is working needs to give Attention or have Intention or take decisions in a particular way'. We were then matching individual movements which had been observed similarly to how we'd observed the manual workers, but usually at an interview or while the man or woman was working on the job.

6. Eventually we came up with a framework for management that could be applied within any situation. We used slightly different terms to assess whether that situation needs a predominance of investigating, or more timing, for example. Whilst we did have a management framework that fitted all, it was used discriminatingly. When one asked a manager what they thought the company particularly needed at a given moment they would always answer with the movement quality that they had a preference for. In our work with teams we always tried to make sure that all different aspects of decision-making were covered so that all different situations could be handled. A successful leader would know how to deploy members of his team to deal with new, unfolding situations.

Steps in the Development of MPA

Laban/Lawrence
'Lilt in Labour'
'Industrial Rhythm'
'Laban/Lawrence Selection and Training
Laban/Lawrence Assessment
Laban/Lawrence Test

Lamb
Aptitude Assessment
Action Profiling
Movement Pattern Analysis

Related Document: A Yardstick for Personality
[Reprinted from BUSINESS The Journal of Management in Industry, November 1953]

ALL businessmen, at one time or another, are faced with the problem of filling a vacant post, either by promotion from within or recruitment from outside the staff. It is always a difficult task. For even when the technically incompetent or unsuitable applicants have been weeded out, there always remains a "short list" of candidates between whom there is little to choose.

A final selection involves a series of interviews with each of the "short list" candidates. Such interviews, however, are at best unsatisfactory. Their success depends ultimately on the intuitive judgement of the man conducting the interview, and this may be affected by many extraneous factors. Prejudice may play a part—many a firm has lost a good employee because the managing director did not like his tie. Memory, too, comes in; the last candidate to be interviewed is inevitably seen more clearly in retrospect than a man who was interviewed some days or even weeks before.

Hence, in recent years, have grown up a whole series of tests aimed at providing an objective basis for the description of a man's whole personality which would act as a guide to management in finding the right man to fit any particular job.   One of these, now finding increasing use in British industry, is the Laban-Lawrence test.

Began with Ballet

The genesis of the Laban-Lawrence test lies in the work of Rudolf Laban. Laban was connected with the ballet, and devised a system of shorthand, still widely used by choreographers, by which the movements of a man's (or woman's) body could be rapidly and accurately noted.

But he did not stop there. He became interested not only in movements of a deliberate nature, such as those in ballet, but in the habitual, half-involuntary movements involved in such ordinary actions as smoking a cigarette, sitting in a chair for a period in conversation, and so on. And he reached the conclusion that there was a very definite connection between such movements and the personality of the man or woman making them.

It was at this point that Laban came into touch with F. C. Lawrence. Lawrence, a Manchester businessman, had sought for years for some means of assessing capacities which would be (a) at least 90 per cent. objective, (b) concentrated upon industry's needs, and (c) capable of expressing results in a simple report facilitating direct action. In association with Laban, he developed the latter's conclusions to meet these requirements.

In any appointment, there are two factors—the man and the job. Each needs to be specified accurately, and Lawrence's first task was to devise a method of specification that could be used to describe any job accurately, without overlooking any aspect of it.

Thus a particular job may be sub-divided into anything between fifteen and forty carefully defined sections, each section describing the capacity needed by the man who will carry it out. The specification for the post of departmental manager in one firm, for instance, ran to eighteen sections, including:—

Determining priorities to be given to the scheduled improvements.

Setting quality standards and standards of output which maintain the company's reputation.

Controlling the availability of materials, purchasing to specified standards.

Persuading outside contacts to accept consequences of work situation—tact and facility of expression.

Once the job specification has been made, any number of candidates can be measured against the capacities set out and a report made on whether they can actively carry them out; or, if not, whether they can develop them through training or experience; or, failing this, whether they lack the capacities for all practical purposes.

Almost anyone will have actively one or two of the capacities; it is extremely rare for anyone to have them all. Men of equal technical qualifications and similar experience will, when measured against the job specification, be found to have a different arrangement of the capacities.

The test of the candidate is made in a personal interview of about one and a half hours at which a trained examiner sits as a third party inconspicuously making observations of the candidate's behaviour. It appears simply as if he is taking notes.

Movements Only

The interviewer may, or may not, ask questions about the candidate's technical qualifications, experience, social background and so on (depending upon the circumstances). If he does, this information is kept completely separate from the report of the test.

The examiner does not listen to the conversation; in fact, he has to concentrate on his shorthand to an extent that would make it impossible for him to do so.

The examiner thus obtains a record showing the movements habitual to the man or woman observed. He cannot, of course, record all movements that occur (people keep up a continuous flow of movements, even when appearing to be still) but he knows that a certain number of observations, whenever or wherever derived, will be a equate for assessment purposes.

The observations taken during the interview are then analyzed.   The different "elements of effort" are totalled, their sequence noted, correlations worked out, and the result of the analysis ultimately expressed in those "phrases of effort" which epitomize the constant behaviour of the individual. This same analysis would result from sets of observations taken of the same person in other circumstances even when his behaviour might be very different.

A report is then prepared stating clearly:—

Capacities of the candidate which can be utilized immediately in carrying out the job. Capacities which can be developed by training and practice to become active Capacities which are to all intents and purposes lacking and will therefore require (if the candidate is appointed) supervision or the provision of specialist advice or the delegation of duties.

A final section gives the candidate's "general aptitudes," i.e., the manner in which he will apply his active capacities or respond to the development of his latent capacities.

Tests are often made of a single individual, perhaps a general manager, to help him towards a better appreciation and use of his personal capacities. He can refer to the report without becoming at all introspective and, if he wishes, reserve judgment upon its findings. More generally, however, tests are commissioned by a manager of a member of his staff, usually someone with whom there is a special problem. The report might be, but is not customarily, divulged to the employee himself.

Similarly, tests can be made of all the members of (say) a department for the jobs they are already doing, so as to rearrange duties and make better application of the people's capacities and promote better team work.

One of the most valuable uses of the test is to determine people's potentialities. The talent, or latent talent, for a responsible position may be found within the company by testing possible candidates against the job specification for the position. Prospective trainees can be tested before embarking on a course and those who lack the capacity to "make the grade" are discovered before expenditure on training is incurred.

Perhaps one of the most obvious uses is in making a new appointment, when those candidates who are short-listed can be tested at the same time as they attend the normal interview, and without other arrangements.

The following are brief case histories of the application of these tests:—

1 A production manager who was having trouble in his job was found to have equally divided active and lacking capacities, with only one latent capacity. He was quite fixed in his methods and incapable of adaptation. Training being out of the question, it was decided to define a restricted sphere of activity in which his active capacities could be effective. This was done; certain duties were delegated to others and some he was

required to execute more thoroughly. There was a vast improvement in working relationships with the rest of the staff, and particularly with the secretary of the company. They were able to carry out a scheme of reorganization which previous antagonisms had prevented.

2 A number of men were tested to find out whether a company possessed a successor to the general manager. The reports revealed that the highest potentiality for the job was possessed by a young man, who had been included among those to be tested as an afterthought, more to learn something of his capacities than to consider him seriously as a candidate.   A course of training was prepared for him and in a matter of weeks a sceptical general manager was convinced that he was the best man for the job.

3 A chief clerk's inability to supervise an office of forty meant the whole staff were at loggerheads. Excessive overtime was being worked and general inefficiency caused many complaints from customers. It was not suspected, until after a number of the staff had been tested, that the chief clerk was the cause of the trouble.   It was arranged to delegate his supervisory functions, leaving him to concentrate on the commercial aspects of his work. At the same time, an assistant was appointed whose latent capacities showed that he was capable of developing a good team spirit. After six months, the management called the change "staggering" and reported that no overtime was being worked, the atmosphere in the office was "a pleasure to encounter," the chief clerk had improved noticeably in health and was much more popular and the department had become the showpiece of the organization.

Although there is no final statistical proof of the tests' validity, some results may be quoted.

In 150 recent tests, 35 of those tested were applicants from outside the companies and 115 were employees of the companies. Of the total, 79 were designated as suitable applicants or employees, 32 recommended to seek occupations other than those for which they applied or which they held, 39 deemed unsuitable, and 26 recommended for training to develop their latent capacities.

For the 115 employees, the employers confirmed or have since confirmed the validity of the results of the tests, as also for the 10 applicants who received appointments—a total of 125 out of 150, the other 25 of whom could not be confirmed because they were met only at the interview and test.

PART FOUR ~ WARREN LAMB'S METHOD DESCRIBED IN DEPTH

Introduction to Part Four

This part of the study consists of a detailed consideration of Warren Lamb's fully developed theory of Movement Pattern Analysis. In conversation he stated that his major intellectual breakthroughs took place in the early 1960s, since when he has spent his time applying, promoting and teaching his system. But this isn't entirely the case. *Posture and Gesture* (1965) was certainly a landmark publication (and the only one he has written by himself) but it didn't contain the final three elements of the assessment - Dynamism, Adaptability and Identifying - that we find in *Management Behaviour* (1969). Nor does his third published book – *Body Code* (1979) - that he wrote with Elizabeth Watson cover the same ground as the two earlier ones. It may be useful therefore to begin with a brief account of these three books so as to give an idea of Lamb's thinking in the sixties and seventies. I should also point out that his split with Pamela Ramsden and Action Profiling International didn't happen until 1992, and therefore he would have described his work of this period as Action Profiling and not Movement Pattern Analysis.

Posture and Gesture was written at the suggestion of Lord Horder, Chairman of the publishers Duckworths, who didn't feel that he could publish *Kinaesthetic Approach*, but, Lamb recalls, 'he was fascinated by the chapter entitled Posture and Gesture which he thought was a wonderful title. So in about 1962/3 I was commissioned by him to a write a book – *Posture and Gesture* - which was published in 1965.' The resulting book was as wide-ranging as his early manuscript *Movement and Personality* and includes reflections on health, sport, education as well as fleshing out an assessment that brings together Shape and Effort, and is based on two types of movement – Posture and Gesture. The pages in chapters four and seven on Flow are his first sustained attempt to grapple with this very elusive element of movement. The graphic form of his assessments in *Posture and Gesture* will be carried over in the later two books, and most of the terminology will remain the same throughout his subsequent writings. The book concludes with a description of two Individual Training Courses in Physical Behaviour that Lamb designed for a Sales Manager and a Sculptor – the last time such courses will be mentioned in his writings.

As the title indicates, *Management Behaviour* is a much less philosophical book and concentrates purely on the application of Lamb's nearly-complete system of movement analysis in the context of the boardroom. There are no expansive discussions of education, or sociological reflections – the job is purely to explain how Lamb's movement analysis can assist a management team in making the best use of their personnel and recruiting the right people to join the team. But where *Management Behaviour* departs from *Posture and Gesture* is the formulation of a direct connection between movement preferences and a decision-making process. While in the earlier book the focus had been on Aptitude Assessment, now the emphasis is on how executives make decisions. The emphasis still remains on the selection and development of effective management teams, but the decision-making framework becomes a much more accurate means of achieving this. Interestingly, readers are referred back to *Posture and Gesture* on the question of Flow.

Body Code was clearly an attempt to write a more accessible book on movement analysis and the job of his co-writer, Elizabeth Watson was to translate his ideas into language that the non-specialist reader would be able to follow. To this end the pages are interspersed with a number of cartoons which more often entertain than enlighten. The familiar diagrams are still present, and the scope of the argument is far wider than *Management Behaviour*. There is a fascinating chapter on the relationship between posture (or what they call 'body sculpture') and clothing, and some perceptive observations on how keeping up with fashion affects our sense of movement. They start from the premise that certain kinds of posture conform to a socio-historical convention while others don't.

> The emphasis will be different in different generations and the severity less in tolerant times, but the pressure to conformity is always present. In this conformity test, it is particularly true that 'every dog has his day'. In war-torn times the man who looks 'every inch' a soldier, in times of feminine dependency the appearance of the sweet idiot, in times of social inequality the grandly authoritarian, and in democratic times the popularly co-operative, have the individual posture characteristic that bring approval. [*Body Code*, p.32]

They repeat the claim later that 'the power of clothes to assist the individual in moving further towards conformity explains the continuous preoccupation with what women, on whom the pressures to conformity are greatest, and to a lesser degree men, ought to wear'. Posture is also defined in terms of generation:

> Since posture is partly determined by the conventional postural norms, and since these change from generation to generation, while adjustment to them does not change, it is easy to understand how postural expression widens the generation gap before young or old open their mouths. [Ibid., p.38]

The argument of *Body Code* can be summed up in the following sentence:

What this book can do is to express as clearly as possible how you can understand the self-expression that is conveyed through the PGM patterns, whether your own or others. [Ibid., p.128]

When it comes to explaining that elusive phenomenon of Posture Gesture Merging (PGM), the writers take everyday situations to which a reader could easily relate. Their approach is to help the reader feel what these movements are like – to attempt to describe the kinaesthetic sense in words is a tall order, and I think they manage to pull it off. So, Lamb's writing comes full circle, ending with a wide-ranging discussion of how movement is central to our everyday lives and could play an even more important role in our lives if only we realised how little we understand and how little we develop our kinaesthetic sense.

Following my own Movement Pattern Analysis in summer 2004 and with a growing understanding of his method, I began to appreciate just how difficult it is to explain Lamb's discoveries about the nature and effects of movement awareness to a non-specialist. So, throughout 2005 I conducted our conversations in such a way as to get Lamb to explain in layman's terms how he made his discoveries; what it was that made him realise that Laban's terminology and approach required refinement and development; in short, how he came to realise that there was a correlation between movement and decision-making.

Reading through the transcripts of our conversations I now realise, in mid-2006, that although I managed to get Lamb to talk about his ideas and principles in an informal and hopefully accessible way, this inevitably means that we have missed out much of the detail that you will find in his books and manuscripts. Hence the need for these synoptic overviews at the head of each section where I can fill in the necessary gaps. I shall begin by offering definitions and discussions of Posture and Gesture, then move on to patterns of Posture Gesture Merging. Following that I will discuss Lamb's preference for creating assessment or profiles, over tests, before examining how he correlates types of movement with modes of decision making.

In *Body Code* the authors give a very accessible account of the distinction between Posture and Gesture:

Imagine you want to point out a parked car. All you need do us to raise your arm and hand into a pointing movement, while the rest of the body remains still. This is a gesture. But now imagine that the car is careering towards an unconscious friend. Immediately the pointing movement takes on urgency, and the tension involves the whole body, even if the movement throughout the head, trunk and limbs remains slight. You have adopted an attitude, or posture, of warning and the movement is no longer confined to a gesture. [*Body Code*, p.3]

Later in the book they make an interesting distinction between the two types of movement: you *have* a posture, you *make* a gesture.

Between us we make, as a result of this 'having', well-planned journeys, scrambled accounts ... and a disaster of the bathroom decorations. What we make depends on what we have; the making derives from the having. In just the same way, gesture is dependent on, and derives from, posture. [Ibid., p.22]

The suggestion that postural movement is part of us while gestures are acquired or learned is something constant in Lamb's thinking, from Movement and Personality through to the present day.

In the transcripts that make up this part of the book there is a wealth of detail on how he came about the terms Posture and Gesture, and more particularly the merging (not integration) of a gestural into a postural movement. Earlier we recalled how Lamb demonstrated the difference between Posture and Gesture by waving goodbye. As with many of the images that Lamb uses, this has been a favourite of his for many years. Here it is in *Posture and Gesture*:

A good example of the merging between Posture and Gesture is when people wave farewell to each other. Their physical behaviour almost always involves an arm action of raising, a hand action of waving and a lowering of the arm. If this is being done with any sincerity it will involve Postural adjustment. This will arise at different points in the process with different people. [...] If the farewell is confined to Gesture alone, it is likely to be felt as a purely conventional action, without anything 'behind' it. [*Posture and Gesture*, p.32]

In our conversations Lamb insisted upon the significance of the distinction between *integration* (where the two kinds of movements lose their respective identities for ever) and *merging* demonstrates just how subtle, how precise, is his understanding of movement. It is for this reason that I feel it is important to offer a detailed examination of all his shifts in terminology – they always correspond to a leap in his understanding of the meaning of human movement. Note the care with which he describes the *process of merging*:

It's not a question of observing a gesture and then a second and unrelated posture, but it is actually in the process of the movement itself that a gesture may become a postural movement, or a postural movement may revert into a gesture.

So I coined the concept of merging. It came from a lot of thinking, observation, anguishing and differentiation between the static and the dynamic, between a rhythm or phrase and a movement on its own; trying to avoid generalised concepts.

I was motivated by the need to be accurate in my observations but also objective and practical; for example, when you've got the analysis, in some way or another to try to interpret what it means rather than getting the two fields of observation and analysis mixed up. I think that this term 'merger' is the right one and that's what really happens. We can make different parts of our body do anything if we are physically capable, and determined enough to master some particular skill but we cannot contrive mergers.

I shall return to his notion of contrived movements below. Posture Gesture Merging can be calculated on the seesaws as the area in which they overlap. One can see the range within which movements merge.

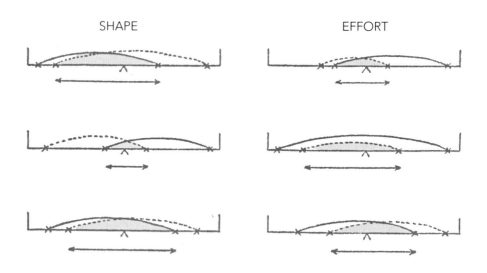

SHAPE   EFFORT

Figure 8. Posture – the continuous line
Gesture – the dotted line
The shaded area shows the degree of merging

This method gives the extent to which Posture and Gesture ranges overlap, i.e., the limits within which the subject is prepared to allow Posture and Gesture movement to merge. There is evidence to show that these are areas of special individual significance. They remain fairly constant. Analyses made of the same people after an interval of ten years have shown ranges of the same relative proportions. [*Posture and Gesture*, p.66]

We then turn to a discussion of the relative merits of assessments and tests, a hugely important preoccupation for Lamb since it gets to the heart of his method and its function. In a business context a movement profile is a means by which a person can understand what their aptitudes and preferences are, and how to make maximum use of their talents and potentialities in a given situation. A profile is an impartial description of certain aspects of a person – how they move and how they go about making decisions - and is not in any way a judgement of that person. If Lamb takes such pains to make the analysis methodologically rigorous, it is only to be able to offer a profile that is all the more accurate and reliable. To understand this we only have to remember Lamb's guiding principles: that there is no one way to do a job, or, put another way, each person has their unique way of doing a job. Thus there can be no question of him setting a person an examination or test which will mark their performance of a task on a range of 1 – 10. Lamb *might* suggest that a particular task is inappropriate for them, given their range of talents and aptitudes, and that they consider tasks to which they would be more suited – but that is an entirely different matter to a test. A movement pattern is as unique and should be as free of value judgement as a fingerprint: both simply serve to identify you as a unique being.

Discussing the question of how we move, the authors of *Body Code* refer to television programmes where humans are compared to animals (again one thinks of Desmond Morris). They point out that unlike animals, we can *choose* the arena in which we act and move:

> We may have sexual drives like apes, covet territory like robins, or destroy competitors like wolves, but the way in which we express these drives is another matter. We are compelled to act out our PGM patterns, but we also choose the circumstances in which we act. [*Body Code*, pp.126 - 7]

They broaden this argument about what movements can say about us, by drawing on the work of psychologist Abraham Maslow - who proposed that cultures can be classified according to a hierarchy of needs, beginning with the satisfaction of reproductive needs - eating, drinking and sex – to the highest need, which is self-realisation – and the theories of behavioural psychologists Skinner and Pavlov.

> On the one hand, the Skinner-Pavlov school emphasises the importance of conditioning as the determinant of behaviour. Maslow, on the other hand, says

that a hierarchy of human needs motivates behaviour. This school asserts that we must be free from stress occasioned by hunger, domestic problems, and crises of self-esteem in order to achieve self-actualisation. The PGM pattern offers a link between these two theories. It is a mode of self-expression which is achieved most fully when the individual is free from stress, but, when it is not fully understood, we fail to avoid stress and to achieve personal fulfilment. Fortunately, the existence of our distinctive patterns actually conditions us to seek situations in which we can achieve such fulfilment. If we learn really to understand our PGM patterns, we can assist such conditioning by making creative choices wisely according to our circumstances. [Ibid., p.127]

In *Body Code* Lamb argues that a test based on the pattern of a person's PGMs is more efficient than an intelligence test 'because its roots go deeper into the personality'.

No assessment of intelligence can tell you to what use that intelligence may be put, no rating of skills tells you where they should be applied, and the prediction of actions has the hit-and-miss quality of fortune-telling, or the ambivalence of the Delphic oracle. An understanding of individual motivation, the driving force that decides behaviour, gives a basis for prediction of a quite different order. From accurate analysis of the PGM pattern, you can tell not only how an individual will choose to behave whenever circumstances permit his freedom of choice, but also indicate the circumstances which he should choose for himself wherever possible in order to make the most creative use of his individual characteristics. [Ibid., p.114]

What you choose to do with your talents and aptitudes is your own business, but Lamb and his associates can help you by demonstrating the range of choices that lie before you. A consideration of assessments and tests leads logically into a discussion of the function and application of Movement Pattern Analysis. It is no surprise that an MPA is about Finding the Right Person for the Job. Following this Lamb describes how he will use the MPAs of a group of executives to help them understand the decision-making dynamic of that particular team.

It may appear that Lamb is presenting a person's movement *pattern* as something that necessarily *limits* their capacities as human beings: because a movement pattern is a selection from all the total possible movements that a human can make, therefore it limits their freedom to explore and experience that full range of possible movements. Behind this question lies the rather romantic assumption that freedom of expression means freedom from all structure. However, as we shall see later in this overview, the only way to achieve this totality would be to possess a freedom to move in all planes with *equal* ease whilst exerting *equal* Effort initiatives – in other words in an entirely balanced and almost neutral way: the movement profile would suggest someone who has absolutely no character at all. It is like considering someone as limited because they are *only* right-handed. Although Lamb doesn't say this in so many words, I'm sure he'd agree that in order to move there has to be some functional asymmetry in our pattern so that we can move. Complete equilibrium is static, not dynamic. This explains why Lamb considers that our freedom to move comes from an understanding of how we move, of the potential for movement that is implied by our pattern. From this conclusion follows Lamb's observation that this unique pattern in which we merge gestural into postural movement could be considered as our core behavioural self – where we feel comfortable in ourselves.

Movement Rites

Throughout Lamb's writings he has described what he calls movement Rites that we all perform to get into this zone of optimal personal movement. We do this in order to settle ourselves, to feel confident, to get ourselves into the appropriate state before we undertake an important task. In *Kinaesthetic Approach* he describes how pianists will go through a series of seemingly meaningless preliminary shuffles and actions before they address the keyboard. In p. 48 – 49 of *Posture and Gesture* he argues:

The purpose can also be viewed under two headings:

Appropriateness: for example, the mood fervour, intensity of application, drive, participation, identification, likely to create the conditions.

Efficiency: for example, the accuracy, delicacy, firmness, speed, precision, care, actually to achieve this purpose. [p.48]

Later on he describes an office manager who

was observed five days in succession to arrive and go through a performance of stroking his chin and shrugging his shoulders before actually getting down to opening the pile of letters in front of him. This was performed with exact repetition of carefully composed Posture/Gesture mergings and Shape/Effort matchings. His attitude at the end was different from that at the beginning. It obviously gave him a good start to the working day and it was important to this man to do it. To have stopped him doing it would certainly have reduced his efficiency in opening the mail. [p.49]

Lamb returns to Rituals in *Management Behaviour*:

> If the term 'ritual' is to have a meaning beyond a repetitive act, then it may be more correctly applied to the sort of everyday performances illustrated than to procedures inside a church. The one quality which a religious ceremony and an everyday ritual have in common is exactness of the physical detail of performance. […] A primitive war dance actually teaches skill in aiming spears more forcefully and accurately at an enemy. By the same token it is worth questioning whether some of the rituals of management behaviour have this result of making individual managers more effective at their jobs. [*Management Behaviour*, pp.36 – 7]

Fresh examples are offered in *Body Code* where they describe how at Wimbledon one player 'will bounce the ball four times with decreasing force before serving, another will settle to serve with two hitches of his shorts, while the receiver will prepare for the expected serve with three revolutions of the racquet, a swing of the hips, and four quick jumps'. They go on to insist that we all have these little rituals which 'reveal personality involuntarily', later asserting that 'These body movements say in a concentrated way "This is me".' [pp.120 – 121] I shall return to the connection between personality and movement pattern below.

Although Lamb hasn't made this connection, in *Posture and Gesture* his description of a development lesson bears striking similarities to a personal movement ritual:

> The full sequence, which must have the quality of a whole composition, would look to some people like a form of physical exercise, to others like a dance, to others like a rite, when given an enlarged performance, i.e. to the fullest extent of physical reach. [*Posture and Gesture*, p.175]

Note also in this description that he stipulates, 'to the fullest extent of physical reach'. This should discourage anyone thinking that there is a similarity between our pattern of movement and what is called our 'comfort zone' (that self-limiting zone where we feel safe and at ease). The whole point behind Lamb's Individual Training Courses in Physical Behaviour was to help develop a person's *potential* movements. While it is true that we cannot achieve total freedom of movement, equally he argues that we all have a great deal more potential than we realise. Apart from helping us become ourselves, these courses can also help us from getting in our own way; that is, helping to avoid generating tension by acting outside of our natural movement pattern.

> The course can be used as a sort of thermometer to measure whether or not you are accumulating tension. [Ibid., p.180]

His development lessons are a practical example of Lamb's educational quest – an ethical quest - to enable people to realise their full potential. The first step towards this is the understanding he furnishes through making your MPA; the next step is the development lesson which helps you experience the wider range of movement within your pattern.

With this dialectic between freedom and restraint in mind, let us return to a set of ideas that I discussed in the introduction to Part III – Strengths, Latent Capacities and Inert Capacities.

> The features themselves which were being put in one of these three categories did come from the matching process, if one of these capacities was focusing on the essential elements in the work in hand. If that person did show a lot of directing and not so much timing, then that would be rated as a strength. If the person had a lot of timing then that would be rated as a strength. If the person didn't have much directing then that would be rated as inert (or a limitation or weakness). I did worry and puzzle over this as to whether it should be called this. When we said that something was a limitation or inert I came increasingly to believe that we weren't saying that the person could never do it. Quite early in this process, and I believe this to be quite significant, I felt that if the incentive was enough, people could make themselves do anything. But what we were concerned with was that people were not only doing a job but also doing a job within a satisfactory career growth.

In *Body Code* he uses the term Aptitude to describe a person's suitedness for a particular type of movement or role in the decision-making process.

> Aptitude, which the teacher instinctively sizes up, depends on the degree to which the essential qualities of movement required for an activity match the innate quality of the student's PGM. If there is close correlation, there is real aptitude; if not, the teacher must expect difficulties, especially if he has no idea how to compensate for the missing quality in the PGM, and is impatient or intolerant of its absence. [*Body Code*, p.103]

This matching of the specifications of a job with a person's PGM pattern is one way of understanding movement in the context of work. Another is to consider it from the worker's own perspective: what happens when they are doing something outside of their pattern? They feel uncomfortable and the inevitable result will be an accumulation of stress. If we return to the opening question in my general introduction

- How can decision-making relate to movement? – I think we are already getting one step closer to an answer. With his analysis of the PGM pattern Lamb is making a very close connection between the way a person moves and their personality or identity or character. In *Body Code* Lamb states the case unambiguously:

> It is clear that the pattern represents some 'core' of individual behaviour, so that when it is applied, the individual acts out his distinctive personality in his unique pattern of movement, saying silently 'this is me'. It is, however, his compulsion to act in this way that is of vital importance. An individual must reveal himself in this manner. Whenever circumstances allow, he will express his personality through his PGM pattern. So great is this power and pull of the pattern as a motivation to action, that no one can successfully resist, withhold, or conceal it. The PGM pattern is always there, always struggling, as it were, to get out. If it is constrained in one direction, it will escape in another; if it is forced to hide, it will find a thousand secret ways for its expression. [*Body Code*, p.114]

So, to paraphrase, you are being true to yourself when you are allowed or allow yourself to act within your own pattern. To look at the question from the other side, what happens when you try to deceive someone by not acting like yourself? In conversation, Lamb insists that you cannot *contrive* to merge gestural into postural movement.

> We can make different parts of our body do anything if we are physically capable, and determined enough to master some particular skill but we cannot contrive mergers.

Put another way, contrived movements can be detected precisely because there is no PGM in their movements:

> When I have observed a lack of PGM I have said that people are contrived, that is, putting on an act. It may warrant some more investigation into a person's background.

It may be that an overbearing parent has forced a child to sit up, walk with a straight back, or whatever, and this has prevented them from walking in their own way. It could be that they swagger or slouch in a particular way because they feel it looks cool or manly. Or it may be that they are trying to make a good impression at an interview. One reason for insisting that the interview for a MPA lasts two hours is that Lamb reckons that no one can repress their natural way of moving for this period. 'It will out'. There are two sections in *Management Behaviour* called 'Contrivance' and 'Spontaneity', and which deal with this question. If at a job interview the interviewee 'shows only Gesture, and then occasionally makes a Posture adjustment entirely divorced from preceding or succeeding Gesture actions, then we can assume that his behaviour is contrived by rehearsed conscious control.' They offer possible reasons: 'It may be through nervousness, intent to deceive, or because his PGM has been so restrained as to be impossible to detect.' They go on to note that confidence tricksters have been exposed 'by further inquiry following assessment of 'contrivance' in physical behaviour'. [pp.80 and 81]

The discussion then turns to acting and they note how theatre in England is moving away from the intellectually-driven gestural theatre, to a more physically-driven postural theatre.

> In England the theatre appears to have been developing away from an intellectual and literary approach to one where the audience is invited to sense the physical inter-relationships of the actors in the play. [*Management Behaviour*, p.81]

This is essentially the same argument that he made in the diagram in *Movement and Personality* reproduced in the Introduction to Part III where he charts a shift from naturalism which relies on Shadow Movements, to physical theatre which is expressed through Body Attitudes. In *Posture and Gesture* we also see Lamb allowing himself a couple of remarks about theatre: again we see him picking up on our tradition of literary as opposed to physical theatre, noting that British actors 'give much greater priority to the words they speak than to the physical attitudes they communicate. The result is that we often detect inconsistency.' [*Posture and Gesture*, pp.127 - 8]

Although Lamb and Turner admitted that 'This is not the place to advance theories on styles of acting', we should remember that Lamb came to find out about Laban through the work of Joan Littlewood's Theatre Workshop and that he performed well into the 1950s with Hettie Loman's British Dance Theatre. I would argue that Lamb's distinction between Posture and Gesture is an amazingly useful means of understanding the arguments of practitioners of mime, physical theatre and dance theatre. Lamb's ideas help us understand Decroux's comment that a movement that doesn't involve the spine is merely 'anecdotal'. I have already referred to Grotowski in my introduction to Part III. Now I shall quote from Clive Barker's *Theatre Games*. The relevance of Barker to this discussion may not seem obvious, but he was a member of Theatre Workshop in the 1950s and 60s which explains why he drew so much inspiration from Laban's ideas. Barker notes how part of his training was to learn how to observe people's walks. He argues that 'This is a part of the actor's work, to observe behaviour patterns in others and to try to recreate them in himself imaginatively.' He goes on:

When first working in this area, the actor Brian Murphy and I spent many hours standing on railway stations and street corners, in libraries and art galleries watching people, and then putting ourselves imaginatively in their situations. [...] We isolated activities in the bodies of the people we observed, and from this we learned the primary importance of the connections between head, neck, spine, and pelvis. [*Theatre Games*, pp.56 – 7]

Barker agrees with Lamb's distinction between movement that is consciously contrived and movement that is generated from a developed kinaesthetic sense. When reading Barker we should remember that Lamb began his first attempt at a book by arguing for a training of the kinaesthetic sense:

...*the kinaesthetic sense* ... is the sense by which muscular motion, weight, position in space, etc., are perceived. The kinaesthetic sense, or body/think is the process by which we subconsciously direct and adjust the movements of our bodies in space, either in response to external stimuli, or to intentions arising in the mind. [Ibid., p.29]

Conscious control, when properly directed, often improves details here and there, but intellect is no substitute for vitality. A sense of futility of life, tiredness and a wish to give it all up is the result of over-taxing the conscious control with the tasks the reflective nervous activity is better suited to perform. [Ibid., p.31]

To end this brief reflection on acting, I want to return to a quotation from Lamb:

By significant is meant that movement which is an integral expression of your personality (and which can be isolated by analysis) as distinct from movements which consists of habits and mannerisms which have been assumed and which may restrict exploitation of significant movement. *[Posture and Gesture*, p. 177]

Although Lamb is writing about movement in everyday life, I would argue that the above quotation applies equally to acting, or more generally, performance movement. A meaningful movement is one that involves all of the performer, as Barker says – from head to pelvis. If it is simply a gesture it is empty – semiotic rather than kinaesthetic. These are huge topics, and I cannot do justice to them here, but there is a long-overdue study to be done on the relation between Lamb's ideas and actor-training.

A very important part of Lamb's reflections concern the elusive question of Flow, one that still seems as open as when he wrote about it in Chapter 7 of *Posture and Gesture*. Then he noted that the most immediate problem is the difficulty in actually observing it.

Much of the imaginative conceptions about Free Flow and Bound Flow cannot be substantiated by observation of what actual body parts do. Whereas a group of observers agree with each other fairly well as to Shape and Effort processes, it is very rarely that any degree of correspondence is achieved in the observation of Flow. [*Posture and Gesture*, p.95]

He continues by noting that it is equally difficult to understand.

We must therefore be particularly careful in examining a phenomenon which is still little understood. It would appear that Flow changes can happen with great rapidity and beyond the capacity of the human eye to observe. They may be difficult actually to separate from Shape and Effort, suggesting that there is a Flow of Shape distinct from a Flow of Effort, seen respectively as growing-shrinking and freeing-binding. There are obviously different thresholds of Flow – some babies show more Flow variation than others and it might be that they are accordingly more dynamic. [Ibid., p.95]

When he turns to Flow in *Management Behaviour* he has little more to add to his analysis, other than associating Flow with control:

We cannot see voluntary or involuntary control. We can, however, distinguish between movement which shows obvious exertion and movement which appears to happen of its own accord - movement which is made to happen and movement which is allowed to happen. [*Management Behaviour*, p.73]

The distinction between movement which is made to happen, and that which is allowed to happen is a particularly helpful one in defining at least the Flow of Effort. He also defines Flow of Shape as 'Variation in the size of the sphere of movement', and Flow of Effort as 'Variation in the potential to fall', which is equally useful. In the consideration of the complete assessment framework below, we will see how he creates a bi-polar seesaw for the Flow of Effort and the Flow of Shape. Since his terms for the polarities of Flow of Effort are slightly different in *Posture and Gesture* to those in *Management Behaviour*, I have put the early terms in brackets.

Flow of Shape

Inflated   Withdrawn

|____< Growing _____ Shrinking >____|

                                    ^

Flow of Effort

Abandoned   Rigid

|____< Free Flow (Freeing) _____ Bound Flow (Binding) >__|

                                 ^

As we shall see below, it was an appreciation of Flow that decided him to add the twelfth item to the assessment framework – Identifying.

The Complete Framework

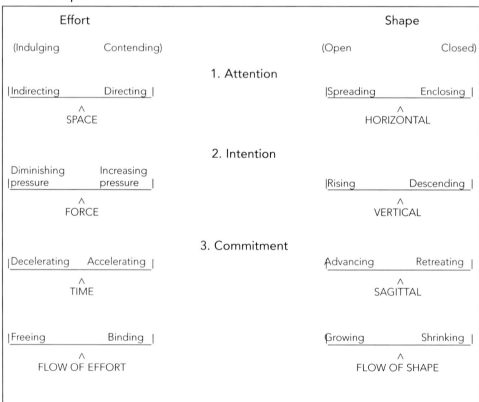

Figure 9. The Components of Movement

This isn't something that is covered in these reflections, simply because Lamb had already made a Profile of me and all this material is in the DVD ROM *Movement and Decision-Making*. But nowhere has Lamb really given an overview of how he came to create his 11-point assessment. This is necessary for a reader to have a complete picture of Lamb's development and his achievement as a pioneer of movement studies. To begin this detailed exposition let us return to the already-familiar Lamb 'seesaw'. This bipolar line allowed him to express four types of information about a person's movement.

In Fig. 8, page 154 the shaded area shows the degree of merging and its position on the bipolar scale, and the arrowed, lower line expresses the average range of the person's merged movement and its position between the two polarities. Once one understands that this sequence is always represented in the same way the person's profile can be represented with the ranges alone, but always showing where they pass through neutral. eg:

Effort   Shape

———————————   ———————————
         ^   ^

      ———————   ———————
         ^   ^

      ———————   ———————
         ^   ^

We would recognise from this profile above that the person had a preference for moving in the Attention area, with markedly less in the Intention and Commitment. As we'll see below, this person would be described as having a preference for Investigating and Exploring. You will find these diagrams in all of his published books. We must not forget that there would also be another graph representing the Flow of Effort and Flow of Shape as mentioned above.

What we have seen above is how Lamb has developed an extremely economical graphic means of representing the results of his observations. At a glance you can see the entire range of movement made by the person being observed.

Now we move on to some evaluations of this information – the decision-making framework itself As we've seen in Part II there are six simple Effort or Shape Components:

When someone moves they have either the tendency to

1. Direct or Indirect (Effort);
2. Spread or Enclose (Shape);
3. Diminish or Increase pressure (Effort);
4. Rise or Descend (Shape);
5. Decelerate or Accelerate (Effort);
6. Advance or Retreat (Shape).

In the framework these are correlated with the following aspects of decision-making:

Investigating (how you direct your attention) - Effort
Exploring (how you go out into the space around you) - Shape
Disciplining (how you exercise your authority, or throw your weight about) – Effort
Confronting (how you place yourself vis-à-vis others) - Shape
Deciding (just when you make your move) - Effort
Anticipating (looking out for the consequences of your decision in the future) – Shape

To the three stages in the process of making a movement there correspond three stages in the process of making a decision:

Attention corresponds to Communication
Intention corresponds to Presentation
Commitment corresponds to Operation

This accounts for the 9-point framework that we find in *Posture and Gesture*. There are some small variations in how these items are described in his three published books, but for the most part the descriptions are the same. Below I reproduce 1 - 9 from the framework as described in *Body Code* (which you could compare with the one on p. 96 of *Management Behaviour*).

Attention

1. *Investigating* = defining, categorising, fact-finding, establishing method, defining standards and principles, extracting information in a defined area.

2. *Exploring* = assessing scope of information, looking for alternative possibilities and approaches, questioning assumptions and reasons.

Intention

3. *Determining* = having firmness of purpose; showing determination, persisting against odds; resisting pressure.

4. *Confronting* = crystallising issues, establishing importance, challenging; recognising immediate needs realistically; accepting hard facts in a forthright manner.

Commitment

5. *Deciding* = having a sense of timing, setting off action implementation at the right moment, settling timing priorities, seizing opportunities, being good at being flexible, on the spot programming.

6. *Anticipating* = looking ahead, foreseeing consequences of action, evaluating practicalities, continually anticipating future developments, systematic future planning. [*Body Code*, p.148]

7. *Communicating* = establishing and maintaining reciprocal communication; approachability; imparting and inviting knowledge and information; harmonising, including sympathising; sharing own process of investigating and exploring.

8. *Presenting* = maintaining confidence, making a positive demonstration, declaring intentions, influencing, persuading, emphasising, insisting, resisting; sharing own process of determining and confronting.

9. *Operating* = on the spot organisation of people; creating sense of urgency or slowing down the pace, spurring people on or delaying activity with awareness of objectives; controlling the action; sharing own process of deciding and anticipating. [Ibid., p.171]

These nine Items are common to all three books, but by the time we get to *Management Behaviour* they have been joined by a further three – Dynamism, Adaptability and Identification each of which are calculated on the basis of a profile. In our conversations Lamb pointed out No 4. 'Confronting' is now called 'Evaluating', and No.5 'Deciding' is now called 'Timing'.

Dynamism

This is a concept that Laban called Loading, and refers to the number of responsibilities an executive can take on at any one time. If in a person's profile there is something like 25% Investigating, 30% Disciplining and 45% Deciding then:

Such a man will appear to be fairly thorough in sizing up the ... situation, resolving what he should do, and particularly decisive in carrying it out. The decisiveness predominates, but other components are by no means inevident. Such a man is dynamic in his application of effort, defining dynamism as the amount of effort actually applied in total relative to a norm. [*Management Behaviour*, pp.92 – 93]

Adaptability

This is a feature of the harmonising between Shape and Effort initiatives.

> There are of course, many gradations in adaptability and evaluation of their significance must take into account the logical sequence of the Attention, Intention and Commitment stages. As Attention is the logical first stage, not to be adaptable in this has a different sort of effect from when absence of adaptability is confined to the Commitment stage. The former often seems to be the case in people who have preconceived beliefs and somewhat brittle standards but will adapt their methods of operation. The latter describes people who are prepared to consider seriously a variety of possible beliefs or variation in standards but in action impose their own timing and can never take orders from anyone else. [Ibid., pp.99 – 100]

Identifying

> It is clear that the Flow components have much to do with the physical readiness to participate in the activity situation. Relative to management a low retention of the Flow components means unreadiness to participate, and colleagues will feel (depending on their own Flow retentional factor) that such a person is aloof or remote in the personal work relationships, however friendly or otherwise cooperative he is. A high retention shows obvious readiness to participate, a factor which could, in some situations, cause embarrassment in personal work relations. [Ibid., p.101]

The three are summed up in *Body Code:*

> There are three qualities which apply to the entire profile overall and which allow comparison on a rating scale. You can say that a profile has a greater, or less, *total potential activity measure* as shown by the degree of *dynamism, adaptability and identification* present. [...] *Dynamism* is the measure of movement-intensity in a PGM pattern and is best thought of as a person's drive. *Adaptability* is the measure of a person's willingness to apply his PGM pattern in a new situation, where different customs, traditions and principles apply, and not to relapse into gestural or puppet-like behaviour. *Identification* is the measure of a person's willingness to participate in current activities – some people always want to be involved... and others always remain aloof, even though they may want to be involved. [*Body Code*, p.173]

However, an indication of how Lamb's method is still open to change is the fact that in 2002 he decided that Adaptability was too much of an inference based on the Profile, and that although they could advise on a person's adaptability, it would no longer be part of the profile itself. Therefore he opted for an 11-point Framework.

This final part of the book brings us up to date with Lamb's thinking about Movement and Decision-Making. We have seen him progressively refine Laban's terms in order to create a logical means of representing a person's movement preferences (i.e. by means of seesaws) and then create a correlation between that person's preferences for decision-making. *Posture and Gesture* was a landmark publication in that it set out as its object of study a completely new sense of movement, one that begins in one part of the body and then progressively involves the rest of the body. We should not underestimate the subtlety of this conception of movement: he is not describing movement (which can be very efficiently done with labanotation) he is investing significance in a particular moment in our movements – when a gesture merges into a posture. It is precisely because this type of movement is so personal, so telling, that ultimately (but not in *Posture and Gesture* itself) he could link the pattern of PGM with decision-making. Although less well-known (perhaps because it was so specifically addressed to a business readership), it was *Management Behaviour* which made the link between moving and decision-making. After that it was simply a question of testing and refining the framework through constant practice. Writing these pages has made me aware of just how logical Lamb's method is. And it is precisely this logic, this methodological clarity that might blind us to the implications of his thinking. For this reason, in the conclusion I shall discuss some of the broader principles involved in Lamb's research, and look at how some of his ideas have been or could be developed.

FRAMEWORK OF MANAGEMENT INITIATIVE

THE MOTIVATION TO ACT

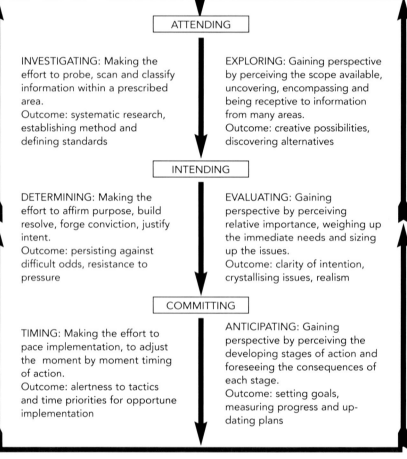

The Decision Making Process in Action

ATTENDING

INVESTIGATING: Making the effort to probe, scan and classify information within a prescribed area.
Outcome: systematic research, establishing method and defining standards

EXPLORING: Gaining perspective by perceiving the scope available, uncovering, encompassing and being receptive to information from many areas.
Outcome: creative possibilities, discovering alternatives

INTENDING

DETERMINING: Making the effort to affirm purpose, build resolve, forge conviction, justify intent.
Outcome: persisting against difficult odds, resistance to pressure

EVALUATING: Gaining perspective by perceiving relative importance, weighing up the immediate needs and sizing up the issues.
Outcome: clarity of intention, crystallising issues, realism

COMMITTING

TIMING: Making the effort to pace implementation, to adjust the moment by moment timing of action.
Outcome: alertness to tactics and time priorities for opportune implementation

ANTICIPATING: Gaining perspective by perceiving the developing stages of action and foreseeing the consequences of each stage.
Outcome: setting goals, measuring progress and updating plans

OVERALL FACTORS
DYNAMISM: The number of novel or non-routine cycles of decision-making the manager will simultaneously initiate and continue

ADAPTABILITY: Willingness to alter basic attitudes to fit in with changed situations

IDENTIFYING: The readiness to respond, participate and become involved in the action

© Warren Lamb Partnership

Figure 10. Framework of Motivation to Act

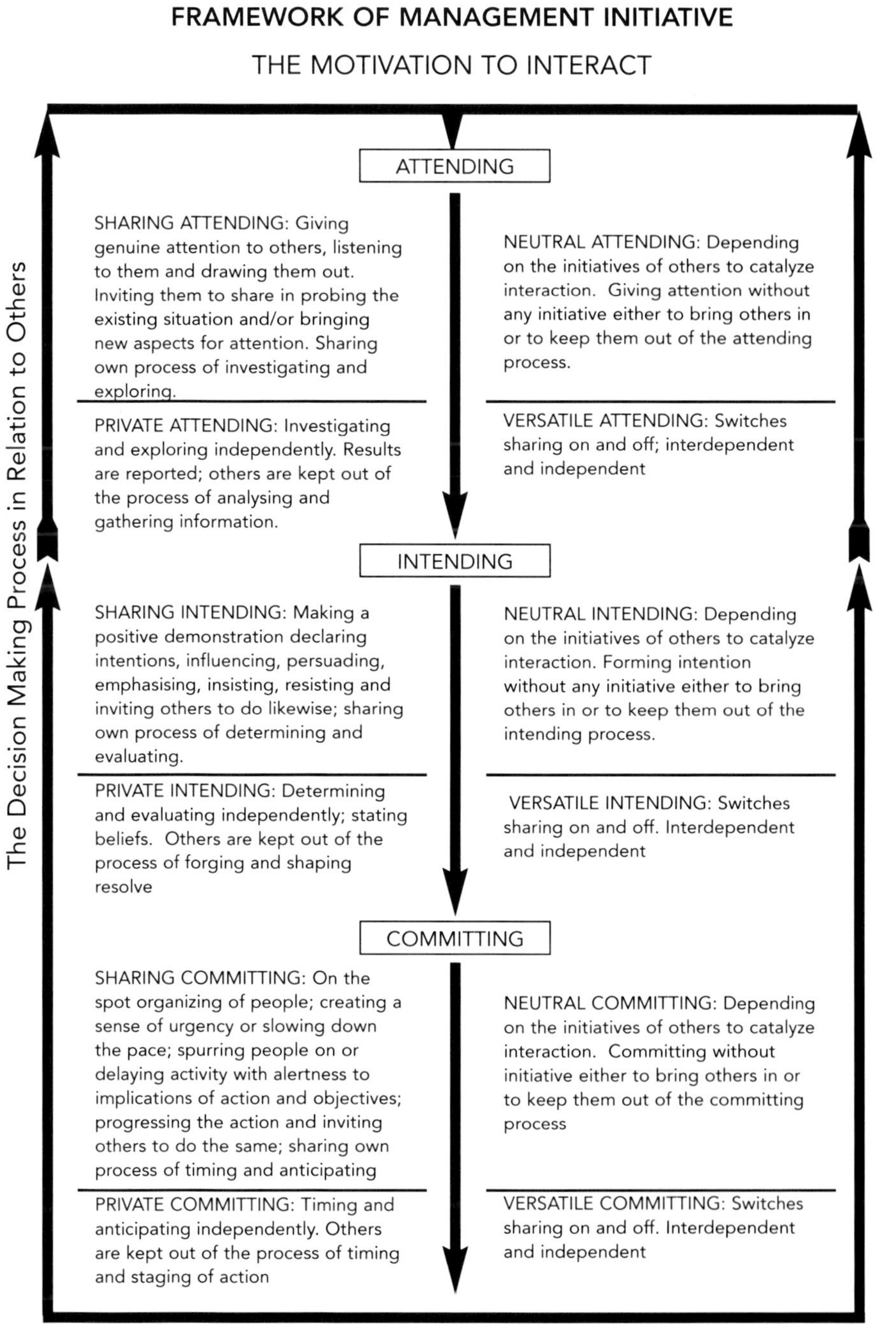

FRAMEWORK OF MANAGEMENT INITIATIVE

THE MOTIVATION TO INTERACT

The Decision Making Process in Relation to Others

ATTENDING

SHARING ATTENDING: Giving genuine attention to others, listening to them and drawing them out. Inviting them to share in probing the existing situation and/or bringing new aspects for attention. Sharing own process of investigating and exploring.

NEUTRAL ATTENDING: Depending on the initiatives of others to catalyze interaction. Giving attention without any initiative either to bring others in or to keep them out of the attending process.

PRIVATE ATTENDING: Investigating and exploring independently. Results are reported; others are kept out of the process of analysing and gathering information.

VERSATILE ATTENDING: Switches sharing on and off; interdependent and independent

INTENDING

SHARING INTENDING: Making a positive demonstration declaring intentions, influencing, persuading, emphasising, insisting, resisting and inviting others to do likewise; sharing own process of determining and evaluating.

NEUTRAL INTENDING: Depending on the initiatives of others to catalyze interaction. Forming intention without any initiative either to bring others in or to keep them out of the intending process.

PRIVATE INTENDING: Determining and evaluating independently; stating beliefs. Others are kept out of the process of forging and shaping resolve

VERSATILE INTENDING: Switches sharing on and off. Interdependent and independent

COMMITTING

SHARING COMMITTING: On the spot organizing of people; creating a sense of urgency or slowing down the pace; spurring people on or delaying activity with alertness to implications of action and objectives; progressing the action and inviting others to do the same; sharing own process of timing and anticipating

NEUTRAL COMMITTING: Depending on the initiatives of others to catalyze interaction. Committing without initiative either to bring others in or to keep them out of the committing process

PRIVATE COMMITTING: Timing and anticipating independently. Others are kept out of the process of timing and staging of action

VERSATILE COMMITTING: Switches sharing on and off. Interdependent and independent

Figure 11. Framework of Motivation to Interact

171

xxiii. *Posture and Gesture*

A year or two after Laban's death I developed the idea of Posture-Gesture and Posture-Gesture-Mergers. I don't know how the words 'posture' and 'gesture' sprang into my mind, I was just looking for a term that had meaning. It seemed to me that we were looking for a means of matching up movement capability with a particular job.   To get that match and to get some understanding of why a person was or was not suited to a particular job needed clarification as to what movement was significant for an individual character, as distinct from those movements which were not. Of course, there is never only one way of doing a job and I always explored whether a candidate in applying his own Movement Pattern Analysis might do the job differently, but with a good prospect of success.

Gesture is commonly understood as a movement that has little significance – as in the phrase, 'to make a gesture'. Quite often the word 'posture' would be used to convey something that is more permanent. These terms came to me as I was looking for a terminology that could adequately describe what I was seeing. At that time I wrote a text with the pianist Ronald Meachen who had come to me for a development course which he felt had been of great benefit to him in his actual playing and in his teaching. We wrote a book called *The Kinaesthetic Approach to Piano Technique* (now available from Brechin Books) in which, using the experience he got from me, he makes an argument for incorporating movement training into teaching piano technique.   I then wrote about posture and gesture.

My Posture Gesture Merging (PGM) principles apply to the Kinesphere just as they do to Effort. We can see that there are certain Shapings where there is a merger and perhaps other Shapings where there is Gesture. In other words, Gestures where there is no merger. Everyone experiences the Kinesphere, it is just a question of whether you experience it with your body as a whole or whether you are observing gestures, even gestures happening simultaneously in different parts of the body. The concept of opening and closing is quite familiar to everyone, so it is just a question of being specific as to how it occurs, what parts of the body are being used, and whether they merge, and of course of getting all of that as a record of this before you go to any judgement – as so often we do – that one person is closing away from another because they don't like them. There are all sorts of interpretations that people will give to their perception of what the opening and closing means and many misinterpretations occur. We talk about someone being open to us, or not, as the case may be.

It's not a question of observing a gesture and then a second and unrelated posture, but it is actually *in the process* of the movement itself that a gesture may become a postural movement, or a postural movement may revert into a gesture. So I coined the concept of merging. It came from a lot of thinking, observation, anguishing and differentiation between the static and the dynamic, between a rhythm or phrase and a movement on its own; trying to avoid generalised concepts. However it didn't really click until about 1964 when I was writing *Posture and Gesture*, which was 6 years after Laban had died. I don't think that there was a Eureka moment when I leapt to the ceiling and rejoiced but I do recall feeling that I had made a discovery, or form of discovery. It was derived from Laban, but the more that I worked with it, the more it made sense.

xxiv. Posture Gesture Merging

Integration (A precursor to Merging)

Very often people are referred to as being integrated or not integrated. Laban had a favourite term for people who were in need of some kind of therapy: they were 'lopsided'. In the present day I hear a lot of people in the field of therapy talking about integration and integrated movements, although I am not often secure as to quite what they mean by 'integration'. I think he was intuitively seeing some sort of connection between Effort and Shape. Although I have argued that – with the exception of the Diagonal Scale – in his teaching he kept up this dichotomy between Shape and Effort, intuitively, in his own perception of people's movement he did see the two together. I think I have evidence of this in some of the comments that he made in the Effort assessments of people. By integration, or not being lop-sided, he would see that there was a link between the Effort rhythms that the person was doing and the Shaping of the movement. After all, this is related to our balance: if we don't shape our Effort rhythms adequately then we do begin to look ugly and possibly ineffective, if it is to do with work.

Certainly, we can make the body do all sorts of things if we have the motivation. We can put our body through terrible trials, ultimately even injuring the body – this happens all the time. It happens constantly to a lesser degree when people put themselves under bodily tension, something for which they don't perhaps get sufficiently compensated. Whether that would qualify as showing a lack of integration or whether Laban would define that as 'lopsided' I am not quite sure. I think that there is a general acceptance in many disciplines and theories that integration is good and fragmentation is bad.

So, one is trying to define forms of integration – for example, speech which is not integrated with bodily movement could be bad. You quite often see actors doing this: you see their voice being produced but it really conflicts with their movement. Speech is a result of movements – for example, gesture movements of the larynx, tongue and mouth - and they do need to be integrated with the trunk. I am just using this as a simple example. One cannot really see these gestures, but the same is true of gestures that you can see – movements of the hands, face, arms, feet. In these cases you can check whether these gestures are integrated with the body as a whole. Only a proportion are likely to be integrated: particularly in this day and age, particularly in contrast with one hundred and fifty years ago: we just have so many things to deal with - computer keyboards, wires, plugs, all sorts of stuff that we are fiddling with all day long. It would be impossible for all those fiddling movements to be integrated with the body.

If we understand the process of integration as one process merging with another (that's really how the term 'merging' arose) I think we really have an understanding of integration which can firstly be analysed, observed and measured – depending on how accurately we can observe. Secondly, we realise that integration is something practical and has no spiritual or emotional resonances. Thirdly, we can see the extent of the integration which may cover some Efforts and Shapes, but not others; this means we can begin to have a differentiation in the nature of integration. I think this is what movement observation and analysis can do for us in a much more specific way than many other disciplines where integration is referred to, but not always understood in precise terms.

From Integrated Movement to Posture-Gesture

I still prefer to talk about Posture-Gesture Merging, rather than what people in the movement world call 'integrated movement' which has more to do with psychological aspects. I wanted to make an observation which had no overtones of psychological interpretation. It just showed that some Efforts do get merged into posture Efforts and others don't; similarly with the shaping of movement. This has remained so for the past forty years. Finding out how Posture and Gesture related, how the one merges into the other, was a particularly significant discovery. You can probably fake a posture or attitude, or particular phrases of posture movement, and we can fake gestures if we concentrate hard enough but we can't really fake the quality of the Effort and Shape during the merger. It's not just Posture and Gesture but the merging element of the two which is the crux of the matter. That really was crystallised when *Posture and Gesture* was published in 1965.

I had always felt uncomfortable with the metaphysical side of Laban's thinking and wanted to be practical and to avoid in the observations I was taking any interpretative element. Laban mostly used to give an interpretation which was perceived as being very, very meaningful, and I'm sure it was. Although I've never regarded myself as a true scientist I have really tried to differentiate between what you've observed, between what you have and haven't seen, and to analyse that. I was motivated by the need to be accurate in my observations but also objective and practical. I feel it is very important not to get the two fields of observation and analysis mixed up. I think that this term 'merger' is the right one and that's what really happens. We can make different parts of our body do anything if we are physically capable, and determined enough to master some particular skill but we cannot contrive mergers.

All of that helped to develop a theory that we all have a pattern of Posture Gesture Merging which eventually got translated against a decision-making model and that's how it is now interpreted. I remember interviewing candidates for a job and I claimed that it might be possible according to the concept of PGM to check whether a person is being truthful or not, because there are a number of occasions, it was subsequently found, that they had been lying about their CV. I found that when a person was talking if he or she used only gesture and you didn't see these gestures merge into a posture – they might be smiling and making very convincing gestures, and so on – then when the interviewer took over the conversation, you would see mergers happen as he or she relaxed. If during the time that the candidate was conversing all that you saw was gestures then that person could, possibly, be untruthful. Then again this might be because the candidate was nervous, so one should be careful in saying this. But I did raise questions in several cases. When I have observed a lack of PGM I have said that people are contrived, that is, putting on an act. It may warrant some more investigation into a person's background. I remember one person who had created a very good impression in interview, actually having a criminal record.

This idea of Posture-Gesture Merging (PGM) is becoming more understood in recent years. A number of theses have been done on PGMs and I am encouraged that people like Dr Frances La Barre has picked up on this concept. This does seem to have substantiated that there is such a phenomenon and that I haven't just imagined it. Her book *On Moving and Being Moved*, published by the Analytic Press in 2001 has added to the literature on non-verbal behaviour and communication. Going back thirty or forty years or more there was a spate of books by disciplined researchers like Charles Darwin, A.E. Shefflin, W.S. Condon, Paul Ekman, Alan Kendon, E.D. Chapple, G. Allport, Erwin Goffman, and Ray. L. Birdwhistell. And then Desmond Morris, who isn't considered a very serious contributor, entered the field; but since then hardly anything has been published. I am hoping that *Moving and Being Moved* will revive the study of non-verbal behaviour. I am sure it's going on in various university departments but I don't hear of much being published in the field.

It may be that the person giving the impression of 'flicking' is moving only part of the body, rather than the body as a whole – the trunk, for example, may not be involved, it may just be peripheral. Therefore it seemed to me that in order to get a fuller, richer, more accurate meaning, we had to distinguish between movements that we put on or acquire - maybe as mannerisms - as distinct from movement which is really important to us individually.   I eventually made the distinction between Gesture movement which I defined as an act of a part or parts of the body as distinct from Posture which is a movement where the quality of the movement is consistent throughout the body as a whole. We have to be careful that we aren't just saying that the whole body is moving because the whole body might be moving, like some kind of one-man band, who through an act of conscious concentration can move different parts of his body. This is the same as when a child pats her head and rubs her stomach simultaneously: through concentration you can make two parts of the body move differently from each other with different effort. However, it seems to me that these are movements that can be assumed and then let go.

Quite often a person has a gesture mannerism. I remember seeing a senior business executive at a lecture and he kept putting his finger to his nose as he was lecturing and it seemed to be that he was almost picking his nose. This was just a gesture that he had got into and of course there is a sensation that it gives him. Somehow or other it may have a sort of a meaning that has helped him overcome some hesitation while he was lecturing. Although he denied that he ever did it, it was easy to prove to him that he did and it was quite simple to get him to use enough discipline to correct it. That mannerism disappeared from his repertoire. However, I also remember a woman who used to pick spots on her cheek and make them bleed: she used to get into situations where she did this compulsively and didn't know she was doing it. Actually it was not just a gesture, it was linked with a change in her posture and it required a very, very considerable redevelopment, rather than a simple correction.

One can distinguish an isolated gesture - which can involve the entire upper part of the body - from a movement which is integrated or coordinated or congruent in its qualities of effort and of shaping. If there is congruence in the movement then there is much greater significance – or a different form of significance. What I am calling 'posture-movement with congruence' has to be differentiated from how we normally use the word to describe somebody who is erect or slumped, or has good or bad posture; that is, when a static position is usually being referred to.   Even people with what some 'body workers' might call 'bad' posture, are able to move their body and are likely to move it so as to merge the movement with gestures, or maybe make a gesture which merges with the body as a whole. It is during this point or phrase of the connecting of gesture with posture or posture with gesture that it appears that movement is meaningful enough to the person, that it is very difficult, almost impossible, to eradicate it completely. I theorise that if this is the case, then we can relatively easily change gestures and relatively easily work on this through training. We can relatively easily work on bad posture. But it seems that if we cannot change the quality of movement at the point where gestures merge into postures, or vice versa; then it has a particular significance.

Any definition of Effort, but also of Shape, does need to take into account whether it is a gesture, in the colloquial sense in which it is often used, or whether it is a movement that is congruent or merged. In terms of defining Effort, these movements are obviously different for the person. To make an Effort, to apply effort, to be effortful, is going to be different – it is going to give different feedback and have a different significance for the individual when it concerns posture-gesture merging (PGM) as distinct from gesture only.

There is no distinction when observing a manager's movement, between personal, behavioural and functional. A person can falsify their movement or move in an uncharacteristic way and what you will then see are more gestures. When they begin to deal with a particular situation and take decisions then you will see that if this requires movements that are not part of their predominant pattern, then these movements will be mostly gestures. The posture-gesture mergings will come as they relax. With somebody who is really fitted to what s/he is doing you will find that the posture-gesture mergings happen even more when s/he is working as well as relaxing.

Gestures can be assumed socially. We move according to how we think we are being required to move. If people are able to get those gestures merged into posture then they look very comfortable doing them, but very often they appear stilted because they have not become merged. It is fairly similar with posture. If someone slouches along to a meeting, they might straighten up as they enter the meeting: how long he or she can maintain this straight position will depend on how long he or she has to. In both cases one has to consider the process of the movement. Unfortunately the word posture is often used to describe a certain physique, a static pose. I use it in terms of the phrasing of the process of movement itself. We can look at gesture and posture alone, to a certain extent: but very soon we will need to look at their merging.

PGM and Acting

People might have been brought up in certain cultures where some gestures do start merging with the posture, and they are probably going to find it very difficult to escape from that cultural movement. An actor might even find it difficult to escape from it. It may be wisest not to try to escape from it but to utilise that cultural influence to positive effect. Just as a manager may be comfortable to take on a certain range of jobs, so an actor may interpret or re-interpret their role to be within their movement range. There may be roles that in terms of his or her movement that they cannot accomplish: they only succeed in looking rather uncomfortable and unhappy. If the role is just within a range of movement then with guidance and through the process of rehearsal they may adjust their performance so that they overcome any sense of being ham or wooden.

I think that the idea of PGM does have some application in the field of theatre and I have worked with a number of actors. I remember an actor who was playing Othello who felt uneasy about one of his speeches, and it seemed to me that he was making gestures that strayed too far away from the posture and when I made him aware of this, he was able himself to get a merger with his posture and he felt very much better and I do believe that that improved his performance. All of this encouraged me in 1964 to think that this discovery of PGM was valid and worth pursuing. Although I have no reason to challenge the validity of that discovery 40 years later, I do acknowledge the difficulty in observing the PGMs. An actor who makes too many gestures without merging them into a posture makes me think of Hamlet's advice to the actors not to 'Saw the air'. That is really indicating an isolated gesture which is very applicable to stylised performances, but if you get too many isolated gestures and there's not enough merger going on it did seem to me at the time like ham acting.

The Observation and Notation of Posture-Gesture-Mergings

What I have done in Movement Pattern Analysis is to take observations of a person to a degree to what we know will be a fair sample. We analyse those observations as to the Effort and Shape processes that have appeared in PGMs and then match the results of that analysis against a decision-making model and we come out with what we declare is the person's preferred way of going through a decision-making process. A person might not be able to follow the preference, but nonetheless the preference is there. The preference will pull the person to want to go through the decision-making process in the way that is comfortable for him or her: this defines their comfort zone. This would not be possible without a form of notation and having got a system of notation, it can be adapted in one way or another. But none of this would have been possible had it not been for the original concept of a notation based upon a codification of the components of movement, and this came from Laban. His notation is just one example of his genius.

The method has held good and I have been immensely encouraged by the confirmation that has come over the years. The only Achilles heel of the whole procedure has been the observation reliability. A lot of effort has gone into trying to get reliability and validity not only in terms of observation but also in terms of movement meaning what I claim it to mean. When we train in Movement Pattern Analysis it used to be very difficult to establish criteria for observer-reliability. Carol Lynne Moore has set up very strict procedures for measuring the correlation between different observers. From time to time practitioners take sets of observations which are then sent to independent specialists in this work who calculate a measure of correlation and determine what correlations are acceptable and when they are not. I have been encouraged by the extent to which they do come within an acceptable correlation. However, I also preface any of my reports by stating that they are not 100% scientific. I have the hope, or expectation, that one day these observations can be taken electronically, rather than relying on the human eye.

About eight years ago I visited a biomechanics laboratory in Minnesota, one of five similarly- equipped laboratories in the world. These laboratories are affiliated with or located in hospitals, but they have been used in other fields, such as analysing sportsmen and women. I looked at data being fed into a computer which resulted in a picture of the person being generated on a screen. While I was there they were studying a long-distance walker who competed in the Olympics. This was being analysed and matched against different criteria such as efficiency. It was the means of getting the data which interested me. They have an area where this man was on a gravity platform walking on the spot (which I thought at the time might falsify the data) while four cameras recorded him at some incredible rate of frames per second, and he had electromyography sensors attached to every joint. All of this data from the cameras was fed into the computer. I think that this could be adapted to recording movement. The shapes of the movements are fairly easy.

Electromyography[17] (see p.180) gives rhythm and the gravity platform gives pressure variation, so I felt that this would be something that could help us differentiate between posture and gesture. This electromyograph simply gives a bleep when the muscle is active. We did an experiment once in the University of California with about twenty students who had fourteen electrodes placed on different parts of their bodies. Signals were fed into a computer for several hours as they went about their daily activity and then we had literally miles of print-out. While there would be moments that one or two different muscles bleeped in each of the participants, there would be moments with all of the participants, and this is what excited me, when all fourteen would bleep simultaneously across the page I think that this would be a PGM.

xxv. Building up the Framework – The final three items in the framework

In *Posture and Gesture* I did talk about Interaction in that the first six items of the framework revealed the independent initiative that the person would take. But nobody is an island, therefore in what respect can this method contribute to an understanding of relationships? People share in their Attention, they create what I call a Communicative mode. If they share the Intention then it is more a Presentational mode, and if they share their commitment then it is an Operational Mode. People could understand this quite clearly. That added three more factors to the framework: the first six were the independent initiatives and the next three were the interdependent initiatives. And then there are the final three which I always think need to be subdivided at some point. There can be both Effort Dynamism and Shape Dynamism. Depending on how confident someone is with an MPA they may go into that.

Identifying

Identifying is drawn from an observation and analysis of the Flow pattern. As Kestenberg has revealed there is an immense body of knowledge that is contained in the concept of Flow that still needs to be developed and made more precise. It was not until 1960 or 1961 that I began working with her. But this work certainly had an influence on me, especially my understanding of Shape Flow, which I incorporated in *Posture and Gesture*. There is, it seems to me, a lot of evidence, particularly from the work I did with Kestenberg, that there is a loss of Flow during childhood growth as the Effort and Shape components are developed It can be linked to the extent to which a person identifies, that is in the way that they participate in other people's activity. All we are reporting on is physical, it is to do with movement. It is not just an intellectual identification. This has been quite meaningful to many people. It is about growing up so as to remain childish and have a sympathy with children. When I began my career I would work at home and I was always interested in how clients interacted with my four young children: they could hardly ignore them as they almost fell over them getting to

---

[17] Electromyography is defined as the study of electric currents, or voltage, in the muscles which is detected by means of electrodes attached to the body.

my office. Some clients would pat them on the head or squeeze their cheeks, but the children weren't taken by that at all. Whereas other people hardly did anything at all and yet the children really got into their field, and there was a real interaction between. When I looked at their movement these were the people who had retained relatively more Flow than those people who didn't strike up that rapport. That was partly the reasoning behind it. There is a lot to Identifying which we can subdivide, but I have deliberately avoided following Kestenberg who has subdivided and then subdivided again, making more and more refinements, until it becomes more inordinately complex that it is only now becoming more popular because Susan Loman, the main Kestenberg trainer, has simplified the system. At some point a whole book could be written about Identifying alone.

Adaptability

This came into the Profile Framework when I was still working on my own in the 1960s when it was obvious that executives particularly were interested in adaptability and frequently asked me about it. I struggled to try and find out if I could help them. What I was advising on was the initiative people take. Not that they were ready to conform to a process of change but rather who initiated the process of change. They take the initiative to create the change. These are the change-makers who were actually responsible for something new. From just looking at people's profiles, I realised that those who were primarily attention-oriented and less intention or commitment oriented, were more adaptable, more the agents of change in the world. They would always look at the situation as to whether they could change it or add something different to it. The commitment-oriented people would tend to say, "This is the situation, how can I exploit it? How can I make something of it?" They may be visionary perhaps in what they can make of something but primarily they accept what they find. Attention-oriented people want to investigate and explore whether something different might be better. It seemed to me that those people who have the highest level of preference in both the Effort and Shape aspects of Attention, and that their medium level of preference was Intention, with the lowest being Commitment would be the truly research-orientated change-makers in the world. Much depends, of course, on what position of power they have, along with many other factors. So after all this I added Adaptability to the profile and it was added to the framework when I wrote Management Behaviour. It was only recently when I was at an MPA conference that we discussed the fact that it is different to all the other items in that it is something that we read from the profile as a whole and not something that is a result of the process of analysis. So we have omitted it, though recognising that adaptability is something that we can advise on.

Dynamism

In contrast to Identifying which required that Shape Flow was complementary to Effort Flow, Dynamism came directly from what Laban referred to as Loading, which he only related to Effort, of course, but it also occurs in shape movement where there can be a greater quantity of variation if you move three-dimensionally rather than one-dimensionally. Similarly with Effort, if you do a basic Effort like a punch which is strong, direct and quick, there is more movement, more loading, than if it was just a strong movement but there was no directing or speed. Basically, all your Efforts include three elements and if all the Shape initiatives are simultaneously in action with them, then that would be maximum loading or Dynamism. If you only ever move one component at a time, then that would be minimum loading. It is a very interesting concept which I feel that we have translated in accordance with Laban's view. If we habitually load our movement relatively more than other people then it must have some sort of meaning. When you are translating this in terms of a decision-making model then it must mean readiness to engage in more decision-making. That's a way of understanding the quantitative aspect of what we're doing.

Pamela Ramsden did devise an arithmetical calculation for Dynamism. Some of our people tried using it and I do think that it has some merit. Otherwise we tend to estimate it. To be able to calculate it your observations have to be precise enough. Basically one has to judge the proportion of basic Efforts to single Efforts, also with regard to Shape. I do make a calculation, but I feel that our assessment on a ten-point scale can't really be justified to within one or two. Maybe we should say that it is High, Medium or Low. To summarise: an action has more loading or Dynamism if it involves three elements simultaneously rather than just one.

But what does this mean if someone is more loaded in their activity? Simply that they will take on more decision-making processes than somebody who is lower in Dynamism. I find it has a lot to do with responsibility. I find this often to be the case that someone with relatively lower Dynamism will say, 'I can't take that on, I've got as much as I can cope with.' That doesn't mean that they can't achieve a lot. Someone with high Dynamism will say, 'Sure I'll take it on'. But they may have taken on more than they can handle: of course what happens then is that they'll delegate or someone will step in and take over some of their responsibilities on their own initiative. It certainly gives a very interesting topic to discuss with executives, because they all like to think of themselves as dynamic. Though I am always a bit nervous if I report to them that they aren't highly dynamic, more often than not they agree, saying, 'The trouble with many people is that they take on more than they can handle'.

xxvi. The degree to which an individual can change their movement pattern

The last stage in an MPA is what we have called a development course through which I make you aware of those relatively less emphasised parts of your movement profile. From the feedback that I get, one way that it is helpful, it seems, is that we become more aware of the pattern aspect of our profile rather than individual initiatives. We become more aware of the relationship. This has the effect that we draw more upon the relatively lower initiatives. If you are effortful and you tend to have a lower use of the shape initiatives then you may just become aware that exploratory, evaluative, anticipatory activities are possibilities. You then utilise more of what you've got without it necessarily assuming a bigger part of the total picture. It is like looking at a picture from the point of view of colour and suddenly noticing a tiny patch of blue: having recognised that, you never look at the picture in the same way again. Maybe you recognise that this small touch of blue is significant in what the artist was trying to portray.

As I sit here I am now looking at a painting which represents the myth of one of the North American peoples – it concerns the figure of the white bison. Someone else could paint a picture on the same theme and it would be different. The artist could change this traditional mythical scene by making the sun a little bigger, the bison a little smaller – but these would be changes in detail, marginal changes. In a similar way, Dick McCaw is basically who he is, and he can change in some detail, and there may be big changes relative to the achievement of harmony in personal relationships and so on but it is still the same Dick McCaw who will be recognised in twenty years' time. It behoves us not to expect to change all that much but to examine to what degree we can change marginally while being happy with the basic picture. I think that is the problem with a lot of New Age claims that they hold out to people – the myth that they can change fundamentally. I think this is a disservice.

It is the same in our movement: one can realise, 'Yes I do have that small amount of exploratory initiative and I can see now how it relates to my determining or timing.' That is one benefit that can influence decision-making. It also has a benefit in the very fact of being an education about the nature of that initiative, certainly in the case of people where that initiative is very low, they really don't have much perception of it: they don't really know what it is. They get to recognise that initiative when other people are taking it and become more appreciative of it when they see it. There's also something which I can confirm from my own experience: as you get older you tend to utilise the bigger initiatives more and the smaller initiatives less. Part of the crotchetiness that older people get is because of this: they over-specialise in the use of their resources.

When I offered individual training sessions I wasn't working on either posture or gesture but their merging. I was trying to help people extend their range. Nobody's pattern of movement is so rigid that it doesn't move to some degree, but I suspect that certain things about the way we move don't change very much unless we have an extreme traumatic event like a car accident. The scope available for a person's development of range is similar to an increased vocabulary: it increases the vocabulary of movement that you can apply in decision-making so that you can be comfortable in taking responsibility and initiative over a broader scope of circumstances. Posture has a lot to do with one's sense of self, with what is and is not 'me'.

I incorporated this notion of development into personal courses that I gave in the 1950s. I used to prescribe ten sessions and people would come on the basis that it would be useful for them to be more aware of their individual movement. Even at that time I was saying that everyone had their own individual movement pattern and that one could be aware of it and develop it. The phrase that did get used a lot was to discuss with people how they 'could extend their range' - almost like having a repertoire of movement and yet this repertoire often gets frozen by the circumstances of life. That concept of extension of range was I think something that matched Laban's own thought, indeed it came from his thought. It linked with the aesthetic principle that if we could extend our range then we would have more movements to choose from; that there was more choreography that we could do, appropriate to different situations that we find ourselves in.

In terms of the component parts that make up a personality the ability to change someone's mental behaviour through how they move is going to be marginal, but it does have an effect. It can be particularly significant in reversing a process. Again, I tend to look upon everything as a process, so I would ask whether it is tending to get worse or better, on the assumption that it is not going to stay the same. It is often reversing the process that is so difficult; if the process has become established then it requires a major therapeutic procedure.

My career has included taking on individuals and I have had a number of individual students who worked in the arts: sculptors, violinists, pianists. I worked and continue to work with a lot of people who aren't in the field of management, though less than in the 1950s and '60s but it still remains of interest how people can develop, how they can change. I am particularly interested in the fact that we are constantly being told that we have to change and that if we don't change we will be left behind because the pace of development is so fast. If this is learning about computer technology then I agree, but if it is applied to personality development then I have my doubts.

People are constantly being exhorted to change, but are never informed about what they should be changing into. Very often it is little known about what they should be changing from. There's a lot of vagueness in this. So I am interested in trying to get a little more definition into how we can change significantly. People do go to gurus and think they have changed and then relapse, and note that there has been no change. This has to be related to one's position in life at any moment in time. People often want to change because they are miserable, or because of distress or disturbance in their life. All sorts of changes are possible: in attitude, temperament, politics, philosophy – all of which can have significance, though the change may not be as significant as people think. Politicians change party but seem to go on the same in terms of the sort of person that they are. Really significant personality change is likely to be marginal and from the standpoint of movement it can be demonstrated that we don't change significantly. I am very interested in the way people change as they age, not least because at my age I have noticed how you contract rather than develop. In all that I am declining I am desperately looking for something in which I might be progressing!

xxvii. On Assessments and Tests

What is one testing? Mental or Physical Actions?

Carol-Lynne Moore talks about Mental Effort in her book *Movement and Decision-Making* and outlines the history of how Laban got into Mental Effort. It always troubles me a bit because everything that I do is based on observation and you can't observe mental Effort, all that you can see is a body. The body does all sorts of movements: it can frown, it can smile, it can fidget, there can be a big variation of effort and shape. From your observation and analysis of movement you may then discover some correlation with thinking, with the mind. One theory is that there is no such duality of mind and body – in fact we just have a body that moves and that mind is movement. I think, subconsciously, that has influenced me right from the very beginning although I didn't talk about it. I think I see now the sort of Cartesian segregation of mind and body still applies when people use the word mind-body; although this is outmoded, there is still a great element of the duality in the way they talk about mind and body. I start from the premise that we just have a body. Maybe if we just start from the observation and analysis of movement, you may be able to talk about intelligence: about how harmoniously, how dynamically that person is moving.

I think all action is about how you are motivated to act in the world. There are many variables involved which is why I am so keen to identify what is constant in our movement. Emotion, temperament, recent events - all have a bearing upon our movement. It is the patterning of movement that is more constant; that applies to a much longer period of time which is the significant element upon which to base the sort of understandings that we've been talking about. On what can I rely in this particular person? Even then, we have to take into account the question of how much scope one has to act according to that pattern. Are you so desperate to maintain some particular activity that you may not be acting according to your pattern?

How do we understand a person's unique way of going through a decision-making process? Whatever a person develops in that respect can be understood as a motivation to act according to that person and this will lead that person in taking an initiative. This is only a small part of the total picture of which you will be taking an account. If you are wondering why did that person show that emotion, that anger; why is this person so joyful at the moment, why has this person changed his views? These sorts of changes in emotion, temperaments, attitudes, beliefs, opinions, are constantly being influenced by all sorts of factors – what you read in the newspapers that morning, what your wife said to you – and I am not suggesting that these sort of things are trivial, they are not. They can be very, very influential. These things do have importance. However, out of all these variables we can differentiate a certain patterning of activity which remains more or less constant – but it's not the be-all and end-all of everything. I've never made this claim but some people choose to make this claim on my behalf.

Tests, Assessments or Profiles?

Maybe there is something in my psychology that predisposes me against making any sort of assessment or rating because I feel sure there are many examples of where people have been misjudged having failed some sort of test or other. Certainly in the Navy there were a lot of stupid officers who must have been rated as well-educated and others who were not so well educated but seemed much more sensible. I was also interested in the distinction between common sense and whatever sense is exhibited by people who pass exams. When Laban and Lawrence imposed upon me the 'Laban-Lawrence Test' – and I think they did this because it would sell better, it would be recognised, people would know what it was - a conflict did develop which led to a break. I must have felt very, very strongly about it. That may be exaggerated – it is, after all, a question of definition, but the intelligence test I felt was particularly vulnerable to having a negative influence.

As I have already said I feel that mental and physical are really one and the same and therefore any mental activity is not the result of bodily action. One is always influencing the other. The way I would prefer to express it is that the two are basically the same, it is a unity. As to whether your movement is intelligent, this should be evident. I have talked to psychiatrists who were interested in intelligence, and there was some agreement that there is a link between movement and intelligence. Some move like a hulk, in a King Kong way, and this is assumed to indicate little intelligence. However, I think that we struggle in our definitions of intelligence. Intelligence testers will say, 'Intelligence is what I measure with this test.' Other people would have different tests. It now seems to be the view that intelligence tests estimate timing and speed in being able to answer particular types of questions. Other people might be able to do other intelligent things but not at the same speed. I know one intelligence test included how quickly one could look up an entry in a telephone directory. I don't think that the issue of what intelligence is has ever been settled. But if you align intelligence with some sort of perceptivity, with some kind of brain activity, something linked with the neurones, and how that is linked with the actions of the rest of the body then we can make a differentiation between someone being more physically active or more mentally active. Or is it a question of not making it a dichotomy in the first place and seeing that all physical and mental activity are interlinked, it's only that the degree of perceptivity may vary.

Over the years there have been various types of tests. We take driving tests – that is truly a test. The outcome of any test is always expected that you pass or fail – or you get a mark and there is a level below which you fail. Whilst I've always recognised that there are many areas where a test is appropriate, I have felt that recognition and understanding what people can do, as distinct from what they can't do, doesn't have to be part of a test. They do not have to be rated as relatively good or bad in terms of understanding what they are capable of. In terms of capability, I am not pronouncing on their capability but on what comes naturally to them. Everybody is different.

One has to recognise that there is no one way to do a job, therefore a person might be given a test as to whether he or she would be able to do a job efficiently, but that test would be inadequate because it would be based on just one way of doing the job. Most jobs can be done in a variety of ways – there's no one way of being a prime minister or being a road sweeper. Everyone can bring his or her own pattern of activity to doing it. Very often there are people who offend the established, prescribed wisdom by doing something quite differently and succeed at it better than anyone has before. You see that particularly in sports. I have always felt that there is scope in this life for understanding people without giving a rating. I fall over myself to say that the movement pattern analysis is not good or bad. It is an analysis and therefore an assessment is made, but it is an assessment done on the basis that whatever we come out with does not have to be rated as good or bad. When we move on to other forms of rating, for example, of relative balance or imbalance, scope or lack of scope, much of what we get led into saying about people describing the pattern that comes naturally to them – their movement pattern – can be interpreted as being either a good thing or a bad thing. The way someone explores can be good in one context and bad in another. Then the notion develops that whatever may be good in one context may be bad in another. That has been the basic principle on which I've pursued analysis or assessment – that nothing is really bad. To what extent can one pursue this?

The MPA can be something of a revelation. It is difficult, I know, to get away from an element of testing in what we do, but on the other hand one could say that we are being tested all the time. If you see someone being attacked you are being tested as to whether you would be public-spirited enough to act, or would be overcome by fear. This is just to dramatise the statement that we are under test in everything that we do. In terms of what is known in personality tests and vocational tests I think it is important to differentiate Movement Pattern Analysis from the Cattel 16 point PF, or Myers Brigg's Test and many of the tests that are used to differentiate students applying for university places. These tests which do give a score need to be distinguished from an analysis which attempts to account for individuality. In most tests it is impossible to avoid the conclusion that if you have a lower score than someone else then you are inferior to them.

A qualitative rather than a quantitative approach

Let's take the example of dynamism. This is something that used to get me in trouble. I remember once telling someone that he wasn't really very dynamic, and he seemed to interpret this in terms of his sexual potency. Maybe I've got better at explaining it, but just a few weeks ago I was explaining to someone that he wasn't dynamic (in the sense that we assess it in the decision-making process) – but he preferred to assume that all decision-making processes were of the same degree and level of responsibility. Comparing him with someone of higher dynamism, I then explained to him he would prefer to handle fewer decisions, and someone else would take on more. He felt this was absolutely right. This probably tends to make you more sparing as to the amount of responsibility that you are prepared to take on. I'm quoting that to pose the question as to whether that is good or bad? In some contexts it could be thought that the Movement Pattern Analysis tests your dynamism. It's the one thing where we do seem to have a score. We do give people a rating on a ten-point scale, so nine could be rated as a good and three or four as bad. But when you get it right it is fascinating how people are very enthusiastic to agree with it. People who understand lower dynamism as being more sparing, not taking on more decision-making responsibility than you feel confident of handling, then are delighted.

We never know when we start observing for a Movement Pattern Analysis to what goal it may ultimately be applied (if there is a goal at all). Whereas most tests are concerned with some defined goal or with some actual achievement, and people who get a high score on the test are deemed able to achieve more, this is not the case with MPA. It may be recognised that something can be achieved by a person because of their skills or intelligence (however that might be rated), but if it requires movement that might be antipathetic to that person's pattern then we know that although the achievement may be made, the maintaining of that achievement is going to be threatened, and that decision-making will become progressively less efficient or effective. When a decision-making process is being achieved by making movement that is predominantly outside someone's range, the capability of being able to do so is a result of his or her high motivation to achieve. The absence of movement-motivation can cause increasing ineffectiveness in decision-making, along with all sorts of stress.

This goes right back to what Laban observed about factory workers on production lines. He challenged the Time and Motion principle that the more you reduced the operations people did, the more economically they did the job. This proved false. People broke down, became stressed, and there was a very high labour turn-over. When Laban allowed people to find their own individual rhythm in doing highly repetitive jobs, they often took a little bit longer but overall production increased because absenteeism, illness and labour-turnover all reduced. I have applied the same principle.

MPA is about Finding the Right Person for the Job

It is a matching, but one that I've always thought has to be flexible because I've always believed that there's no one way to do a job. If you're matching a person against a job how do you specify the job? Certainly in working with managers there's always enough scope in whatever the nature of the management job is to look at possible different ways of doing it. You're not looking at just one job as a set number of items - that list of requirements that you see in job advertisements – this is a very crude, arbitrary way of making a selection. If you're going to do it properly you've got to look at every application and think that the most unusual and even eccentric person will make the best appointment. Most appointments are made on the basis of who is most unexceptional, who best conforms to what has been regarded as the right way in the past.

One thing that team leaders have to do is adapt to new appointments. I think Carol-Lynne's new book – Movement and Making Decisions – deals with this aspect of decision-making. It is important that a team be able to adapt to new situations by asking workers to take on new responsibilities and roles. It is remarkable the extent to which people are often kept within the watertight boxes of their roles. The finance director may be able to make a contribution to marketing: you can understand that there might be territorial imperatives which discourage people from crossing boundaries, but I am amazed that opportunities to contribute to the company in this way are not encouraged. On the basis of the understanding that we get from MPA we can fight this sort of restriction by demonstrating how people are going to benefit from such initiatives: the Marketing Manager will benefit from the Finance Manager's initiative. The tendency to feel threatened territorially by this sort of thing does disappear when the Marketing Manager realises how he or she can benefit from this initiative. When someone takes an initiative that is consistent with their MPA profile I have found that they usually get accepted, but where a person takes an initiative that he or she has read about in a text-book, and it hasn't really come from their pattern of behaviour, then that tends to be perceived as imposed.

xxviii. The Transmission of Action Profiling and MPA

Pamela Ramsden joined me in 1969. I engaged her because I had been requested to do a research project by my client Trebor. They had recognised the value of what I had done for them for the previous almost 20 years but regarded it as just some special perception or intuition that I had. They wanted to find out whether other people could do it. It's true, I had not attempted to train anybody until she came on the scene. I had given courses in movement observation, but they were one-day or weekend courses. I have already described how I trained Pamela Ramsden in observation using the 'Sitting next to Nelly' principle, in other words, training on the job. Then I introduced her into client work. She would accompany me when visiting clients and she would begin taking observations and we would compare our results. She was herself perceptive and quite naturally a good observer. That's how she became a qualified Action Profiler. She also suggested the change of name from Aptitude Assessment to Action Profiling when she was writing her book, *Top Team Planning*. The name Action Profiling did catch on and it's very difficult to escape from it now - it was such a marketable name. But when the break came in 1992 we thought it would be good to have a name that described what was done. Action Profiling was a bit loose, whereas MPA is what we do. We observe people's movement, we're looking for a pattern, and we analyse it before we interpret it. It's a good name from that point of view but it's not so marketable; commercially it's not such a suitable name. But we're stuck with it now.

Pamela Ramsden trained Carol-Lynne Moore. I came into the Training a bit, but it was primarily Pamela – that's the main contribution that she made to the whole development of Action Profiling. Within Action Profiling International – the professional institute that we formed - she was both Vice-President and Director of training. She developed training materials – very good ones. As Director of Training she had considerable power as to what she introduced. My accountant advised me that I should dissolve the partnership with myself, Pamela and Eddie Bowes, basically because I was providing two thirds of the earnings and she and Eddie between were supplying the other third. I am very glad I did because it was during those 20 years between 1982 and when I semi-retired in 2002 that I managed to earn enough money to provide the pension on which I am now living. After that break, although Pamela and I continued to work together as President and Vice-President of Action Profiling International, she became, it seemed to me, rather weird. Maybe this is explained by the fact that her main job now is as a priest in the Wicca pagan sect. Up to 1982 we had worked together very congenially but between 1982 and 1992 we grew more apart. I had been grateful for and do acknowledge the very great contribution that she has made, especially in the creation of training materials. She continued to train people after 1982 and it became clear to me that she was training people in a changed framework with which I didn't agree. Since 1992 we have had no contact.

Now Carol-Lynne is Director of Training, and while I take part, I leave it up to her. I think that she is also a very good trainer, but whereas Pamela was much more free-roaming, Carol-Lynne is very strict in maintaining professional standards. Carol-Lynne has almost gone to the opposite extreme in that we have independent inspectors who look at the work of all the students, which has to be vetted at all the stages of their training. Primarily I come into this training at what we call Stage Three – teaching people how to apply what they have learned, for example in team-building. To date we have trained about 15 people in Movement Pattern Analysis.

xxix. The Application of the MPA to the Management Field

Movement Pattern Analysis can not *only* be applied to the management field. Of course, it can be applied to wherever people make decisions, and that is everywhere. Apply that within the management field and it does suggest that they will make better management decisions if they have this understanding. And better decisions hopefully means making more profit, which is what most managers have to worry about.

The procedure consists of identifying members of the top team. That sometimes can be difficult because there isn't always a hard and fast dividing line, but usually it's fairly clear that a certain group of people does provide the main initiative to run the organisation. There was an occasion where one man defined twenty-six people who were reporting to him, so I had to argue with him that really you couldn't have a feasible team with so many people. In fact research not only by me but other people too does seem to show that over six people it gets difficult to preserve cohesiveness within a group of people. Over six you get sub-groupings or cliques forming and that's difficult for the leader to handle. I have worked on this problem with some leaders who have had more than six people and it's important that they should understand the risks.

Having identified the team the project then consists of meeting each individual person, separately of course, for a minimum of two hours and conducting the interview from which I can take the movement observations. Then I go away and analyse the results and match them against a decision-making model. The result is a movement pattern analysis, or a measure of the person's unique pattern of preference for coming to a decision. Then I go back and give each person feedback – a counselling session. At the end of that session I invariably ask whether they would be willing for their profiles to be used and made known to other people in the company for the purpose of a team-building seminar. I've only once had anybody who has demurred. Usually they are extremely enthusiastic, not least because they are very eager to see what profiles their colleagues have. Then I see the leader of the team and I believe that he or she is the main person to have what positive information has come out of the project.

So, having got the permission of all the participants, I talk with the leader and explain what kind of group he or she has. They may well have problems in certain places but in others there are certain opportunities, for example, for a person to be utilised more fully, or a subgroup to be formed, or responsibilities to be changed. I then get to talking about the leader's own strategy. After I have given my own findings on each person, then the leader may give me his or her opinions. In some cases I may disagree, in some cases I may understand the way he or she thinks the way they do because I already have their profile. This is a very significant meeting that can go on for many hours. Eventually we make a plan to get everybody together for a team-building seminar. This includes having a topic for discussion where we divide people into groups and compare the results in their handling of this topic. Importantly, the leader has contributed to setting the programme.

Then we meet, it may be anything from half a day to two days. It could be a weekend spent at some hotel or other. The day after the team-building seminar they may have a strategy or planning session, and sometimes I might stay on for this and make a contribution. The seminar usually starts with a recapitulation of what we are doing and what a Movement Pattern Analysis is, and the Framework of Management Action. Then we go through each individual profile. I like to do this so as to emphasise the strengths or the potential strengths, rather than focusing on the weaknesses. I do so in such a way that I usually succeed in getting people to laugh. As they do so, other members of the team usually recognise in what I am saying something that they have themselves experienced. I refer to them in a particularly constructive way and how these individual features can be contributed positively. Then we look at the team as a whole and I will have done a team analysis. So I say, 'Well there's never been a group of people in the world quite like you, and you are a unique team, you are the sum total of the individual features that make it up.'

Next, we look at the team analysis. I tell them what sort of team they are. One example I can quote was of a team in a highly competitive technical business who regarded themselves as being in advance of their competitors, but who were in fact, not competitive; together they prolonged their deliberations so as to waste time. They were amassing lots of points of view and research and whatever, but they were not taking the opportunities and certain advantages that were available to them. This was a case when I had to say that if their strategy was to be ahead of the competition, then it was not an appropriate way to be acting. Then we worked on what could be done about this – how could they utilise to a greater extent an individual in the team who does have that particular quality that they need. The leader can delegate people, can co-opt people or can recruit somebody new to the team. I've been involved in that being done. If I do get involved in recruiting somebody new to the team, it has usually come out of that sort of team analysis. They may agree to my meeting other people within the organisation to see if there's anybody who could be promoted, or it may be decided that they have to go outside the organisation.

Amongst the laughter and merriment there are also some very serious questions and study on what sort of team they are. Then I usually set a group discussion and divide the team into three groups, if I can – depending on their character. The groups are based on how they react, on their relative privacy or sharing tendency, and as to whether that is concentrated more on one stage of the decision-making process than another. I find a topic or will have agreed on one at a previous meeting which impinges on them all equally – in other words, not something that is only of interest to one department. They may discuss it for half an hour before coming back when a person from each group will give a report. I have always been able to pretty well predict how those reports will be given. It does demonstrate that according to the MPA of the people who make up the team, you will get a different outcome. Some of my clients have used this deliberately because they want a topic to be tackled in a particular way. That usually impresses people and it enables us to look at the significance of interaction. For example, there is usually somebody in the team who is more private than others, and I could say that he or she should not be misinterpreted as not having an interest or being indifferent. It is very often the case that a very sharing sociable person will interpret someone who is a bit of a loner as not being one of us and not being on board. I am very often able to correct that and other misinterpretations that people make because of their personal experience.

Finally, we get on to how the findings can be implemented. I do try to get a programme of action drawn up which might involve different sub-groupings; it might involve some people having other responsibilities; it might involve some people going beyond the boundaries of their jobs – I am always telling them that they are running the organisation, not just their own department. Territorial imperatives get discussed and, hopefully, corrected during this session. The end of that, I hope, is a programme of what they are going to do to implement the findings and I make it my business to follow this up and get in touch with them maybe three to six months later. Of course, I'm quite likely to have been in touch with them anyway because many of my clients did continue for many years.

So, that's what we do. It has a significance with regards to strategy. The strategy of the company or organisation has to be drawn up. Usually senior people feel that they have to have a strategy, even though sometimes they think that they have one, but it is not really viable at all. The seminar is very tied up with strategy and can have a major impact. I know of occasions where as a result of this work that a decision has been taken of major importance where millions of dollars have been involved.

I do like to differentiate what we do from the very worthwhile activity that is often called well-being work – the human resources type of activity that really concerns what people are feeling. I personally have never used MPA for that, except when it started way back in the factory days and we were concerned with the well-being of the worker. The first consideration was to get an improvement in the job and something that would satisfy the management in terms of output. It was incidental that when you got the worker to work more according to their unique individual way of working, then she'd be happier but also the output of work would be greater. That is still the case in the project that I've just described. People become happier, basically because they are working more like themselves – this can apply to the leader just as well as it applies to those people who report to him or her. The main thrust is to make the top-team more effective.

CONCLUSION

I'm still working on it …

In our final conversation for this book, Lamb concluded with the words that I've quoted above. Other quotations from it occur throughout this conclusion. The phrase is at once casual, humorous and determined – like every serious researcher he still retains an open mind about his chosen field. Without such openness I doubt whether he could have continued to work in pretty much the same area for sixty years. Lamb's thinking remains indefatigably in motion.

In the same conversation Lamb summed up the structure of this book as a dramatic quest for a framework which could accurately correlate movement patterns with decision-making. I added that the second drama was my struggle to understand this deceptively simple framework. I have included so many quotations from his earlier writings precisely to show how the elaboration of this framework was the result of tireless observations of people moving – both at work and in everyday activities – and reflections upon the best way to notate and interpret those movements. In many of his early writings he justifies his claims by citing how many thousands of people he has observed. The sheer number of studies he has undertaken is itself a considerable achievement: unlike academic research which is reviewed by peers, Lamb has had to sell his framework to hard-nosed businessmen – he has made a living by persuading them to buy his ideas. If there is a drama in the development of Lamb's framework for correlating movement with decision-making, it is because his research has had to be tested out in a much less collegiate environment than academia.

On the wall of Lamb's dining room there is a painting which incorporates the statement 'It is the property of true genius to disturb all settled ideas'. While I might have portrayed Lamb's pioneering work as a dramatic struggle, he has actively resisted being described as a hero, and even less a genius. To make his point Lamb quotes an eminent figure (he couldn't remember which) who said, 'Before I was a genius I was a drudge'. Lamb goes on to say that in his case, 'It's all part of a long process of drudgery.' When it comes to understanding movement Lamb clearly feels that he's still working on it …

This conclusion will begin with a review of Lamb's achievements and then addresses some broader headings, which will suggest possible extensions to his thinking. Although there is a considerable cross-over between the headings, I want to make some summary statements about Lamb's approach to education, tests and examination, and what is now called personal development. Next I shall point out the differences that we have seen in the way that Laban and Lamb approach the theory and discipline of studying movement. Finally, I shall revisit the themes of aesthetics, dance and drama.

Establishing the Framework: 1952 - 1969

In 1980/1 Lamb wrote a series of articles under the title *Developing Action Profiling* where he describes his split with Laban and Lawrence in 1952 which prompted him to set up his own consultancy where he offered Aptitude Assessments.

> When I set up my own consultancy base from a bedsitter in West Kensington I received a note in Laban's rambling scrawl asking me to give him 33% of my earnings. Such was the compelling power of the man that I recall treating it seriously. Had it been 10% I would probably have agreed. The demand caused me to argue that I had well repaid Lawrence's subsidy and out of the work I did under his banner I knew that Laban got a share. So eventually I put these arguments to Laban, and told him I did not think it right for him to get any percentage of my earnings at all. He shrugged (I can picture the movement now) in acceptance. We continued to be in touch, right up to his death, and the matter was never referred to again.

> It did mean, however, that I was confirmed from all points of view in my independence. And I was successful in getting clients. With at least two, Trebor and Eversheds, I brought in Lawrence and he earned fees for doing his own stuff.

> If I rejected 'Test' then what was I to call the work? My reports became 'Aptitude Assessments'. I reasoned that, O.K., everyone has to do his job, but he would have more aptitude for some part of it than for others. For years I was dedicated to the idea that what could be read from movement was aptitude.

> This conviction helped me to establish some basic principles underlying what I was trying to do (apart from earning a living):

> There is no one way of doing a job.

> Everyone has his own way

> Each person has a distinctive pattern of action

> We should try to pursue whatever we have aptitude for

> Maybe we can find a new way of doing a job which is in accordance with our aptitude

If it is impossible to find such a way relative to a particular job, then we are unsuited to it.

These six principles underpin all his successive work. *Movement and Personality* indicates that throughout the fifties Lamb devoted his energies to creating a more systematic approach to Aptitude Assessment, continually testing it against the actual work he was doing for clients. Twelve years of him continually testing hypotheses in working situations – the drudgery of his work - resulted in him establishing the basis for his framework.

By 1965 my main creative input to the development of Action Profiling had already been made. It included:

1. The concept of a decision-making sequence enabling emphasis to be put on the process as distinct from the content of a decision.

2. The isolation of posture-gesture-merging (integrated movement), containing the relatively enduring features of a person's individual movement as distinct from the transitory.

3. A systematic matching of Effort (assertion) with Shape (perspective).

4. The notion of affinities between Effort and Shape having significance for interaction.

5. The distinction of two types of Flow, Flow of Effort and Flow of Shape, essential for the concept of 'Identifying' and having significance for the understanding of masculine and feminine qualities of movement.

6. The Framework which divides the three-stage decision-making process into six basic actions and the three interactions together with three overall factors (Dynamism, Adaptability and Identifying).

7. The recognition that Flow (of Effort and Shape) diminishes during childhood growth while the Effort and Shaping movement of the three stages of the decision-making process are being developed.

However, 1965 did not start as a year of achievement. For three months I was unable to obtain any earning work. Early in April I was on a selling trip to the north of England when my car, having done 70,000 miles, exploded and had to be left by a deserted mountain road. I returned to London drearily by train, wondering where all my intensive developmental activity had got me, and wondering how I was going to pay the rent, or the next term's school fees. [*Movement Man*, Ch. 3]

The above list has been called Lamb's Seven Creative Principles and I want to explore some of them. I shall begin by considering his distinction between Posture and Gesture, and their merging, and then consider how Lamb's principles helped psychiatrist Judith Kestenberg elaborate her own framework (The Kestenberg Movement Profile). Like so many great truths, now that the difference of posture and gesture has been pointed out it seems so obvious – it was a truth just waiting to be put in so many words. I don't feel that even Lamb accords it the importance it deserves in his list of Creative Principles. This obviousness shouldn't blind us to the fact that this elegant distinction is one of Lamb's important discoveries. Although the everyday sense of word 'posture' doesn't suggest movement (it evokes the sense of a fixed position), an early definition of postural movement (in *Kinaesthetic Approach*) relates it to a shift of weight, or change in balance, which he defines as a 'core of stillness, around which the body moves like a gyroscope' [p.20]. In the context of teaching movement (especially for students of theatre) I find this a hugely useful distinction, and can imagine teachers in future giving a note, 'Your movement consists only of Gestures – risk taking it into Posture!' An even greater discovery was his conception of posture-gesture merging – that moment when a movement becomes personal. I think that this discovery may be undervalued for a different reason – because it is so much about the process of movement, and because the concept of movement as a process is so little understood.

I want to select a few passages from *The Meaning of Movement*, by Kestenberg and colleagues to demonstrate how she both confirms and develops some of Lamb's core principles. We begin with her explanation of why a gesture (like crossing one's arms) can reveal far more when broken down into its 'elementary qualities of movement'.

> The focus on elementary qualities of movement contributes to the KMP's range of application. Because the terminology describes universal qualities of movement it is applicable across cultural boundaries and with individuals of diverse backgrounds. It does not classify movement according to culturally specific labels though the meanings attributed to movement also permits discovery of subtle variations in meaning and in an individual's style of completing an action. For example, it is often suggested that crossing one's arms closes oneself off or distances oneself from others. Describing a gesture using more elementary qualities would allow us to differentiate individual ways of performing the same action. [*The Meaning of Movement*, p.11]

This is a crisp restatement of one of the first principles of movement analysis: that although one can offer generalised interpretations of a gesture, one can find out so much more, and in a more objective manner, by examining exactly *how the gesture is performed.* The difference between the Movement Profiles of Kestenberg (KMP, for short) and Lamb is that hers has nine to his two graphs. But this isn't complexity for its own sake – as a developmental psychiatrist she has to report on a far greater range of mental and emotional activity than just decision-making. Were there space I would argue that many of her graphs (for example, of what she identifies as pre-efforts) are hugely revealing of aspects of human behaviour which simply aren't relevant to Lamb's sphere of interest. Each researcher has created a framework that corresponds to their own field of research.

Next we see how Kestenberg can confirm, after observing many hundreds of infants both in New York and in Anna Freud's clinic in London, Lamb's claim that decision-making follows a necessary sequence of Space, Weight and Time, and also follows the infant's intellectual development.

> Whereas in the earlier phases, children learned the concept that an object is likely to be where it was last seen (object constancy in space), that objects have weight and mass which remain consistent (object constancy in weight), now they are able to conceptualise that the object retains an identity over time, even when it is no longer in its place (object constancy in time). Thus, in the third year a child can anticipate a parent's return and more easily accept a parent's absence. [Ibid., p.43]

The fact that our decision-making process is echoed in our development is interesting enough, but it also poses a research question: is the sequence a culturally transmitted construct, or part of our neural hard-wiring, or a mixture of both?

Turning to Kestenberg's development of the idea of Flow, let us begin with her distinction between bound and free flow:

> The control achieved through bound flow protects and the release achieved through free liberates. Bound and free flow are responses to feelings which arise out of conditions which are perceived as dangerous/threatening or safe/reassuring. Thus bound and free flow are responses to both internal emotions and external reality, but with an emphasis on internal reality or subjective experience. [61]

In other words, flow deals with the primordial aspects of human behaviour – those emotional drives and appetites that are with us from our birth: for example, hunger, laughter, anger, fear. Kestenberg relates flow to some of our most basic rhythms of life, all of which are regulated by the older, more emotion-driven part of the brain – the limbic structure. As in Lamb's analysis, a binding flow in an infant's rhythmic movements indicates a degree of conscious, intentional control of a movement: that is, rather than indulging in a rhythm, the infant will change it.

> The degree to which emotions are regulated is revealed by comparing the number of tension flow attributes with the number of tension flow rhythms notated. The more a child (or adult) engages in repetitive rhythmic behaviour, the less her impulses and emotions are being controlled. The more she uses tension flow attributes, the more she modulates her impulses perhaps in adaptation to changing contexts. [Ibid., 72 - 3]

The amount to which an infant will control or modulate different rhythms is what Kestenberg, following Laban, calls the **load factor** and which in a different context (that of Effort-Shape) Lamb calls Initiative.

> If a person uses two or three different tension flow attributes in various combinations, this offers them a larger range of response and has the potential to produce more adaptive behaviour than if someone only uses one attribute at a time. Following Goleman, we might call this an 'emotional intelligence' measure... [Ibid., 73]

In Part IV we saw Lamb admit that Identifying in his framework is a result of his work with Kestenberg:

> Identifying is drawn from an observation and analysis of the Flow pattern. As Kestenberg has revealed there is an immense body of knowledge that is contained in the concept of Flow that still needs to be developed and made more precise. It was not until 1960 or 1961 that I began working with her. But this work certainly had an influence on me, especially my understanding of Shape Flow, which I incorporated in *Posture and Gesture*.

Lamb was right to realise that Flow is an entirely different movement factor to Focus, Pressure and Timing (Space, Weight, Time) – and he is right to suggest that an entire book could be written on the subject.

To offer a first step towards this broader consideration of Flow, I want to quote from Daniel Stern's *The Interpersonal World of the Infant*. While I am not suggesting any direct influence of Kestenberg on Stern though he does quote her research in his introduction. Like Lamb and Kestenberg he realises that a huge amount can be learned about humans (and in his case, infant humans) by looking at how they move; like them, he has elaborated his theory after the observation (and video-recording) of hundreds of infants and their mothers. He focused on the changing modes of non-verbal communication that infants from the age of one to eighteen months have with their mothers. From these observations he has been able to draw some challenging conclusions about an infant's ability to communicate (they are not born autistic as some child psychologists have suggested) and how this generates a core sense of self from a very early age. The communication of emotional states is achieved through the use of different rhythms of movement – and these have to be named.

> It is necessary because many qualities of feeling that occur do not fit into our existing lexicon or taxonomy of affects. These elusive qualities are better captured by dynamic, kinetic terms, such as 'surging', 'fading away', 'fleeting', 'explosive', 'crescendo', 'decrescendo', 'bursting', 'drawn out', and so on. These qualities of experience are most certainly sensible to infants and of daily, even momentary, importance. It is these feelings that will be elicited by changes in motivational states, appetites, and tensions. [*Interpersonal World of the Infant*, p.54]

He goes on to describe how parent and infant understand each other through attuning to each other's movement qualities: 'how the mother picks up baby, folds the diapers, grooms her hair or the baby's hair, reaches for a bottle, unbuttons her blouse' [Ibid., p.54]. As with Kestenberg the focus is on the qualities of movement rather than their functional content. Frances La Barre, a psychoanalyst interested in movement, has written a study – *On Moving and Being Moved* - about the physical communication between therapist and patient: how the process of transference or non-transference can be understood in terms of physical attunement (what Lamb would call Identifying). I hope these two examples demonstrate the rich research potential there is in exploring the dynamics of interpersonal relations through the flow of Shape and Effort. I also hope that they demonstrate how theories about human communication, development and behaviour can be generated through the close observation of movement, and that hypotheses about the meaning of movement come after rather than before observation and are then tested through continuing observations.

On Laban, Lamb and transmission

> I just wonder if 50 years after his death that he might have thought that he would be almost completely forgotten. Would that have upset him? Or would he be pleased by the modest resurgence in him today. He isn't a well-known name now, but he wasn't then. It's difficult to fathom what he thought about the continuation of his ideas. Did he believe in an afterlife? Probably he did. He is probably revising God's laws and principles. Just as he tried to do with the Freemasons, when he got thrown out for his troubles!

Possibly with a mind to hand something on of their knowledge of movement, both Laban and Lamb wrote books. With Laban, one thing is clear: he totally resisted the notion that he had created a system. This may be that he didn't want his thinking to be hemmed-in or second-guessed by other people – he always wanted to have the last word. Lamb pointed out that had Albrecht Knust not taken on Labanotation then it would never have been a system that anyone else could have used. Lamb and Laban have completely different approaches to method and system: for one the quest was for a system that was objectively verifiable, for the other, the quest was for truths that were more personal, more mystical, and that couldn't be confined within a system.

A second difference between them lies into how they approached their movement research. Laban was fascinated by the implied movement patterns within the Platonic solids (Tetrahedron, Cube, Icosahedron, Dodecahedron). He devised intricate Scales and Rings that linked different points in these solids: many of his drawings follow his imaginary tracings within these spaces. In other words, part of his research began with a pre-existing theory, which he then tried to relate to an approach to aesthetic movement. As Lamb puts it, this was to achieve a union with some universal principles of movement and structure. Where Laban was interested in unbounded philosophical reflection Lamb was interested in finding accessible and intelligible terms that made up a coherent and logical framework. Lamb takes an empirical and inductive approach whereas Laban takes an idealist and deductive approach. If the lines that Laban drew were prescribed within given spaces, Lamb imagined vapour trails left in space by people making real movements – he is trying to understand the phenomenon of movement through observation and description: 'I base everything I do on an attempt to observe objectively'.

This difference could be expressed in terms of the two men's systems of thought. Both held that the meaning of movements lay in how they were patterned. Laban subscribed to a theosophical view of the world (his interest in Gurdjieff and Rudolph Steiner has already been noted) in which these patterns are common to all matter – the universe forms itself in certain shapes. For the ancient Greek philosopher Pythagoras (from whom Plato took much inspiration) harmony was a question of both space and sound: ratios like 3:2 were part of the harmonious structure of the cosmos. Theosophists sought to find a unity between man and these universal principles of construction. This is clear from a passage in *Choreutics*:

> We can understand all bodily movements as being a continuous creation of fragments of polyhedral forms. The body itself, in its anatomical or crystalline structure, is built up according to the laws of dynamic crystallisation. Old magic rites have preserved a great deal of knowledge about these laws. Plato's

description of the regular solids in the *Timaeus* is based on such knowledge. He followed the traditions of Pythagoras who was the first, as far as is known, to have investigated harmony in European civilisation. [*Choreutics*, p.105]

He goes on to explain how the icosahedron which consists of 20 equilateral triangles is a more sophisticated form than the cube. This explains why the triangle is one of the fundamental forms of all matter. Later in this discussion Laban excitedly explains how he discovered that the lateral rotation of our joints is 60 degrees, the same as the angle of any of the triangles of the icosahedron: quite literally, we 'fit into' the icosahedron! The meaning of human movement for Laban ultimately derives from its affinity with cosmic principles of construction – to move is to enact, and to join in with this harmony.

So did Lamb conceive of Movement Rites in the same way? The pattern he describes in his writings and conversation is something utterly personal – it is that type of movement which is unique to the individual. The meaning is something that the individual invests in the movement. The whole concept of PGM is that moment when a movement takes on a uniquely personal meaning. For Laban it is the pre-existing, indeed the eternal, System which contains the truth about movement – organic and inorganic. For Lamb the meaning is in the human movement itself – in its intention to make connection with other humans. His System, his method, is something much more humble; elaborated through painstaking effort, to try and describe and define the quick of the movement objectively: 'quick' meaning both life (in a more ancient meaning) and fleeting. For Laban the Truth lies in a Universal and eternal principle. Lamb is for the particular and the verifiable, as opposed to generalised assertions. It is for this reason that he rejects the unverifiable generalisations offered by 'Body Language' specialists. His implicit questions are 'How do you know this is true of all people at all times?' True Laban had a great eye for movement observation, and a keen instinct for what that movement might signify. But with 'Body Language' there is the risk that one might simply be perpetuating cultural stereotypes, and therefore imposing meanings on movements that, when considered in the context of an individual's pattern, might actually mean something entirely different. Lamb finds meaning closer to home in the unique way each of us moves in our everyday lives. And he offers a framework whose methodological transparency allows everyone to understand how those everyday movements correspond with our decision-making.

Lamb admired many things about Laban, chief amongst which were his skills of observation – his eye for movement - and his creation (if not the systematisation) of dance notation. Their difference of approach was in how to interpret those movements after they had been observed and notated. Lamb sought to create a methodologically rigorous framework relating movement to decision-making from Laban's mercurial musings. Lamb did not begin his quest by rejecting Laban's terminology – the lengthy and elaborate schema he uses in *Movement and Personality* is based entirely upon his teacher's terms – rather, he tested these terms through endless practical experiments. If there is a hero that Lamb resembles it must be Sisyphus who was condemned by Zeus to push a heavy boulder up hill, and once reaching the summit, to see it roll all the way down again. Lamb took everything he had inherited from Laban as a hypothesis which he then subjected to painstaking examination. An example of this arose when we were doing final corrections for this book. Lamb pounced on a term that had been used in *Management Behaviour:* in 1969 he had described one of the polarities of movement in the Sagittal plane as Advance and Retire, but this was later refined to Advance - Retreat. For Lamb the difference is not semantic, it is to do with his search for methodological clarity. Maybe that is the best word to describe Lamb's process – one of ever greater refinement through ever more precise differentiation between terms. Where Laban would use his uncanny powers of intuition to interpret a movement, Lamb narrowed his focus on to a very specific range of meaning (decision-making), in a specific context (business management), which correlated with movement in a very specific way (through his 11-point framework). Maybe Lamb began his career tackling something as broad as personality, but for the purposes of a decision-making framework he had to select only one aspect:

In some ways I shouldn't shy away from the word 'personality': it's just that decision-making doesn't say everything about a personality.

As concerns the creation of an intelligible framework it was necessary to remove all elements which might detract from its utility. He may not have been able to have made such wide and sweeping claims as Laban, but he could always back them up with solid argument and observation.

While I have never claimed to be scientific I have always been disciplined and practical, to be able to know and demonstrate what I have seen.

One important thing to bear in mind is that Lamb's framework and the terms he chooses are not metaphorical. Not to mince words, the relation between physical movement patterns and mental-emotional actions are related in a literal way. We should recall that in Part IV Lamb rejected the notion of 'mental action', arguing that everything takes place within the human organism (possibly a more inclusive term than 'body'). He notes that 'you can't observe mental Effort, all that you can see is a body.'

The body does all sorts of movements: it can frown, it can smile, it can fidget, there can be a big variation of effort and shape. From your observation and analysis of movement you may then discover some correlation with thinking, with the mind. One theory is that there is no such duality of mind and body – in fact we just have a body that moves and that mind is movement. I think, subconsciously, that has influenced me right from the very beginning although I didn't talk about it. I think I see now the sort of Cartesian segregation of mind and body still applies when people use the word mind-body; although this is outmoded, there is still a great element of the duality in the way they talk about mind and body. I start from the premise that we just have a body.

Once again we see Lamb distinguishing his thinking from Laban's, and exploring the meaning of movement and human choice from a neuro-physical rather than a metaphysical point of view. In his search for the meaning of movement Lamb never went *beyond* movement – he has always tried to understand its dynamics by remaining *within* it. Where Laban sought for the harmony between the inorganic structures of crystals and the structure of the human movement, Lamb sought to understand human movement by watching humans moving.

The above comparison with Laban might give the impression that Lamb's thinking and writing is narrowly focused upon the development and explanation of a particular method of matching the right person with the right job in the context of top management. While this might have been true of *Management Behaviour,* we have seen that this isn't true of his other two published books, and his many (I now feel uncertain as to just how many there might be) unpublished manuscripts. From *Movement and Personality* through to *The Movement Man* Lamb has ranged over a bewildering variety of subjects – the training of athletes, piano technique, the history of fashion, health and well-being, psychology (Jung versus Freud), therapy, education and philosophy, and there are more. I want to finish by considering four subjects: the philosophy of movement; Education and examination; aesthetics and physical wellbeing; and, finally, drama.

Seeing patterns of movement in all things

Whatever their philosophical and methodological differences, both Laban and Lamb understood the importance of understanding movement as a process of variation, as a phenomenon that involves constant change. On several occasions Lamb mentioned that one of Laban's favourite words was 'flux'. To understand the work of either man it is necessary to grasp the elusively obvious truth that movement can not be understood as a fixed thing. It seems obvious because we think in snapshots, therefore we think we have understood a movement because we have grasped its process by freezing a few significant moments – classically, the beginning, the middle and the end. This procedure is good for understanding the functional content of the movement, the 'what', but it cannot grasp the quality of movement, the 'how'. The narrative, functional approach doesn't begin to grasp the life of the movement, as it goes through these different points: for example, where is there an acceleration, where an increase in pressure, where does the gesture merge into a posture? All these questions were first posed by Laban and then developed by Lamb. You cannot even begin to ask these questions if you still think of understanding as a process of pinning-down, of arresting, of framing. To fully understand the meaning of a movement you have you be able to identify at what moment and how it changes - when and how and in what combinations the Effort and of Shaping alter. This is what I mean by understanding movement in dynamic rather than static categories – an effort of imagination which probably requires a finely-developed kinaesthetic sense. Lamb's thoughts about our current grasp of movement are summed up in the following reflection:

> Everybody moves and yet the extent of understanding is pitiful and I just wonder whether one day there will be a breakthrough when the scope and possibility of studying movement will become recognised.

Lamb has consistently demanded that it is time for movement studies to be established as a discipline in its own right, one freed from the apron-strings of dance. If he has proved anything, it is that human beings can be understood through the way that they move. And yet, for many it is still 'too great a leap' to connect psychology with movement:

> A lot of my research has been met with a great deal of respect, but nobody has known quite what to do with it. This has been especially the case in psychology. It has been just too great a leap from what is happening.

It may have been too great a leap in the past but recent advances in research into the brain – driven by empirical experiment, rather than speculative interpretation of discourse – means that Lamb's own researches may be of some help.

> I need to be more up to date to answer questions about psychology. It did seem that psychology as a discipline was in the doldrums. Now it seems revitalised by the new research into neurological and neurophysiological research. This will be helped by movement pattern analysis. People are aware of the physical but not of movement.

A possible revolution in our understanding of movement may come from the field of neurophysiology which is gradually offering an ever more detailed picture of the functions of the brain. Consider, for example, the possibility of the information being yielded by the different forms of brain scanning (MRI, CAT, PET) being combined with data from electromyography (to which Lamb has frequently referred in our conversations): potentially you would be able to map the process by which a person makes a move (attention, intention, commitment). This reflection brings us back to one of his early hypotheses about the 'psychological' – it is, I think, more of a neurological question – the connection between gesture and posture that he posed more than forty years ago in *Kinaesthetic Approach*:

> It is significant for each individual how he composes the great many actions involved and how he relates the different gesture movement with posture movement. For example, a certain effort and shape of hands 'feels right' when coinciding with a certain effort and shape of the posture. The movement of most intense 'feeling right' is the recognition kinaesthetically of an integration between the two processes of movement (posture and gesture). These points of contact are individually extremely important and significant. Psychologically it can be hypothesised that they are points of contact between afferent discriminatory sensing by way of response to environment or stimuli and efferent appropriate sensing by way of adjustment. [*Kinaesthetic Approach*, p.34]

Not everything to do with movement is in eternal flux – at least not in human movement. There are identifiable patterns in each person's way of moving – patterns as individual and as recognisable as their handwriting (itself the result of a process of movement). Were this not the case then there would be no point in Lamb having spent his life looking for constant movement patterns. At the risk of labouring I repeat a point that I have made earlier, the subtlety of Lamb's analysis is that it is based on the pattern of our posture-gesture mergers: that moment when a movement shifts from being local and peripheral to more general, when it 'gets personal'. Although the examples given above (waving goodbye to a much-loved friend) convey some sense of this principle, it is by viewing and re-viewing the film on Lamb's DVD ROM that you will really start to appreciate the originality of this conception. In the paragraph above I was arguing that you can't grasp the meaning of a movement through its function, or content, alone – you need to understand the process of its variation, how, when and in what way it changes. This, precisely, is the patterning that Lamb sets out to observe, notate and interpret.

> It is the patterning of movement that is more constant; that applies to a much longer period of time which is the significant element upon which to base the sort of understandings that we've been talking about.

For a Movement Pattern Analysis to have any lasting value it has to address constant aspects of a person's decision-making and movement preferences. After the observation and analysis of many thousands of people over more than fifty years – a large enough sample to satisfy the criteria of any programme of research – Lamb can surely claim that his analysis has demonstrated its validity. Moreover, think of his clientele: hardnosed business men and women who would not continue to use his MPA unless it demonstrated its value.

Education of the Individual

We have already seen Lamb state that 'There is never only one way of doing a job', an optimistic philosophy which echoes Laban's belief that everyone could dance or move in their own, unique way. Optimistic but not utopian:

> There's no utopian sense behind my use of the word freedom. Unless you are aware then you can't be free to choose, because otherwise you don't know what there is to choose between. There is always a development aspect, so that you can know how to extend your range.

This brings us back to the concept of a range: if the specifications of a job fall within our range of movement or decision-making then we can undertake it without stress. We could force ourselves to do the job (it's the only one available and we have a family to support), but we won't feel 'at home' in it or fulfilled by it. It will be stressful. However, we might not realise that the job is actually within our range because we have a very limited conception of 'how far we can go'. This is where the aspect of development comes into play – Lamb would argue that many of us operate within a self-restricted range, and that we are capable of so much more. It may be we limit ourselves according to societal and familial pressures.

The limitation of potential may come from the other side of the interview table. Rather than challenge the existing team – the status quo – the interviewing panel will opt for the least challenging option:

> Most appointments are made on the basis of who is most unexceptional, who best conforms to what has been regarded as the right way in the past.

The notion that there's no one way to do a job cuts both ways: one can consider this from the employer's perspective, who might limit the potential of his or her team by not seeing just how a prospective candidate could bring the oxygen of new ideas to their rather jaded management culture. Lamb may not be utopian, but he insists that we have many more options than we imagine. The question of appointment can be much more than matching the right person to the right job – this is to think two-dimensionally. A three-dimensional approach is to think how the whole team could be reconfigured by the appointment of this multifaceted person – creating new challenges for everyone. So if Lamb can't be called 'utopian' then you have to create a term like 'radical pragmatist': while he always works from what is there, the point is that his trained eye sees so much more.

Lamb's early writings dwelt with some considerable passion on how education (like employment) limits rather than develops a child's capacities. His preferred model would be one that encourages a child to be exceptional, not to conform, to be different. He explained this in our final conversation.

> Everybody is different and we need to be discerning and specific about what those differences are. An ideal would be to encourage the child to grow up understanding more about him or herself in all the different subjects that are taught. You need to learn about yourself in the process of learning about the subject matter.

Again, this demands a very different attitude from the person at the other side of the desk: a teacher needs to use the subjects on the curriculum as so many different means to enable the child's understanding of what he or she is good at – their underlying range within which they can excel. It boils down to a choice between coercion and conformity or education and creativity.

Throughout his writings and conversations we have seen Lamb militantly opposed to tests and examinations which only serve to demonstrate that one person is inferior or superior to another – we are simply different. Whether he is writing about school education or the presentation of a Movement Pattern Analysis he insists that it is about demonstrating and celebrating the uniqueness of the individual. He offers no judgement about the individual, simply a profile or portrait of what they are and could be – based on careful observations of their movement preferences matched against a tried and tested framework. The theme, once again, is one of freedom, difference, and development:

> I would hate to have presented you with your profile and state that you have scored so many points in such and such a category, that you are good at this and not so good at that. Instinctively people look at the scores and start thinking how they can improve it. I have a different approach: I go out of my way to say that there is nothing good or bad about a profile; you are who you are and let us rejoice in who are. Let us simply try and understand how you are different from

other people. I believe this is very characteristic of Laban.

Maybe it is simply about the exercise of power and authority – the protection of vested interests. The teacher or expert hands down their wisdom that takes no account of an individual's specific needs and potentials. Everything remains unchanged – the knowledge being imparted, the teacher imparting it, and the student – it is in every way impartial.

This leads us directly to the theme of wellbeing and aesthetics.

> Currently there is a lot being written about happiness. Most people think that this is airy fairy and not much can come from this. It doesn't go much beyond the fact that money isn't the source of all happiness. But you could be happy with yourself whatever arises, irrespective of whether your neighbour earns more than you. In other words, what none of the researchers into happiness seem to think about is being happy with yourself whatever the outside circumstances may be. The main question is being happy in yourself, feeling right, being OK. And movement helps!

Although dealing with a different aspect, the argument remains focused upon a person being happy because they know that they are going about things according to their own individual pattern. It probably doesn't need stressing, but we should be clear that when Lamb talks about 'being happy with yourself whatever the outside circumstances may be', he isn't referring to us remaining within our comfort zone. Our range of movement is something for us to actively explore rather than passively experience in a self-contented way. You learn to recognise your pattern, through the exercise of it; you find out what it permits you to do (just as learning an academic subject is learning what you can make of it): a pattern is not something inert and given – a thing - but something heuristic, something by means of which you can discover new things about yourself, something which brings you into new relations with other people and the surrounding environment. Even to think of the pattern as an 'it' is dangerous, since this suggests a thing separate from you, rather than a dynamic principle which shapes the way you live.

The aesthetic dimension returns us to his early and abiding preoccupation with the kinaesthetic sense. Lamb echoes the Polish director and pedagogue Jerze Grotowski when he observes someone who moves according to their personal pattern has a certain beauty, a certain truth, and how someone who moves with no sense of themselves is, to be blunt, ugly. Like Grotowski, Lamb demands that we shed socially-acquired tics and mannerisms and get in touch with our own principle of movement. Both men present the process of maturing into adulthood in terms of an expense/gain ratio. By accepting the limitations, distortions and disguises that make up contemporary life, you gain acceptance as a rule-observing and compliant adult, but you lose your range of spontaneous and creative movement – you fit yourself into a mould that denies you much scope for individual expression. Lamb used the expression 'puppet-like' to describe gestural movement that was purely acquired: this image conveys precisely the lack of personal autonomy in the person's movement – someone else is pulling the strings. In his analysis of movement rites we have seen a direct correlation between certain personal types of movement and personal happiness. Both Laban and Lamb (and Grotowski, for that matter) would argue that you would live a more fulfilling life if you expanded your own personal potential for movement – not to become a better dancer or mover, but as part of your own means of self-realisation. There is a functional link between kinaesthetic re-education (un-learning some of the bad lessons of adulthood), discovering aesthetic pleasure in everyday living, and thereby happiness.

The mention of Jerzy Grotowski leads me to the final theme in this introduction – theatre. Lamb's entry into the world of Laban movement was via Theatre Workshop and theatre provided a constant point of reference throughout his writings. Although Lamb was more closely involved in Dance Theatre (Laban must have been the pioneer for this movement-driven form of theatre), I would argue that his ideas and principles have application for any kind of theatre – from the most naturalistic to the most physically expressive. In everyday life we recognise our friends from how they walk, and we can recognise even a stranger's mood from how they move. But this is to talk about the importance of movement generally. What Lamb has grasped is that the drama comes when some element of a movement changes: suddenly the pressure increases, the shape encloses and the movement accelerates – then, just as quickly, it dissipates. The drama is in this sudden change – the more elements involved, the greater the effect (a dramatic equivalent of what Laban calls, Loading). An actor can be helped to choose that range of roles which match his or her movement range (what the French call an actor's 'Emploi'). But maybe most useful is the inherently dramatic notion of a Posture-Gesture Merging – that crucial moment in which a person's character fully embodies a movement, endowing it with a significance that communicates with the audience kinaesthetically. Even if one is dealing with a less representational form of theatre – that of Grotowski, or Barba, or Joseph Chaikin – these PGM moments are those which will be endowed with maximum expressiveness and personal investment of meaning.

From the 1920s through to the 1950s Laban must have had hundreds of students whom he encouraged to develop his ideas and start up their own schools or practices. It was this rather carefree, almost careless, approach which has meant that there are so many conflicting and contradicting Labans in the world. Lamb has developed the work of Laban by rigorously testing his concepts and terms, rejecting those which he couldn't use, and developing (and often renaming) those he could. Lamb has arrived at a form of theory that has been informed by practice. Rather than engaging in purely theoretical speculation about movement, or confining his transmission to 'on the job' training (what he calls 'Standing next to Nellie'), he has constantly tested the one against the other – a theory of movement that moves in the process of its elaboration. Lamb hasn't always worked in the spirit of Laban, because that isn't part of his own pattern – they really are two very different men. What we are left with is a body of work that is still being refined and which has added immeasurably to our understanding of the meaning and value of movement.

Appendix

Warren Lamb's Profile of Dick McCaw

Career Guidance Dick McCaw		% of total initiative	Extent of interaction initiative		
Assertion	Perspective			Sharing	Private
Investigating		14	Communicating		
	ATTENTION			75%	70%
	Exploring	8			
Determining		25	Presenting		
	INTENTION				60%
	Evaluating	18		40%	
Timing		29	Operating		
	COMMITMENT				
	Anticipating	6		35%	30%
Assertion/Perspective ratio		68 : 32			
Dynamism on a 10 point scale		8			
Identifying		High			

213

Index